Literary Folkloristics
and the Personal Narrative

Literary Folkloristics and the Personal Narrative

Sandra K. Dolby

Trickster Press
Bloomington, Indiana

Library of Congress Control Number: 2008906615
ISBN: 978-0-915305-48-3

Cover photograph courtesy of Carol Dolby Shenefield: the figure in the center of
the photo is Loretta Dolby, circa 1935
Cover design by Adam Shlian
Technical Consultant Arle Lommel

Published by Trickster Press,
A division of Folklore and Ethnomusicology Publications
504 N. Fess Avenue
Bloomington, IN 47408
folkpub@indiana.edu

Advance Praise for
Literary Folkloristics and the Personal Narrative

"In less than twenty years after its publication Sandra Dolby's seminal work on *Literary Folkloristics and the Personal Narrative* has become a classic in folklore and narrative studies. In fact, no scholar or student can be engaged in the study of personal narratives without this ground-breaking work. Dolby's pioneering work has won international acclaim with its theoretical discussion of literary folkloristics, its detailed definition and analysis of the personal narrative as an oral literary genre, its methodology of interpreting personal narrative texts, and its analysis of actual texts. As such, this book has guided the advancement in personal narrative studies over the past two decades in scholarship worldwide. For its much needed and desired reissue Sandra Dolby has added an erudite and informed preface reflecting on the progress that personal narrative studies have made, including comments and resources on the history of the personal narrative genre and its study from the point of view of its audience and reception, performance, cultural frame of reference, cultural identity, themes, values, and worldview. Both Sandra Dolby and Trickster Press are to be applauded and commended for making this invaluable study available again for a new generation of folklorists, cultural historians, and literary scholars who will benefit greatly from the informed content and the lucid style of this brilliant book."

—Wolfgang Mieder, Professor of German and Folklore, University of Vermont

"The reprint of Sandra Dolby's influential work, *Literary Folkloristics and the Personal Narrative*, is a most welcome event for folklore studies. With a handful of other brave scholars, Dolby reminded folklorists that narrative is often local and embedded in life worlds. Dolby's work emphasizes that—in many ways—the personal is traditional. It is a happy moment to have this recent classic back in print."

—Gary Alan Fine, John Evans Professor of Sociology, Northwestern University
Editor, *Social Psychology Quarterly*

"When *Literary Folkloristics and the Personal Narrative* first came out in 1989, it had an immediate impact on folklore studies by defining the personal narrative as a genre and giving direction to the scholarship through in-depth interpretation of specific stories in context. I'm pleased to see it back in print; Dolby's new preface undoubtedly will be just as influential on future oral narrative scholarship."

—Patrick B. Mullen, Professor Emeritus, Ohio State University

Contents

Illustrations

Figure

Dedicated to the memory of my parents,
Charles E. and Loretta Dolby

Foreword

The other day, as I was thinking about how to frame my Foreword to this new edition of *Literary Folkloristics and the Personal Narrative*, I heard a piece on National Public Radio featuring Ms. Trudy Henry, an elderly woman from Kansas, recalling the day, back in 1933, when Bonnie and Clyde visited her family's home in Dodge City. Ms. Henry's mother was Registrar of Deeds for the county, and Clyde came to the house seeking information about some property in the area while Bonnie stayed back at the car, smoking a cigar—a shocking and memorable sight for young Trudy and her sister. On discovering the identity of their notorious visitors some time later, Ms. Henry reports, "we really felt like we were something, getting to see Bonnie and Clyde." The radio piece featuring Ms. Henry's story was produced by an outfit called StoryCorps, working in partnership with NPR and the American Folklife Center at the Library of Congress, where the stories they record from narrators all around the country are archived. StoryCorps, according to its website, "captures and defines the stories that bond us," that make us feel, as Trudy Henry aptly puts it, like we are something. Listening to each others' stories, StoryCorps suggests, "is an act of love." "Well," I said to myself, "they have nationalized Sandy Dolby's personal narrative project." Would this national enterprise have come about if Sandy hadn't opened the eyes and ears of folklorists to personal experience narratives? Who knows? But the American Folklife Center is guided and staffed by folklorists and "personal experience stories" and "personal histories" are prominently featured in their definition of folklife and their guide for collectors. And no one played a more influential role in the recognition of personal experience stories as grist for the folklorist's mill than Sandy Dolby, beginning in the mid-'70s and culminating in the publication of *Literary Folkloristics and the Personal Narrative* in 1989. Sandy herself has filled in this history in the Preface that follows, as only she can, and contextualized the book vis-à-vis subsequent scholarship on personal narrative.

The field has become an enormously complex and heterogeneous enterprise, distributed over an impressively large number of disciplines. In my view, though, reconfirmed by reading it again over the past several days, *Literary Folkloristics and the Personal Narrative* remains a unique and special work. What I value most about this inspiring book is the admiration and respect with which Sandy celebrates the stories people tell about themselves. She holds the stories up to us as complex, affecting, artistic achievements, as true works of verbal art: meticulously crafted, densely packed with associational meaning, anchored simultaneously in the collective richness of our lives in common and the unique qualities of individual experience and imagination, and offered up by their authors for the enhancement and intensification of the sociable moments in which they are told. No other scholar that I know of has come close to the interpretive fullness and resonance of Sandy's critical readings of personal experience stories. Every scholar committed to an appreciation of vernacular creativity should know and learn from this book. We owe thanks to the author and to Folklore and Ethnomusicology Publications for bringing it back into print.

Richard Bauman
Indiana University
May 2007

Preface to the 2008 Reissue

Personal Narrative:
Reflections on an Enduring Resource

These true stories grow out of reminiscences of the past, and events, hearsay, rumor, gossip, and personal experiences of the present.
   —Linda Dégh, "Folk Narrative" (1972:78)

Discursive forms—especially narrative forms—for the construction and representation of the social self have risen to unprecedented prominence in anthropology, linguistics, folklore, and psychology in recent years.
   —Richard Bauman, *A World of Others' Words* (2004:82)

A Little History

In the early 1970s, the oral personal narrative was not to be found among the genres of folklore listed in introductory surveys of the field, such as Jan Harold Brunvand's *The Study of American Folklore* (1968). Distinctive features of these tales—such as their non-traditional content, limited circulation, and obvious authorship—suggested that the personal narrative should not be considered "folklore" and was not useful in folkloristic research. However, several decades earlier at least one influential folklorist had seen value in collecting and studying examples of the genre. In *Bloodstoppers and Bearwalkers* (1952), a book of tales from the Upper Peninsula of Michigan, Richard Dorson included narratives of "the sagamen"—and these were stories of personal experience. Little wonder, then, that in 1975, at the helm of Indiana University's Folklore Institute, Dorson was receptive when I proposed to write my dissertation about "The Personal Narrative as a Folklore Genre." For me, the topic was an exciting way to explore the definition of folklore and challenge the canon of accepted folklore genres.

   These two questions—are true stories folklore? and is the personal narrative a genre?—were the subject of two articles I wrote in 1977: "The Oral Personal Narrative in Its Generic Context" and "The Personal Narrative as Folklore" ([Dolby] Stahl 1977a, 1977b). Although these issues were prime topics in the legend course taught by Linda Dégh at Indiana University in the early 1970s, few people today worry about whether personal narratives are folklore or whether they constitute a genre of oral narrative. I like to think that my early work helped those issues recede in favor of other, more contemporary questions. By 1986, Richard Bauman's *Story, Performance, and Event* had successfully demonstrated how useful the genre was in exploring issues of performance, artistry, and context. By 1987, in *Storytelling Rights*, Amy Shuman had explored how both written and oral personal narratives were used to negotiate reports of fights in an urban middle school. And by 1989, when I wrote the book I am reflecting upon here, a growing number of studies depended upon the personal narrative as a textual base for research. Along with the original publication of *Literary Folkloristics and the Personal Narrative*, the year 1989 saw the publication of at least two important articles addressing new research directions associated with the personal narrative. In the first of these, Kristin Langellier reviewed the growing literature on the topic for *Text and Performance Quarterly*. Here she introduced the idea of viewing the personal narrative as a "boundary phenomenon," a kind of discourse that scholars have typically positioned between conventional categories—for example, between literary and social discourse or between public and private spheres of interaction. Another influential 1989 article was Barbara Kirshenblatt-Gimblett's essay "Authoring Lives," published in the *Journal of Folklore Research*. There the author raised the issue of appropriation—the claiming of the teller's voice—something that has become a central concern of more recent research. In 1989, this issue was just beginning to emerge in discussions about how personal narrative should be elicited and presented.

Furthermore, in that same year, a scholarly consortium called Personal Narratives Group edited *Interpreting Women's Lives*, a collection of nineteen essays that adopted a feminist stance to speak about life stories, biographies, and autobiographies. Clearly, the personal narrative had emerged as an identifiable kind of discourse able to serve a variety of analytical purposes and theoretical perspectives. As the years have passed, the personal narrative's status as a subject of folklore research has only become more solidly assured. The genre has flourished in its supporting research role across disciplines, largely because of its obvious ties to the individual, its seeming truthfulness, and its simple artistry. As might be expected, much current personal narrative research is, following the lead of British social historian Paul Thompson (2000), primarily descriptive and tied to oral history and cultural documentation (Allison 2004; Boenisch-Brednich 2002; Estes 2005; Hinkle 2006; Minchin 2004; Rouverol 2003; Ryan 2004; Scuro 2004; Sebre 2005; Tranguyen 2002; Zecker 2002). The abundance of scholarship on the more inclusive category of life stories and life writing is reviewed annually in the journal *Biography* (see Wachter and Schultz 2005). Increasingly, studies use the personal narrative to explore new analytical territory. For example, in their 2001 book *Living Narrative*, Elinor Ochs and Lisa Capps consider how the perspective of telling stories *with* rather than *to* others changes the nature of storytelling as an activity. For additional contemporary analytical studies, see work by Allen Feldman (2004), Camilla Mortensen (2005), Steven Robins (2006), Maria Gabrielle Swora (2001), John Traphagan (2004), Fugich Waco (2002), Kwesi Yankah (2004), and Steve Zeitlin and Ilana Harlow (2001). Other recent studies consider the personal narrative in relation to other genres, such as the legend (Gabbert 2000; Goldstein 2004), or like Charlotte Linde in her 1993 book *Life Stories*, they analyze stories of personal experience in an effort to refine narrative analysis. Work of this type can offer insights that would be difficult to discover using more traditional or written texts (see Abrahams 2005; Goodwin 2004; Katz and Shotter 2000; Marander-Eklund 2002; Meyer 2000; Quah 2002; Schiffrin 2003; Wolf-Knuts 2003). The cross-disciplinary usefulness of the genre is also increasingly evident; for instance, scholars have explored the role of personal narratives in corporate culture (Brown 2005) or education (Dominicé 2000).

Contemporary work on this genre also recognizes its influence in a range of media, from the electronic to the oral. The personal narrative has emerged as the text of choice in studies of internet blogging and posted home pages (Killoran 2003; Langellier and Peterson 2004). In his 1999 book *How Our Lives Become Stories: Making Selves*, Paul John Eakin reflects on the written tradition of autobiography, and more recently (2004), he ponders, "What Are We Reading When We Read Autobiography?" In answering his own question, Eakin suggests that, among other actions, the autobiographer creates a narrative identity—an "extended self" that combines memory and anticipation. Other scholars consider many of the same questions with regard to oral narratives and the representation of self and identity in community; authors such as Russell Frank (2003), Deborah Golden (2001), Joseph Gone (2006), Marsha Kelly (2005), Elaine Lawless (2001), Suzanne MacAulay (2004), Kgafela Oa Magogodi (2002), Margaret Mills (2004), Lynne Miyake (2001), Martha Norkunas (2004), Chaim Noy (2007), Dorothee Schreiber (2004), Maria Yelenevskaya and Larisa Fialkova (2004), and Rosemary Lévy Zumwalt and Isaac Jack Lévy (2002) have all addressed these issues in different ways.

The 1997 special issue "Oral Versions of Personal Experience: Three Decades of Narrative Analysis," edited by Michael Bamberg for the *Journal of Narrative and Life History*, pointed the way toward this growing interest in the relationships among personal narrative, identity, and historical or social contexts. Earlier, in *Story, Performance, and Event* (1986), Richard Bauman had anticipated attention to how a storyteller shapes and reshapes a "self" while telling narratives. For instance, as he analyzed Texas storyteller Ed Bell's variations on a tall tale over a period of eleven years, Bauman demonstrated how Bell changed plot and narrative devices in response to context. He also observed that Bell had "transformed from someone who 'never used to think of myself as a storyteller' to someone who is preeminently a storyteller" (1986:106).

Bauman's more recent return to yet more riches in Ed Bell's repertoire is further evidence that the personal narrative remains an exciting subject for folkloristic study. Writing in 2004 (*A World of Others' Words*), Bauman appreciates the growing body of personal narrative research, but his aim in this study is to "explore an alternative strategy" and examine how Bell uses first-person narratives to shape and present "the social self in dialogue with others" (2004:83). In looking at Bell's stories with this new strategy in mind, Bauman guides us through a process of narrative identity formation encapsulated in Bell's cameos of himself as learner and teacher. Bauman's analysis is still very attentive to the text, but his stronger emphasis on the individual life of the teller in community and on narratives as expressions of identity represents a shift in the direction of personal narrative research more generally.

Similarly, in crafting this new introduction to *Literary Folkloristics and the Personal Narrative*, I hope to suggest how some of the ideas I presented in that 1989 book could now be recast and developed in light of recent theoretical and methodological advances. I have chosen not to rewrite the book, in part because I cannot re-interview the storytellers. However, I will comment here on five concepts at the heart of the book that continue to represent exciting areas of research—theoretical perspectives that, I believe, continue to demand the personal narrative as a partner if they are to be developed most effectively.

Audience and Reception Theory

I chose to use the phrase "literary folkloristics" in the title of my book in part because during the 1980s I was very much influenced by European literary criticism. Wolfgang Iser and Hans Robert Jauss were significant theorists at that time, and their perspectives were reflected in a much-cited book that appeared in 1980 and brought together the reception theories of several American and European scholars. This collection, *Reader-Response Criticism: From Formalism to Post-structuralism* (Tompkins 1980), included essays by some of the most influential literary theorists of the day: David

Bleich, Jonathan Culler, Stanley Fish, Walker Gibson, Norman N. Holland, Wolfgang Iser, Walter Benn Michaels, Georges Poulet, Gerald Prince, and Michael Riffaterre.

Most influential for me was the work of David Bleich; I found his 1978 book *Subjective Criticism* especially useful. Bleich and a number of other theorists promoted the idea that the "informed reader" must be attended to when examining a text, because it was the reader's understanding—as influenced by his or her personal and cultural background—that determined what the accepted meaning of a text should be. This idea prompted me to consider the role of the listener when analyzing oral texts. I determined that when studying personal narratives, conscientious application of this analytical perspective would require me to explore my own responses as an "informed listener." Folklorists were also increasingly influenced by theorists who examined dialogic patterns in linguistic and literary materials—scholars such as Mikhail Bakhtin or Roman Jakobson. And because these folklorists were primed to examine oral materials along with written literature, they developed the notion of "the audience as co-author" perhaps more readily than literary scholars (see Duranti 1986).

The concept of audience or reader as a creator of meaning still influences much scholarship in folklore and adjacent fields. While the notion of reception or audience theory has been subsumed, in many ways, within performance theory in folklore studies, the idea of audience is still a separate concern for many folklorists, ethnomusicologists, and media scholars. For instance, the recently initiated online *Journal of Audience and Reception Studies* is very popular, especially in the United Kingdom. Personal narratives have been especially relevant to this research because of their non-traditional content. Typically, a story of this type will not already be known to the listener, so she or he must more obviously "create" meaning along with the teller. I feel comfortable in suggesting that my attention to the role of the listener in *Literary Folkloristics and the Personal Narrative* was timely. What better way to gauge the response of a listener than to present that listener with stories that are presumably the idiosyncratic creation of the speaker? Personal narratives challenge the listener with something new and original and lay at the listener's feet responsibility for a competent response.

The challenge for folklorists and other scholars who attend to reception is still the methodological and perhaps even ethical one it was for me more than fifteen years ago: How can an ethnographer discover the teller's or the audience's natural response? Must they merely presume to know based on simple observation or, on the other hand, must they intrude interpretive questions (see Oring 1987)? Elaine Lawless has tried to address this concern through a practice of "reciprocal ethnography," which brings narrators into the process of representing and analyzing their texts (1993). But again, as for Kirshenblatt-Gimblett in "Authoring Lives," there remains a strong concern that an elicited voice is tainted by the aims of the interviewer. Furthermore, some researchers (see, for example, Scruggs 2001) worry that any analysis of public performance must necessarily select only those messages that the interpreter deems significant, based on interactions among performer and audience. If I had my 1989 study to do over again, I would find a way to record the responses of listeners other than myself, though I'm not convinced that I would feel entirely ethical in subjecting those individuals to the kind of personal interrogation I was willing to accept myself. Nevertheless, I do believe that recording and studying the responses of audiences will be an increasingly important part of contemporary personal narrative research.

Improvisational Narrative Performance

Albert Lord's *Singer of Tales* (1971) is one of the books that have most influenced my thinking about folklore. Granted, I would not have grasped this book's significance without the aid of teachers and scholars who expanded its application. But to me, the realization that people could create poetry by drawing upon oral formulas and traditional themes was ground-shifting. It meant that humans have evolved to be creators, and that careful study can document the process of creativity. Richard Bauman's expansion of this notion in *Verbal Art as Performance* (1977), and his subsequent documentation of intertextuality—the indexing and mixing of multiple texts and varying contexts—as a crucial part of the performance process (2004), have been important to my own perspectives on personal narrative research.

Not surprisingly, scholars continue to find the personal narrative one of the genres most effectively analyzed in performance studies. Once again, it is the personal narrative's obvious ties to the individual storyteller, and his or her creative use of personal and cultural resources, that make such stories so very useful in documenting narrative process. Patricia Sawin, for example, has examined how Bessie Eldreth employed the device of reported speech to such good effect in her storytelling (1992). In *Listening for a Life* (2004), Sawin expanded this analysis of narrative improvisation to demonstrate how this one practice became Eldreth's signature creative device as she used personal narratives to convey a sense of self. Clearly the personal narrative remains a primary source for examining the process of creative narrative performance.

Like a jazz performer, the talented teller of these stories must not only respond to every new context with a new text, but she or he must also dip down, every time, into the well of personal experience.

In my analysis of the tales in *Literary Folkloristics and the Personal Narrative*, I cannot say that I identified any hitherto undocumented narrative devices, nor did I demonstrate conclusively how the storytellers created text in response to context. If I were writing the book today, I would examine these issues in more detail. However, in naming the structural types of the personal narrative, I did examine one especially effective device: the narrative structures learned and used by storytellers are important in their repertoire of narrative tools. In sum, attention to the creative process involved in crafting an experience into a narrative performance is one abiding influence of those who have studied the personal narrative and its many practitioners and contemporary contexts.

Cultural Frame of Reference

An important book in the 1970s was Erving Goffman's *Frame Analysis* (1974). In conjunction with performance theory's spotlighting of cultural resources, Goffman's notion of a "frame of reference" led me to look for "cultural allusions" that corresponded to a listener's cultural repertoire. My analysis in *Literary Folkloristics and the Personal Narrative* called for attention to "generic conventions, themes, folkloric allusions, and personal frames of reference" that allowed the listener to understand narrative content. I would still argue that identifying personal frames of reference is a significant and thorny part of personal narrative research; however, the more manageable task of identifying relevant folkloric or cultural allusions remains both achievable and useful. In a way, researchers who identify cultural materials in personal narratives continue the anthropological practice of extracting "culture" from life stories (see Linde's discussion of Kluckhohn, Kroeber, Simmons, and others [1993:48-50]). However, folklorists studying the personal narrative are interested in seeing how storytellers use these cultural materials to create stories that "work" with varying success within given cultural contexts, rather than viewing the stories as repositories from which to mine more general knowledge.

I believe that "cultural frame of reference" is a concept useful in exploring any kind of narrative. It allows us to see, for example, how urban legends build upon general understandings of microwave ovens or Big Macs and also presume stereotypes, beliefs, and values shared by listeners. In analyzing personal narratives, the cultural frame of reference is especially telling because it reflects much about what the teller assumes his or her listeners already share. The fine line between personal frames and cultural frames is, as I argued in *Literary Folkloristics and the Personal Narrative*, the tantalizing store of information that serves the cause of creating and celebrating intimacy. Cultural frame of reference is what makes Larry Scheiber's trip to the car wash in "Tiny Wires and the Chicken Blood" humorous, but it is his personal frame of reference—including information about Scarborough's and the old township school—that reveals and affirms his friendship with me, the listener. Today, attention to cultural frames of reference—what is shared, and what is not—is often included in examinations of intertextuality: the cultural frame includes "texts" of varying sorts, some of which are not typically viewed as such. In either case, it is the cultural frame or connection between text and culture that brings meaning to this analysis.

Identity and the Cultural Thumbprint

Closely tied to the concept of a cultural frame of reference is the notion of cultural identity. While the study of "folk groups" has long been central to folklore studies (see, for example, Oring 1986), links between individuals and their presumed cultural identities have been increasingly reexamined and further scrutinized. Researchers are reluctant to cast people into categories or to suggest that they are in any way one-dimensional. Nevertheless, there is an abiding view that the various groups to which an individual belongs are significant in determining his or her cultural frame of reference or repertoire of cultural expressions. One area of research that has expanded greatly in the last two decades is the study of life story or personal narrative as it relates to identities. In *Stories, Community, and Place*, for example, Barbara Johnstone examines the narratives of storytellers in Fort Wayne, Indiana, and recognizes the varying effects of place, gender, age, and social class on the tales she recorded (1990).

In *Literary Folkloristics and the Personal Narrative*, my practice was to identify the "folk groups" that seemed to loom large in the storyteller's background and then check to see which of these groups were shared by the listener. To aid my analysis, I created representational "wheel charts" that indicated eight different kinds of groups that typically affect the cultural knowledge of any individual. These included ethnicity, religion, place, age, gender, occupation, family, and social network (or class). Though many other factors could have or even should have been included—education, for example—the charts helped me identify areas of cultural overlap between tellers and listeners.

These charts have continued to be useful for me and my students. I have used the group wheel chart to help students predict the knowledge or content they might learn from the people they interview. And I have expanded the concept slightly over the years. I now describe the chart—or similar instruments that identify an individual's significant resource groups—as a "cultural thumbprint." Once the chart is filled with individually pertinent detail, it becomes a unique record of the cultural resources that have contributed to the information in a person's memory bank. And while most researchers are particularly interested in how an individual's folklore reflects his or her participation in a specific folk group, the student of the personal narrative should be interested in identifying all resources that contribute to a storyteller's store of knowledge and allusions—or at least as many as possible.

No individual's identity is ever tied to only one folk group, nor is identity ever adequately represented by any category or folk group. And yet identity is something researchers try to discover in studying the personal narrative. The challenge is to elucidate viable "personal identities" (see Langellier and Peterson 2004) without relying on the broader cultural identities imposed by stereotyping. The cultural thumbprint idea is helpful in this sense: it shifts attention from the folk group itself to the individual and the individual's unique constellation of significant influences. Since a person's cultural thumbprint is never wholly the same as anyone else's, researchers can use this tool to illuminate unique cumulative repertoires. The value of personal narratives to the study of identity is that no story can be assumed to represent only one of the many groups to which the storyteller belongs; every personal narrative grows out of the multiple combined cultural and personal resources of the storyteller.

Themes, Values, and Worldview

One other important folkloric concept that attracted me when I first started studying the personal narrative was Alan Dundes's notion of the "folk idea." As Dundes explained, the concept was not simply another term for belief, nor was it a synonym for the proverb. Instead, "folk idea" represented a category of worldview that could be expressed in any number of forms—proverbs, songs, stories, even games or quilts (1972). Other disciplines had already explored some concepts very close to this idea. Psychologists had studied values, anthropologists had studied beliefs, and literary scholars and musicians had studied themes and motifs. For me, the literary idea of a narrative theme was useful in studying the personal narrative, but these themes became more immediately relevant to the storytelling context when viewed in conjunction with the anthropological concept of worldview. In other words, for the teller of a personal narrative, an important resource is the store of themes or values that collectively define his or her personal philosophy and approach to the world. One related area of research that remains especially vital today is the study of experience narratives or "memorates"—stories that include at their cores recognizable beliefs or, as Dundes suggested, "folk ideas." In *The Terror That Comes in the Night*, David Hufford argued convincingly against the "cultural source hypothesis," the presumption that storytellers necessarily create their narratives in response to a shared, traditional belief. However, his data also supports a more descriptive claim that personal narratives serve to keep conventional themes, concerns, or values alive in a culture; in other words, stories do document traditional beliefs. A story such as Larry Scheiber's "Koo-Nar, King of the Rats" conveys conventional values and concerns and even a belief about what might happen while one dreams, but the story is not primarily a vehicle for a particular belief about nightmares or "the old hag," as are the stories in Hufford's book. Personal narrative studies highlight how interlocutors influence both narrative creation and interpretation; for instance, researchers may find themselves "eliciting narratives of a type that [an] informant would never have produced on his own" (Linde 1993:47). Typically, it is the scholar, not the storyteller, who labels a piece of discourse a "memorate" and identifies its theme or embedded belief.

My early work suggested that values or themes constituted traditional content in otherwise idiosyncratic personal narratives (see [Dolby] Stahl 1985); since that time I have looked at how other contexts do much the same. For example, in *Self-Help Books: Why Americans Keep Reading Them*, I found that nearly all self-help books include personal narratives. These narratives, coupled with editorial commentary, are intended to convey themes or values that the authors have drawn from the larger culture and are eager to recycle through this new and popular nonfiction genre (Dolby 2005). However, self-help writers are wary of narratives that appear to express a dominant worldview too clearly (cf. Shuman 2005:54). The aim of self-help writers is to gloss over the shared nature of the themes and values they are promoting and instead offer them as new and necessary. Our goal as researchers, on the other hand, is to make obvious the continuity of themes and values we perceive in the materials we study. Whether in self-help books or in daily life, it is clear that personal narratives use and construct worldview.

Conclusion

The personal narrative remains an especially appealing kind of discourse for scholars in many fields. Thirty years ago Eleanor Wachs found the personal narrative the best way to study the culture of New York City. In 2005, Cornelia Cody found the "New York City Personal Narrative" still among us, loud and strong. This reissue of *Literary Folkloristics and the Personal Narrative* reflects in part a reaffirmation of the important contributions folklore has made to the growing corpus of literature about the personal narrative.

Many research questions can best be illuminated by using the personal narrative as raw data or text. But the concepts that tie the personal narrative to the field of folklore can also help move forward our understanding of folklore theory and research methodology. The concepts of audience and reception theory, the practice of improvisational narrative performance, the cultural frame of reference and its role in conveying narrative meaning, the notion of a cultural thumbprint representing the many groups that have contributed to an individual's cultural knowledge, and the recognizable themes and values that are embedded in personal narratives and inform listeners and researchers about the storyteller's worldview—these research tools have developed most effectively within the context of personal narrative research. My hope is that these concepts, along with the engaging stories recorded in the book, will continue to be useful and provocative to those who read this new printing of *Literary Folkloristics and the Personal Narrative.*

I extend my warmest good wishes and thanks to the volunteer staff at Trickster Press and to Danille Christensen, who read the new Preface, edited it, and offered valuable suggestions. Your faith and hard work are much appreciated.

Bloomington, Indiana
May 2007

Works Cited

Works mentioned in the preceding essay but not found in this reference list can be found in the bibliography at the close of the book.

Abrahams, Roger D.
  2005. Everyday Life: A Poetics of Vernacular Practices. Philadelphia: University of Pennsylvania Press.
Allison, Fred H.
  2004. Remembering a Vietnam War Firefight: Changing Perspectives over Time. *Oral History Review: Journal of the Oral History Association* 31(2):69–83.
Bamberg, Michael G. W., ed.
  1997. Oral Versions of Personal Experience: Three Decades of Narrative Analysis. Special Issue. *Journal of Narrative and Life History* 7(1–4).
Bauman, Richard
  1986. *Story, Performance, and Event: Contextual Studies of Oral Narrative.* New York: Cambridge University Press.
  2004. *A World of Others' Words: Cross-cultural Perspectives on Intertextuality.* Malden, Mass.: Blackwell.
Boenisch-Brednich, Brigitte
  2002. Migration and Narration. *Folklore: Electronic Journal of Folklore* 20:63–76.
Brown, John Seely
  2005. *Storytelling in Organizations: Why Storytelling Is Transforming 21st Century Organizations and Management.* Boston: Elsevier Butterworth-Heinemann.
Brunvand, Jan Harold
  1968. *The Study of American Folklore: An Introduction.* New York: Norton.
Cody, Cornelia
  2005. "Only in New York": The New York City Personal Experience Narrative. *Journal of Folklore Research* 42(2):217–44.
Dégh, Linda
  1972. Folk Narrative. In *Folklore and Folklife: An Introduction*, ed. Richard M. Dorson, pp. 53-83. Chicago: University of Chicago Press.
Dolby, Sandra K.
  2005. *Self-Help Books: Why Americans Keep Reading Them.* Champaign-Urbana: University of Illinois Press.
Dominicé, Pierre
  2000. *Learning from Our Lives: Using Educational Biography with Adults.* San Francisco: Jossey-Bass.
Dorson, Richard M.
  1952. *Bloodstoppers and Bearwalkers: Folk Traditions of the Upper Peninsula.* Cambridge, Mass.: Harvard University Press.
Duranti, Alessandro
  1986. The Audience as Co-Author: An Introduction. *Text* 6:239–47.

Eakin, Paul John
  1999. *How Our Lives Become Stories: Making Selves*. Ithaca: Cornell University Press.
  2004. What Are We Reading When We Read Autobiography? *Narrative* 12:121–32.
Estes, Steve
  2005. Ask and Tell: Gay Veterans, Identity, and Oral History on a Civil Rights Frontier. *Oral History Review: Journal of the Oral History Association* 32(2):21–47.
Feldman, Allen
  2004. Memory Theaters, Virtual Witnessing, and the Trauma-Aesthetic. *Biography: An Interdisciplinary Quarterly* 27(1):163–202.
Frank, Russell
  2003. Folklore in a Hurry: The Community Experience Narrative in Newspaper Coverage of the Loma Prieta Earthquake. *Journal of American Folklore* 116(460):159–75.
Gabbert, Lisa
  2000. Religious Belief and Everyday Knowledge: A Functional Analysis of the Legend Dialectic. *Contemporary Legend: The Journal of the International Society for Contemporary Legend Research* 3:108–26.
Golden, Deborah
  2001. Storytelling the Future: Israelis, Immigrants and the Imagining of Community. *Anthropological Quarterly* 75(1):7–35.
Goldstein, Diane
  2004. *Once Upon a Virus*. Logan: Utah State University Press.
Gone, Joseph P.
  2006. "As If Reviewing His Life": Bull Lodge's Narrative and the Mediation of Self-Representation. *American Indian Culture and Research Journal* 30(1):67–86.
Goodwin, Janna L.
  2004. The Productive Postshow: Facilitating, Understanding and Optimizing Personal Narratives in Audience Talk Following a Personal Narrative Performance. *Theatre Topics* 14(1):317–38.
Hinkle, Maija
  2006. Latvian-Americans in the Post-Soviet Era: Cultural Factors on Return Migration in Oral History Interviews. *Journal of Baltic Studies* 37(1):48–67.
Hufford, David
  1982. *The Terror That Comes in the Night*. Philadelphia: University of Pennsylvania Press.
Johnstone, Barbara
  1990. *Stories, Community, and Place: Narratives from Middle America*. Bloomington: Indiana University Press.
Katz, Arlene M., and John Shotter

2000. For Another First Time: "Instructive Spontaneities" in Dialogical Moments. *Narrative Inquiry* 10(1):253–63.

Kelly, Marsha C. S.
2005. Continuing Maricopa Identities: Gila River Reservation, Arizona. *Journal of the Southwest* 47(1):47–56.

Killoran, John B.
2003. The Gnome in the Front Yard and Other Public Figurations: Genres of Self-Representation on Personal Home Pages. *Biography: An Interdisciplinary Quarterly* 26:66–83.

Kirshenblatt-Gimblett, Barbara
1989. Authoring Lives. *Journal of Folklore Research* 26:123–49.

Langellier, Kristin M.
1989. Personal Narratives: Perspectives on Theory and Research. *Text and Performance Quarterly* 9:243–76.

Langellier, Kristin M., and Eric E. Peterson
2004. *Storytelling in Daily Life: Performing Narrative*. Philadelphia: Temple University Press.

Lawless, Elaine J.
1993. *Holy Women, Wholly Women: Sharing Ministries of Wholeness through Life Stories and Reciprocal Ethnography*. Philadelphia: University of Pennsylvania Press.
2001. *Women Escaping Violence: Empowerment through Narrative*. Columbia: University of Missouri Press.

Linde, Charlotte
1993. *Life Stories: The Creation of Coherence*. New York: Oxford University Press.

MacAulay, Suzanne P.
2004. Diaspora by Degree: Narrative and Performance in Interviews of Expatriates from Wanganui, New Zealand. *Journal of American Folklore* 117(465):262–87.

Magogodi, Kgafela Oa
2002. Refiguring the Body: Performance of Identity in Mapantsula and Fools. *Theatre Research International* 27(3):243–58.

Marander-Eklund, Lena
2002. Narrative Style: How to Dramatize a Story. *Arv: Nordic Yearbook of Folklore* 58:113–23.

Meyer, Rachel S.
2000. Fluid Subjectivities: Intertextuality and Women's Narrative Performance in North India. *Journal of American Folklore* 113(448):144–63.

Mills, Margaret
2004. *Alf Laylah Farsi* in Performance: Afghanistan 1975. *Fabula* 45(3–4):294–310.

Minchin, Timothy J.

2004. "It Tears the Heart Right Out of You": Memories of Striker Replacement at International Paper Company in De Pere, Wisconsin, 1987–88. *Oral History Review: Journal of the Oral History Association* 31(2):1–27.

Miyake, Lynne K.
2001. Interactive Narrators and Performative Readers: Gendered Interfacing in Heian Narratives. *Women & Performance: A Journal of Feminist Theory* 12(1 [23]):23–42.

Mortensen, Camilla H.
2005. (Eco)Mimesis and the Ethics of the Ethnographic Presentation. *Journal of American Folklore* 118(467):105–20.

Norkunas, Martha
2004. Narratives of Resistance and the Consequences of Resistance. *Journal of Folklore Research* 41(2/3):105–23.

Noy, Chaim
2007. *A Narrative Community: Voices of Israeli Backpackers*. Detroit: Wayne State University Press.

Ochs, Elinor, and Lisa Capps
2001. *Living Narrative: Creating Lives in Everyday Storytelling*. Cambridge, Mass.: Harvard University Press.

Oring, Elliott
1984. Dyadic Traditions. *Journal of Folklore Research* 21:19–28.
1987. Generating Lives: The Construction of an Autobiography. *Journal of Folklore Research* 24:241–62.

Oring, Elliott, ed.
1986. *Folk Groups and Folklore Genres: An Introduction*. Logan: Utah State University Press.

Personal Narratives Group, ed.
1989. *Interpreting Women's Lives: Feminist Theory and Personal Narratives*. Bloomington: Indiana University Press.

Quah, Sy Ren
2002. Performance in Alienated Voices: Mode of Narrative in Gao Xingjian's Theater. *Modern Chinese Literature and Culture* 14(2):51–98.

Robins, Steven
2006. From "Rights" to "Ritual": AIDS Activism in South Africa. *American Anthropologist* 108(2):312–23.

Rouverol, Alicia J.
2003. Collaborative Oral History in a Correctional Setting: Promise and Pitfalls. *Oral History Review: Journal of the Oral History Association* 30(1):61–86.

Ryan, J. S.
2004. Oral History, Memory, and the Folklore of Contemporary (Australian) Poverty. *Australian Folklore: A Yearly Journal of Folklore Studies* 19:78–82.

Sawin, Patricia E.
1992. "Right Here is a Good Christian Lady": Reported Speech in Personal

Narratives. *Text and Performance Quarterly* 12:193–211.

2004. *Listening for a Life: A Dialogic Ethnography of Bessie Eldreth through Her Songs and Stories*. Logan: Utah State University Press.

Schiffrin, Deborah

2003. We Knew That's It: Retelling the Turning Point of a Narrative. *Discourse Studies* 5:535–61.

Schreiber, Dorothee

2004. Salmon Farming and Salmon People: Identity and Environment in the Leggatt Inquiry. *American Indian Culture and Research Journal* 27(4):79–103.

Scruggs, T. M.

2001–2. "Come on in North Side, You're Just in Time": Musical-Verbal Performance and the Negotiation of Ethnically Segregated Social Space. *Current Musicology* 71–73:179–199.

Scuro, Jennifer

2004. Exploring Personal History: A Case Study of an Italian Immigrant Woman. *Oral History Review: Journal of the Oral History Association* 31(1):43-69.

Sebre, Sandra

2005. Political and Relational: Autobiographical Narrations of Latvian Women across Three Generations. *Journal of Baltic Studies* 36(1):69–82.

Shuman, Amy

1986. *Storytelling Rights: The Uses of Oral and Written Texts by Urban Adolescents*. New York: Cambridge University Press.

2005. *Other People's Stories: Entitlement Claims and the Critique of Empathy*. Urbana: University of Illinois Press.

Swora, Maria Gabrielle

2001. Narrating Community: The Creation of Social Structure in Alcoholics Anonymous through the Performance of Autobiography. *Narrative Inquiry* 11(2):363–84.

Thompson, Paul

2000. *The Voice of the Past: Oral History*. 3rd ed. Oxford: Oxford University Press.

Tompkins, Jane, ed.

1980. *Reader-Response Criticism: From Formalism to Post-structuralism*. Baltimore: Johns Hopkins University Press.

Tranguyen, Trangdai

2002. From Childhood Storytelling to Oral History Interviews. *Oral History Review: Journal of the Oral History Association* 29(2):119–26.

Traphagan, John W.

2004. Interpretations of Elder Suicide, Stress, and Dependency among Rural Japanese. *Ethnology: An International Journal of Cultural and Social Anthropology* 43(4):315–29.

Wachs, Eleanor

1988. *Crime-Victim Stories: New York City's Urban Folklore*. Bloomington: Indiana

University Press.

Wachter, Phyllis E., and William Todd Schultz

2005. Annual Bibliography of Works about Life Writing, 2004–2005. *Biography: An Interdisciplinary Quarterly* 28:558–676.

Waco, Fugich

2002. Tradition, Memory, Creativity, and the Self in the Personal Narratives among the Borana of Kenya: Conformity and Conflict. *Fabula* 43(1–2):18–34.

Wolf-Knuts, Ulrika

2003. Contrasts as a Narrative Technique in Emigrant Accounts. *Folklore* 114(1):91–105.

Yankah, Kwesi

2004. Narrative in Times of Crisis: AIDS Stories in Ghana. *Journal of Folklore Research* 41(2/3):181–98.

Yelenevskaya, Maria N., and Larisa Fialkova

2004. My Poor Cousin, My Feared Enemy: The Image of Arabs in Personal Narratives of Former Soviets in Israel. *Folklore* 115(1):77–98.

Zecker, Robert M.

2002. "Not Communists Exactly, but Sort of Like Non-Believers": The Hidden Radical Transcript of Slovak Immigrants in Philadelphia, 1890–1954. *Oral History Review: Journal of the Oral History Association* 29(1):1–37.

Zeitlin, Steve, and Ilana Harlow

2001. *Giving a Voice to Sorrow: Personal Responses to Death and Mourning.* New York: Penguin.

Zumwalt, Rosemary Lévy, and Isaac Jack Lévy

2002. Making Atlanta Home: Recollections of Place through Narrative. *Folklore Forum* 33(1/2):67–81.

Acknowledgments to the 1989 Edition

Folklore is a special discipline. This is a subjective statement, and the only real defense I can offer for this claim is a demonstration of why it is special to me. In large measure, that is what this book is about—what a trained folklorist finds so very appealing about the field of folklore study. I enjoy listening to stories, and my training as a folklorist helps me enjoy them even more. In this book I try to lay bare the process whereby I hear and enjoy personal narratives. So my first round of thanks goes to all the people who have been instrumental in my training as a folklorist and student of literature, especially the faculty and students who were a part of my graduate experience at the Folklore Institute.

Less specific but equally important is the debt I owe to the larger academic community I have been a part of over the ensuing years. This study does, I hope, reflect my participation in this larger community. Many of the concerns I address are or have been in the air among my colleagues at Indiana, at professional meetings, and in the pages of publications in folklore and adjacent fields. I am not breaking new ground in attending to text and context, in attempting auto-ethnography, in analyzing the social base of seemingly idiosyncratic stories. Yet, the way these ideas come together in my mind and in response to these particular stories is unique and, I hope, instructive. The constellation of traditions, skills, and ideas that inform my interpretation reflect my personal experience as well as my assimilation of the concerns and methods of literary folkloristics. Folklore studies provide the discipline its own best examples of reflexive historiographic case books.

I am grateful to the many people whose talents and energy benefited me and the project represented by this book. Some were helpful primarily through their own scholarly discourse, both formal and informal: especially, Richard Bauman, David Bleich, Linda Dégh, Alan Dundes, Gary Alan Fine, Robert Georges, and Henry Glassie. Others offered personal support or practical advice when it was needed, especially Richard Dorson, before he died. Mark Workman gave me an invaluable close reading of the manuscript, and I very much appreciate his suggestions, large and small.

The copyeditor at Indiana University Press did a wonderful job. Suzanne Hull and Michelle Rhee did the illustrations. The Folklore Institute secretaries, Ruth Aten, Velma Carmichael, and Syd Grant, all helped with some parts of the manuscript, at least before I finally mastered word processing. Joan Catapano, senior sponsoring editor, and Roberta Diehl, managing editor, were my patient and supportive contacts at Indiana University Press. I thank them and their staffs heartily for their warm and professional interactions. I am grateful to the professional journals that published my earlier research on personal narrative, and I am especially appreciative of the many well-wishing friends who have listened to and commented on my papers at professional meetings. You know who you are, and your interest has made all the difference.

My deepest appreciation goes to the two wonderful storytellers who share their stories in these pages—Loretta Dolby and Larry Scheiber, both of Huntington, Indiana. My sincerest apologies go to them as well; inevitably my uses and interpretations of their stories cannot do justice to their talent and creativity. I am happy to thank my sister, Carol, once again for all of her help in creating an effective fieldwork situation. My husband, Mark, and my daughter, Alexis, have offered a constant supply of support and distraction, whichever was needed. Above all, I thank my parents for the faith and love that nurtured initiative for such a project in the first place.

Prologue

One time we were having a spelling bee and one of the "fine ladies" from the Church was giving the words. Finally she said one word I just didn't know—"ee-MINCE, ee-MINCE"—just like that [said in a high, squeaky voice]. Several people in front of me sat down. Finally there was just me and a bigger boy left. And she said it again—"ee-MINCE, ee-MINCE." The boy couldn't spell it, so he sat down and it was my turn. She said the word again—"ee-MINCE, ee-MINCE." I looked at her, and I said [in a loud, disgusted tone], "Immense—I-M-M-E-N-S-E—Immense!" And I won the spelling bee.

A personal narrative told by
my grandmother in the late 1950s

The saddest day of my life was when my grandmother died. We used to take walks—over to the college woods or past Mollie Cupp's house. And she told me stories—things my father used to do when he was a boy, things her family did on the farm when she was growing up—so long ago—things like making bricks from yellow clay or finding arrowheads in the fields, or some things I never really understood at all, like castrating pigs. Often we would sit on her porch swing—Grandma lived right next door to us in her "little brown house"—and she would snap beans or pit cherries and tell me about how she learned to play the piano just by picking out the chords to match the hymns she had to accompany at Sunday School. And she would come over and pound out "Oh Them Golden Slippers" on our old upright.

Some things always remind me of Grandma—poems by James Whitcomb Riley, the smell of coffee and toast in the morning, certain songs like "Blest Be the Tie That Binds" and "Away in a Manger," the old Seth Thomas clock that used to hang on her wall, the Santa Fe railway that used to carry her out to California to visit Aunt Mary. But most of all, I feel like she is really still here and a part of me when I think of the stories she used to tell. In fact, these stories are perhaps the more precious reminders, since they scarcely have an existence outside my memory. Oh, occasionally someone in the family will refer to one of Grandma's stories, and for a brief time, we indulge an exclusive nostalgia. But, for the most part, I must rehearse them to myself for my own personal enjoyment, for Grandma told stories that nobody else knew, except maybe a few family members who had heard her tell them before.

My grandmother told personal narratives, stories based on real experiences, interesting little anecdotes about herself. Unlike fairy tales or legends or tall tales or jokes, personal narratives are not usually perpetuated in tradition much past the lifetime of the stories' main character. They may for a while enter the repertoire of the extended family or a tight-knit group of friends, but eventually the stories fade, for much of their color came from the animating voice of the person who had the experience. The "personal" is a magic ingredient in such stories. For the teller and the listeners, so much of what a personal narrative means is outside the narrative itself and inside the intangible memories and feelings engendered by the relationship between the teller and listener and the teller's personal world.

Personal narratives are best heard as they live—on the warm breath of the teller, in the resonant shell of the listener's ear. Then their purpose is clear: like any literary performance, they are there to move us, to excite us, to entertain and teach us. In the world outside of academe, the storyteller's responsibility is simply to be an adequate practitioner of the literary genre he chooses. It is the responsibility of the listener or reader to be moved, to respond. Sometimes the narrator takes some of that responsibility upon himself; he is moved by his own story and performance, and his own response leads his listener to a shared emotion. I can tell you that I responded many times to my grandmother's story of the spelling bee. I was amused, I was impressed; no matter how many times I heard the story, I never was bored by it but rather was always intrigued by my image of her as a young woman and touched by her willingness to create a story from her life and share it with me. I can insist that she was an "adequate practitioner" of the genre called personal narrative. And, in terms ill suited to scholarly analysis but nonetheless meaningful in the real world, I can easily defend her success as a "literary" artist. For the one overwhelming and undeniable fact about her spelling bee story is that my memory of it brings her immediately before me, conjures her up, if you will, just as she was known to me when I last heard her tell the story.

When a person tells a personal narrative, he or she invites someone to know him, to know her, intimately, personally. Such a person is very vulnerable; he may be repulsed or misunderstood. Like physically intimate encounters, such verbal encounters carry the risk of rejection along with the promise of pleasure. Usually, however, a person tells personal narratives only to those people who want to know the teller better. This is not a conscious motive, of course, but it is a basic directing strategy of the genre. One gets to know someone else by sharing experience; *intimacy* is our word for the exciting sensation that comes with our perception of someone else in our personal world. We "know" others and assume that they "know" us when we believe we have shared a similar perception of a mutual experience. The knowledge one gains as a listener when personal narratives are told brings with it the sensation of intimacy, our feeling that the telling and the listening are an exclusive exchange where we come very close to seeing each other's reality. The successful teller of personal narratives engages the listener in an adventure—not simply the plot of a story, but rather the shared activity of exploring the teller's world, the teller's identity.

The teller's identity is the listener's treasure; there is a treasure in each story—not the text, not the transcript, but the experience of hearing another voice, of seeing—if just for a moment—someone else in a subjective world. Like my grandmother, people who tell personal narratives celebrate the intimacy that lets their listeners discover their identity. I knew my grandmother very well. As I was growing up, I saw her nearly every day. There were many things I did not know about her. In her stories she never mentioned that her hair had been auburn when she was a young woman, not that it ever really mattered. But I am sure when she told her spelling bee story, she saw herself standing there tall and straight with her auburn hair pulled up into a knot the way girls did then. When I try to visualize the story, I see her with short white hair and gold-rim glasses, about seventy-five years old, standing near the old wooden wash bench she used as a coffee table, and looking east out of the triple-set casement windows in her house across the yard toward our kitchen window. The story happened for me there in her living room; that is where I learned to know a little more about her. I did not learn (then) that her hair had been auburn, but I did learn that she was not easily intimidated. I learned that she was a good speller and proud of her knowledge, that she enjoyed competition, that she was not afraid to be "smarter than a boy." I learned that she had little use for fancy women who tried to project an air of superiority through affected speech. And there were some things she did not talk about in the story that she allowed me to fill in for myself—things which demonstrated subtly how well she knew me and how much she assumed I already knew about her.

The "text" she gave me was a map, a sketch abstracted from the multidimensional reality of her experience, her culture, her self. Critics applaud the novelist's careful development of a fictional character. How much more amazing was my grandmother's gentle artistry that found a way to glimpse reality! For the character in a personal narrative is neither a crafted fiction nor an exaggerated stereotype. My grandmother knew who she was, yet she wished to explore, even at seventy-five, who she was becoming. Her story of the spelling bee was imbued with new meaning each time she told it. And that delicate map—the text—how many invisible fibers of meaning attached to its sticky surface! But I could not see all of those fibers, only those we shared. And like the reader of literature, I must bring to the text my own strands of meaning. The map must be paced by my feet and "read" through my perceptions. Yet the artistry of the personal narrative exploits precisely this dilemma. My grandmother knew tacitly those aspects of our culture, our family's past, her life and my life we already shared. By inviting me to participate, by demanding that I match her unspoken allusions to her personal world, she ensured some correspondence in meaning, some real transmission of the reality she felt. The treasure I gained by pacing the map was a glimpse of the pearl of great price, another person's soul.

1.
Introduction
Literary Folkloristics

Folklore and Literature

It is no easier to interpret a folklore text than a literary text. The process of interpreting is a complex and demanding one in either case. Methodologies that scholars use to interpret literary or folklore texts are increasingly sophisticated and microscopic. Among literary critics, the influence of deconstructive analysis and reader-response theory has assured this hallmark of complexity, and among folklorists, the rise of performance theory has also determined that the interpretation of texts will never again be a simple matter.

Both literary critics and folklorists have developed methodologies that allow them to identify and explore the complex relationships that produce the resonance of meaning in a literary or folkloristic text. In this study I am proposing an interpretive methodology that integrates these two contemporary approaches. This perspective—"literary folkloristics"—is an interpretive scheme that capitalizes upon the complexity of and basic similarity among the theories of folkloristic performance, deconstructive criticism, and reader-response theory. Literary folkloristics is an integrative criticism which identifies the many private or collective traditions that function as meaningful allusions in the reader or listener's interpretation of a literary or folkloric text. Exploring the relationship between these traditions and the listener/reader's interpretation of the text is the objective of this kind of criticism. Its aim is to demonstrate how specific textual interpretations evolve for given interpreters of a "literary" text.

In contrast, earlier folklore-and-literature studies have generally been applications of standard critical approaches either to verbal texts that can be studied as though they were literature—e.g., the ballad, the fairy tale, the fable—or to works of literature that are assumed to "contain" folklore. For example, one might consider the works of Mark Twain and endeavor to identify folklore as (1) the basis for certain mythic themes or motifs, (2) the basis for the plot or subplots, (3) the basis for narrative form (e.g., the tall tale), (4) the source of "local color" in the stylization of each work, or (5) the traditions that are used throughout the works as common allusions. In 1957, Richard M. Dorson proposed a system for identifying folklore in literature, and in the three decades since then, identification studies using some adaptation of this system have made up a large portion of the total research on folklore-and-literature topics (Dorson 1957; for examples, see Jones 1984 and Baer 1986).

Methodological Characteristics of Literary Folkloristics

Literary folkloristics as a methodology builds upon this research background but offers a radically different perspective vis-à-vis the *agent* (person) presumed to be identifying these traditions and the *process* of interpretation. In theory, it is the listener who identifies the traditions, and it is the experience of hearing the text that is translated into an interpretation. Literary folkloristics does identify traditional elements in a text, but it goes beyond conventional folklore-and-literature studies in asserting that the range of traditions significant in the listener's hearing of the story is larger and more inclusive than previously assumed and that the process of hearing the text is a creative act in which the listener's own large store of cultural and personal resources is used to produce a unified resonance of meaning. This perspective does not adopt wholesale the well-established system of literary semiotics (though it does benefit from a number of its insights); rather, it integrates the perspectives of folkoristic performance theory, reception theory, and deconstructive criticism by examining the relationships among (1) cultural and private frames of reference, (2) the allusions growing out of those frames, (3) the text, (4) the experience of hearing the text, and (5) the listener's interpretation of the text or performance.

Critical methodologies presuppose some guiding theoretical inquiries. In this case, literary folkloristics could be characterized by its conceptual concern with the issue of text versus context, by its analytical attention to the practice of hearing the text, and by its fundamental attachment to lore or tradition.

The Issue of Text versus Context

A primary characteristic of this methodology is its ambivalence toward the issue of text versus context. This issue is not one that literary folkloristics presumes to solve; rather, the controversy is simply a primary segment of the background necessary for understanding why this methodology seems an appropriate replacement for earlier analytical schemes. Among folklorists, the issue has grown out of a perception of "oral literary" performances presented within specific situations or contexts. As Alan Dundes suggested two decades ago in his article "Texture, Text, and Context," there are three analytical domains that should concern the folklorist, but it is the text that has most often been the basis of study (1964b). In the late 1960s and early 1970s, the "contextualists" brought a new focus to folklore research, and this new perspective in turn sparked a series of reactions calling for a reappraisal of the importance of the text (see Ben-Amos 1972; Wilgus 1971; Jones 1979; Georges 1980; Zan 1982). In literary studies the controversy has been incorporated into the very fabric of deconstructive criticism. One of the best examples of this is Barbara Johnson's essay on Derrida's reading of Jacques Lacan's reading of Poe's "Purloined Letter," in which each piece of writing serves as a frame for the next (1980:Essay 7). Whether designated a "frame" or a "context," increasingly the surroundings of the text vie for attention equal to if not greater than that given to the object supposedly at the base of the study.

The text/context dichotomy has stimulated discussion of "What is the text?" in both literary and folkloristic scholarship. And it has provoked a much more careful consideration of what the author or teller uses—what he invents or borrows or adapts—and presents through the performance we recognize as a text. Particularly the "rhetorical" literary theories of Wayne C. Booth (1961) and Kenneth Burke (1941) have assumed that the author's use of various "resources" determines what the text becomes. And among folklorists, Roger Abrahams and Richard Bauman have been primary advocates of a textual criticism that assumes cultural and individual control of the rules and resources available to the teller in the performance of a text.[1] Even when it has not been clear what constitutes the text, there has been a consistent assertion that the relationship between the text and the context is intimate and significant. In studying either folklore or literature, the scholar's hope has been that with careful attention one can discover the "rules" and content resources the performer uses to tell or write an effective story in a given context. Like Dell Hymes's research (1960, 1975) into an "ethnography of speaking," performance theory and rhetorical criticism have aimed at the identification of the tacitly shared rules of effective narrative performance tapped by the successful storyteller in either medium.

The problems inherent in this growing effort to identify and demonstrate in the fullest detail what is in the text, or in fact what is going on in the performance *represented* by the text, are impressively addressed by Elizabeth Fine in her book *The Folklore Text: From Performance to Print* (1984). Fine discusses a number of schemes people have tried in their efforts to represent on the printed page the actual, observable behavior involved in the performance of an oral narrative. And she peers below the surface of each scheme to see what conceptual expectations are influencing each scholar to select the scheme he has chosen. She demonstrates and defends her own scheme as well, but in every case, it seems, the printed page inevitably fails to do what the collector-transcriber hopes it could do. No text, not even one weighted with intricately coded analytical information, can demonstrate even the relatively well understood relationship between the specific text and the context of a conventional performance ethnography. And for other kinds of context, the frustrating complexity is even more striking.

It is easy to see why a concern with context would arise as theorists explored those aspects of the text apparent to scholars but not easily made visible to other readers of a given text. In folkloristics, this inadequacy of the text is clearest in studies of proverbs. For example, a proverb such as "Look before you leap" is nearly meaningless without some indication of the context in which it is used. This is context in its simplest, clearest sense. Even more striking is the effect of varying contexts on the actual verbal makeup of a narrative text. Richard Bauman, in his excellent study of Texas storytellers, compares three separate tellings of the same story by one man. He accounts for some of the apparent differences from one telling to the next by pointing to changes in the storyteller himself (over the ten-year period involved), changes in the setting and audience, and changes in the aesthetic requirements of storytelling (1986:78-111).

Literary scholars deal with contexts of an even less obvious sort. Contexts, in this case, are conventionally recognized categories of influence, and for any specific literary performance these contexts will be perceived as exerting pressure within the creative process and ultimately influencing the text. The writer's skill in invoking effective rules of rhetoric, his familarity with his chosen genre, his awareness of current tastes, even the quality of his personal life all affect the performance which becomes the text others read as literature.

The separation of such contexts from the texts under scrutiny, while never achieved in actuality, is continually invoked in heuristic exercises in the hope of learning more about how writers or tellers are able to tell their stories. One significant contextual concern shared by literary studies and folkloristics is the identification of genres or "generic context" and the conventions it implies. For most literary critics, a text must be identified as intentionally representative of a specific genre before it can even be approached for the sake of interpretation. An immediate problem arises, however, one which is directly tied to the perceived relationship between the concept of any genre and its representative texts. Paul Hernadi (1972) identifies the problem as "Müller's remarkable quandary," to wit: "How can I define [a genre] before I know on which works to base the definition, yet how can I know on which works to base the definition before I have defined [the genre]?"[2] For the scholar it is not at all clear *from the text* which came first, the genre or the text. Nevertheless, because of the frame of "text versus context," literary critics are compelled to identify a generic context which has influenced the storyteller. The problem is, as Müller's quandary suggests, that the generic context cannot be known until a representative text is known. The text and context are mutually dependent.

Another kind of context literary critics have in the past pursued with great energy is the biographical context represented by the author of the text. What in the lives of Dickens, Hemingway, Lawrence, Dickinson, or Joyce allows us to understand their texts more fully? In fact, isn't Stephen really Joyce, isn't Nick Adams really Hemingway, isn't the "I" of Dickinson's poems really Emily Dickinson? Or to reverse it, isn't "truth" represented by the author and "fiction" by the works he or she creates? Isn't the author's biography the real text and the works he or she creates simply an "effect" of the text at work in a literary medium? A study such as John Livingston Lowes's *Road to Xanadu* (1955) could be written only by someone who viewed Coleridge's intellectual and personal life itself as the text he investigates.

For critics willing to look to the author of a text, the problem of distinguishing text and context becomes very muddied indeed. For the biographical context of a work is not so much an influence on the work as it is inherent in it and, like poor Antonio's blood, inseparable from the precious pound of flesh it sustains. Any influence study that assumes real historical connections, any biographical study that views the author of a work as anything other than an unconscious medium at the service of some greater god, must finally, or better yet initially, tear through the false membrane that separates text from context. And yet a holistic text, such as that envisioned by Elizabeth Fine or even more ambitiously by Roland Barthes (1970), frustrates even the most painstaking analysis.

One essential assumption in literary studies is that a text may be, in fact must be, viewed within its aesthetic context, the context of contemporary stylistics or taste. Arnold's famous "touchstone" theory is implicated here.[3] The aesthetic context not only suggests what choices are open to the creator of a text but also determines what characteristic choices are deemed "good" by the people who receive and appreciate the text. Thus, a written piece is called literature if it fits easily into the canon representative of a standard aesthetic context or current taste—even at the extreme where a written piece was not intended as a literary work, as in "found" literature, which is simply *perceived* as bound to an identifiable aesthetic context (see Strelka 1978).

Similarly, in folklore studies, texts are often separable from their conversational context only on the basis of the researcher's recognition and use of an aesthetic context. John McDowell (1974), for example, identifies "informal narratives" in the midst of ongoing conversations through reference to the presumed canons of coherency and delight. The stories are described as autonomous narratives through an appeal to the aesthetic context. This context requires that the storyteller make stylistic choices that maintain coherency and produce delight for an audience that has supposedly long since incorporated these same canons as touchstones in their sense of aesthetic preference. Nevertheless, even such a tacitly recognized notion of "style" is not a clear concept. Like genre, style is a domain or context that cannot be identified apart from the text that illustrates it—the "remarkable quandary" once again. As Bennison Gray (1969) has demonstrated at great length, ultimately there is no such thing as style, or more precisely for our purposes, the aesthetic context is simply a heuristic convention that helps us identify an artistic text.

And since the rise of reception theory and deconstructionism, the very notion of "text" has been challenged, or rather transformed, to identify not the printed words or recorded performance but rather the intangible "mind" that reads or hears. Context *and* text, if they are separate in our analysis, are subsumed within the mind of the individual—whether that individual is the creator of the story or the reader/listener. In the past, in anthropology, for example, one spoke of an item in its ethnographic context, its historical context, its psychocultural context. And in folklore studies, a primary consideration has been the context of tradition perceived as maintaining the item within the active memory of at least some individuals. A contemporary holistic study of an item will take into account all of these contexts—ultimately to the effect that the distinctions between text and context become invisible to the researcher.

The contexts do themselves "deconstruct" if they are used too rigorously as tools for understanding the text. Thus Dan Ben-Amos (1972) contends that there is no such thing as "tradition," Bennison Gray (1969) that there is no such thing as "style," Robert Georges (1969) that there is no such thing as "the story." Instead, the context of tradition is, as Ben-Amos suggests, an "analytical construct." Likewise the style of a narration or, in fact, the very notion of a distinguishable item such as a story—these are as well simply reflective of the scholar's *view* of "the item in context." Philosophically both the item and the context are conceptualizations, neither one more real than the other and neither one a more virtuous abstraction than the other.

A question which this unresolved controversy raises for this study is whether the same ambiguity prevails when one considers how a story is *heard* (or read) rather than how it is performed or created. That is, if the methodology is contrived relative to the listener or reader rather than the teller or writer, is there still a problem in identifying what is the text? I would say the problem is indeed the mirror image of the previous one. The historical development of the text/context question on this "response" or "reception" side of the creative performance is closely tied to the emergence of reader-response theory and a recognition of the problems in identifying the text.

Consider, for example, the chain of arguments tied to the essay by W. K. Wimsatt and Monroe Beardsley (1954) titled "The Intentional Fallacy." In criticizing Wimsatt and Beardsley's essay, Frank Cioffi suggests that "once [one is] in possession of biographical data it is difficult to be sure what is in the work itself" (1973:231). Within these "biographical data," Cioffi includes a number of contexts mentioned above, especially as those contexts are conceived of as functioning frames of reference in the author's mind. The distinction between what Wimsatt and Beardsley call "internal" and "external" evidence becomes untenable. If Eliot's notes to *The Waste Land* become internal evidence—"part of the poem"—then what is *not* part of the poem? Cioffi asks, "Does it follow that since the effectiveness of certain lines in *Prufrock* depends upon familiarity with Marvell's *Coy Mistress*, then Marvell's poem should be considered part of Eliot's?" (223). Or, less peevishly, is it a part of our sense of the "meaning" of Eliot's poem if we know that Eliot knew Marvell's poem?

Where is the text and where is its meaning? Literary critics are not yet ready to make the text the inclusive body of internal evidence that helps create meaning, that puts "a field of force round a work," as Cioffi says. Biographical context is in theory still separable from text in literary studies. However, the related notion of "the author's intention" or "the text as repository" (of an intended and permanent message) has come seriously under fire. In other words, though some literary critics, such as E. D. Hirsch (1967), are willing to accept the idea of "authorial intention" as a necessary convention in any interpretation of literature, others—the reader-response critics—are not convinced that the notion is an essential one. They contend that since the "intentional fallacy" prohibits anything but pure speculation about what the author *really* meant, we should turn instead to the reader.[4] Similarly, in developing a literary folkloristic methodology (Stahl 1985), I have emphasized the listener's response as an alternative point of view, one that might benefit our efforts to interpret oral literary performance.

Hearing the Text

Zealots of reader-response criticism argue that meaning *is* in the mind of the reader; that is where meaning is created, and it is there (in the reader's mind) that the critic must look for the meaning associated with a particular text (i.e., meaning does not reside *in the text*). The closest a critic can come to the "seat" of meaning, according to reader-response critics, is in a new kind of text—the critical or responsive exegesis of "the reader." Thus David Bleich (1975) and Norman Holland (1975) solicit new texts from readers of varying degrees of literary sophistication and in turn use those texts (the readers' responses) in their own integrative discussion of meaning growing out of this expanded presentation of the text.

In folklore studies this emphasis on meaning articulated by the audience rather than the author of a text was anticipated in Alan Dundes's suggestion (1966) that the fieldworker collecting texts should also try to elicit "oral literary criticism" in response to the text. Such oral literary criticism, Dundes contends, could come from the storyteller himself or his audience. In either case the implication is that the text belongs to "oral tradition" and that the folk who tell *or* listen to it are—in this instance—the ones who must "read" or interpret the text.

Implicit in this is the assumption that some (not all) significant meaning that can be associated with the text is present and discoverable in the minds of those who receive the text in a natural (typical) situation. Or more precisely, the folklorist analyzing an oral text may—in fact, should—expand his text to include the commentary of typical listeners. We cannot, in other words, simply assume that the significant evaluation of a story is contained in the teller's text. Rather, the meaning is "housed" in the listeners' usually unspoken interpretations of the text. If the fieldworker can elicit these interpretations, then the text he offers will be more complete. Oral literary criticism is not simply secondary or corroborative data to be used by the scholar; it is a real and significant part of the item (text) the scholar must now address.

The inevitable result of such a notion, unfortunately, is that the text appropriate for critical analysis becomes very cumbersome. And this bulkiness is simply increased by the folklorist's sense of fair play. That is, if, for example, folklorist Tom Burns collects a text *and* the commentary of listeners or others who "know" the item and the teller, he is obliged to present the whole interview in which the commentary is elicited. For in fact the new text that he presents to his own readers must exhibit in a straightforward manner the presuppositions that directed his own line of questioning. His own readers must be given the "whole text," to which they in turn can respond with such interpretations as, for example, "at this point Burns was leading his informant toward an articulation of a thematic concern the informant may not have perceived at all; what we really see here is Burns' own response to the text, his assumption that the joke is about infidelity and that the teller projects his own concern with adulterous desires onto the character in the joke."[5]

The "deconstruction" could of course go on forever. There is the danger of losing sight of the critic's goal altogether through such an enterprise, for meaning remains hidden even in an expanded text such as this. The critic hopes to present an interpretation and persuade his readers to accept it. If he does not in some way focus his readers' attention on those aspects of the whole text he considers meaningful, he will have simply presented a larger text; he will not have articulated even the meaning *he sees* in the larger text, nor will he be any closer to the "covenanted" meaning of the folklore item itself. The paradox is, as literary critics have found, that the critic cannot get into the mind of the author or even the mind of the audience or listener, and yet at every turn he cannot escape the encapsulation of his own mind. The critic can no more know the response of the listener than he can know the intentions of the author. His interpretation is ultimately subjective even if he lets oral literary criticism inform his discussion.

In anthropology, this same problem is usually regarded as a conflict between emic and etic analysis. Emic analysis is "from the native's point of view," while etic analysis is from the "outsider's" cross-cultural perspective. Anthropologist Clifford Geertz (1976) admits to a preference for terminology borrowed from the field of psychoanalysis: Heinz Kohut has suggested the terms *experience-near* and *experience-distant* for the concepts of emic and etic respectively, and Geertz adopts these terms because to him they convey more clearly a sense of the *degree* of difference between rather than the polar opposition of the two concepts.[6] Geertz argues that the notion of "experience-near" identifies things as "close" to the informant whenever the knowledge involved is un-self-conscious or covert: "People use experience-near concepts spontaneously, unselfconsciously, as it were colloquially; they do not, except fleetingly and on occasion, recognize that there are any 'concepts' involved at all. That is what experience-near means—that ideas and the realities they inform are naturally and indissolubly bound up together" (224).

A basic tenet of literary folkloristics is that there are numerous conventions or traditions that are thus used—"spontaneously, unselfconsciously"—by the tellers and listeners who participate in a narrative performance. These traditions represent experience-near or emic concepts. People know how to use these concepts, but the concepts are maintained within the tacit dimension.

There is little motivation to recognize or describe the concepts themselves so long as they function adequately. Genre, on the other hand, is one concept storytellers and listeners may well be aware of; they may identify the concept or its subcategories by name, e.g., legends, jokes, anecdotes. More commonly, however, important concepts remain covert functional entities. In this study of personal narratives, one very significant emic concept is what in literary studies would be called an *allusion*. In the academic or etic system, an allusion "is a reference, explicit or indirect, to a person, place, or event, or to another literary work or passage."[7] Within an emic system of narrative performance and reception, the allusion is assumed and relied upon as the fundamental stylistic convention supporting the narrative, its performance, and its reception.

Allusions: Perceptions of Tradition

To speak of allusions is to assume the concept of tradition, and an attachment to tradition or lore departs from the lessons of modern deconstructionism. Actually, the attachment represents the "old" ties to conventional folklore and literature study; it is deconstructionism that is a departure from this fundamental perspective. Geoffrey Hartman, in commenting on Jacques Derrida's indelible effect upon literary criticism, says: "It [Derrida's critical commentary] is so radical that, despite its reference to our dependence on the words of others, the contained (language) breaks the container (encyclopedic book, concept, meaning) and forces upon the reader a sense of the mortality of every code, of every covenanted meaning" (1981:xvi). Deconstructionism alone, in other words, would discount the "traditionality" of folkloristic content. Literary folkloristics serves as an antidote to such a nihilistic perspective.

Because the concept of the allusion remains covert or unnamed in the emic system, there is little conscious resistance to the notion that an allusion is conceptually within the domain of the listener as well as the teller or writer. That is, it is not simply the teller or writer who alludes to something, but the listener, too, hears allusions, perceives references, even (and perhaps often) ones not intended (or alluded to) by the teller. The sophisticated poetry of T. S. Eliot or Ezra Pound, for example, assumes a "cultural literacy" that is shared by the poet and (he hopes) his readers. But as E. D. Hirsch (1987) has pointed out, many contemporary readers do not share the store of very specific knowledge that makes those allusions meaningful. This would not seem to be a problem with the simply told personal narrative. Not, however, because the allusions refer to a less esoteric body of information. The reason it is not a problem is precisely because listeners hearing a personal narrative tacitly recognize the role of the allusion and have faith that they can independently identify an appropriate image or tradition to match the allusion within their own frames of reference. They recognize their responsibility to *perceive tradition* by hearing allusions.

A literary folkloristic methodology capitalizes upon this emic endorsement of the allusion's function. The allusion, whether cultural or private, is heard by the listener as an element of performance style—something that makes the performance an emotionally satisfying experience for the listener. The listener participates in the storytelling by hearing specific and personally meaningful allusions where an analytical outside observer might have perceived ambiguity. The listener's task is to hear a specific text, in this case, one that is uniquely created out of the listener's response to allusions in the teller's performance. The ambiguity semioticians are likely to treat as an etic concept is indeed an experience-near concept assumed by listeners hearing oral narratives. The listener accepts responsibility for dispelling the ambiguity of the text. He expects to choose or hear specific allusions that when heard do simultaneously *reveal* the listener's own personal sense of tradition. That expectation is crucial if the listener is going to be content with what he hears, with his own unarticulated interpretation. The listener is a natural interpreter. The challenge, then, for a literary folkloristic methodology is to document how that natural interpretive exercise is accomplished.

Literary Folkloristics and Naturalistic Inquiry

In the study that follows, I shall present background information toward such a methodology, and then, with what must be acknowledged as the reader's patient indulgence, I shall allow a relevant demonstration to emerge in the last two chapters. The work represents a "naturalistic inquiry" of the sort identified and described by Yvonna Lincoln and Egon Guba (1985) in their study of a new holistic research paradigm. Such a study, they argue, does not pose a general hypothesis and then seek to prove it as would a positivistic study. Nor does it offer any context-free generalizations or empirical definitions. A naturalistic study is more demanding of the reader; it requires participation, patience, responsiveness, and goodwill. However, a naturalistic study does not, I hope, reflect an arrogant disregard for the reader; instead it acknowledges the complexity of the process of understanding. My aim in this study is to guide readers to an understanding of how meaning is created for the listener when an oral storyteller relates a personal narrative.

In the discipline of folkloristics, the new naturalistic paradigm has had its greatest impact on fieldwork methods. Or, perhaps it is the other way around: Folklore research has moved into the new paradigm through its growing interest in context and the essential shift in field methodology this new emphasis has required.[8] In this literary folkloristic study of personal narratives, I have expanded this emphasis on context to include attention to the listener/interpreter who actively "responds" and "practices literary folkloristics" in actual fieldwork contexts. Consequently, this is *not* a genre study with a clear, descriptive thesis. It is a contemporary folkloristic study, a naturalistic study, and it has at best a hidden thesis. Naturalistic inquiries revolve less around a provable thesis and more around a set of axioms that are assumed to fit the needs of people-oriented research such as this inquiry into the telling and hearing of personal narratives. Lincoln and Guba list five axioms of the naturalistic paradigm and contrast these with five axioms underlying most positivistic research. Briefly, the five axioms of naturalistic inquiry are:

(1) Realities are multiple, constructed, and holistic.
(2) Knower and known are interactive, inseparable.
(3) Only time- and context-bound working hypotheses (idiographic statements) are possible.
(4) All entities are in a state of mutual simultaneous shaping, so that it is impossible to distinguish causes from effects.
(5) Inquiry is value-bound. (1985:37)

I believe these five axioms are inherent in the methodology developed in this study. The only one that tugs annoyingly at my own perception of the discipline is the fourth. Folklorists are loath to dismiss tradition as a cause in the scheme of things.

Nevertheless, the essential thing is that tradition be identified—something folklorists do probably better than anyone. The discipline does not insist that tradition be the cause; sometimes it is indeed the effect, and often it is inseparable from its opposite, innovation. This is the basis of the "twin laws" suggested by Barre Toelken (1979:34–36).[9] In a given folklore context, both tradition and innovation (or conservatism and dynamism) are at work. Usually folklorists attend to the performer—the person who tells or manufactures the folklore—and to his or her use of tradition or innovation in the performance. In this study I attend to the listener/interpreter—the person who hears or observes the folkloric performance and, consciously or not, interprets it as a meaningful communication. In either case, the construct of tradition is essential. It is the "sixth axiom" that makes this study *folkloristic* rather than simply *naturalistic*.

However, tradition aside, the emphasis placed upon the listener and the interpretation of narrative brings literary folkloristics squarely into the naturalistic paradigm. While contextual studies have been edging folkloristics into this new perspective for several years, the wholesale adoption of a holistic, subjective perspective has been slow to materialize. By incorporating the emic perspective from anthropology and the subjective paradigm from literary studies into a literary folkloristic methodology, this study demonstrates folklore's natural right to a leading role in the continuing development of this new paradigm.

The book is constructed to allow the literary folkloristic perspective to emerge, each chapter building upon the previous one and each chapter dependent upon the reader's familiarity with the preceding discussion for proper grounding in the issue to be addressed. In chapter 2 the genre of the personal narrative is introduced as a frame that allows a listener to comprehend storytelling, specifically the telling of personal experience stories. The genre itself is both a context and a tradition or resource which serves the teller's performance and the listener's interpretive participation. The genre is described with attention to structure, function, and stable content features, especially values or themes. The personal narrative is then classified according to thematic/structural types.

In chapter 3, perspectives current in poststructuralist literary criticism are incorporated into a folkloristic appreciation of the audience in oral storytelling. The shift of focus from teller to listener is essential to the proposal of a methodology in this chapter. The objective of this methodology is to produce some understanding of how a listener accomplishes a "natural" interpretation of a personal narrative. Interpretive textual studies have not been common in folklore, and the few that have been published have not been particularly well received. In this study, the adoption of a naturalistic paradigm requires that the interpreter's personal perspective be identified, and this I have done by describing the "interpretive context." To accomplish this, chapter 3 reconsiders the folkloristic concept of the "group" and the accompanying notion of a social base for at least some segments of reality (those we call traditional). Folklorists assume that social groups *are* responsible for creating and maintaining cultural resources that the individual then uses to build a personal reality. In this study I combine this folkloristic interest in social groups with the literary interest in biographical context. Together they are largely responsible for the degree of understanding a listener experiences when hearing a personal narrative. It is the particular combination of contributing social groups that is idiosyncratic for each teller *and* each listener. The allusions a listener hears when a story is told reflect both the shared frames of reference growing out of common groups and the intimacy of face-to-face interaction.

Chapters 4 and 5 present interpretations based on this methodology in the form of two detailed instructional texts. In the field of anthropology, the writing of cultural accounts is a growing issue in itself (Clifford and Marcus 1986; Marcus and Fischer 1986). The instructional texts in chapters 4 and 5 are offered as "cultural critiques" borne out of my own folkloristic training and personal interpretive context. The texts are thus both representations and reflexive interpretations, and they propound the fundamental folkloristic principle that all cultural exchanges depend upon shared traditions.

The Epilogue reiterates the importance of tradition as a basic axiom of the literary folkloristic perspective. The work as a whole is intended to build toward an understanding of both the chosen methodology and the subjective validity of the interpretations offered in chapters 4 and 5. Tradition is an essential concept in folkloristics and one that remains essential even within the new naturalistic paradigm. I have chosen to spotlight the personal narrative because it, of all oral folk narrative genres, is most often considered devoid of tradition. From a literary folkloristic perspective, nothing could be further from the truth. The listener hears tradition in the personal narrative. The listener enriches the text by listening and interprets the text by discovering tradition in the interpretive context.

2.

The Personal Narrative
as an Oral Literary Genre

Oral Literary Genres and Narrative Theory

Personal narratives are so common that for a long time researchers overlooked them as a subject of study. And yet they represent a genre that demands creativity and skill in composition and performance and a sensitive interpretive competency in response. In fact, while the personal narrative as a folklore genre builds upon traditional resources, any given example of the genre is by definition a *creative* text. The experiences at the base of personal narratives and the values that are expressed through them are original elements the tellers add to the tradition of the genre when they create their stories. And, as we shall see, the allusions to common or private reality listeners hear when such stories are told are the building blocks of literary folkloristic interpretation. Together the tradition of oral genres and the process of interpretation constitute a fundamental narrative theory, a commentary on the nature of oral literature. In chapter 3 we shall consider how the listener interprets. In this chapter we shall consider the literary tradition of the personal narrative, the formal, thematic, and functional aspects of the genre itself.

The personal narrative is a prose narrative relating a personal experience; it is usually told in the first person, and its content is nontraditional. This definition of the personal narrative is one I offered several years ago (Stahl 1977a), in an article focusing on the place of such stories in the context of established folklore genres. This and similar definitions suggested by other researchers have been dissected, contested, reassembled, sometimes even accepted wholeheartedly over the past decade. Most recently, the definition was taken up again and left at least two-thirds intact by Linda Dégh (1985) in her plenary session paper at the Eighth International Congress for Folk Narrative Research, in Bergen, 1984. The two questions I thought most pressing when that definition was first formulated are implicit in the particular aspects chosen for emphasis in that working description: that is, is the personal narrative an autonomous genre, and is it folklore? Interestingly, though the first question has been answered positively and with relative ease by a large number of researchers, the second question meets with a certain underplayed ambivalence in the discipline.

Can something be an oral literary genre and yet not be folklore? Normally, one would expect a folk narrative genre to exhibit traditional content—not simply an oral presentation mode or a traditional style, or even simply an established niche in the teller's personal repertoire—points I presented earlier (1977b) in defending the folkloric status of the genre despite its nontraditional content. My argument was that even though the narrative content of such stories could not be corroborated precisely (as traditional plots or motifs), still the values or attitudes reflected in the stories are culturally shared and thus traditional. However, claiming that embedded or even generative values are traditional is not the same as identifying as folklore the stories that reflect those values. From a conservative perspective on "What is folklore?" the *stories* themselves would not be folklore so long as their plots were idiosyncratic. A narrative based on a teller's personal experience is not a narrative taken from oral tradition and retold by the storyteller, nor is it a folklore item whose plot or major motif can be corroborated by a folklorist, no matter how alert and patient.

My own perspective is more flexible on this point, but I can appreciate why the lack of traditional content in personal narratives would be disturbing, especially to those who consider a more obvious collectivity central to the definition of folklore. Ironically, from an emic perspective there is ample evidence for the folkloric nature of personal narratives. Fieldworkers such as Joe Graham (1981) and Keith Basso (1984) and theorists such as Paul Helas (1981) have demonstrated that, at least within specific cultures, native taxonomies recognize the collectivity of personal experience stories. But the field of folkloristics has tended to cling to an etic, cross-cultural perspective that requires satisfying first the demands of the analytical framework of the discipline. The personal narrative, in other words, must be seen as exhibiting the essential features of *a folklore genre* to qualify as folklore.

Many studies have identified such features, either in a comprehensive look at the genre or in a narrower consideration, usually, of function.[1] Because much of this research presupposes that the precise distinctions typical of etic classifications are in order, there is often some discussion of differences between narratives dealing with belief (*memorates*) and the secular personal narrative, or between the longer life-history account and the single-episode, anecdotal form. My own emphasis in this study is on the secular, single-episode personal experience story. While I am prepared to argue that this genre is a natural or emic category at least in American culture, I do not feel that its separation from such close relatives as the memorate, the local character anecdote, the fuller life history, the family story, and the local history event is clear-cut or always desirable.[2] However, within an etic system, the personal narrative is easily distinguishable as a particular kind of oral narrative. As a formal, "literary" category, the personal narrative meets at least those requirements essential to its identification as a genre.

As I mentioned in the last chapter, the question of etic versus emic genres can be very inhibiting if taken too seriously (i.e., if it seems to impose an ideology). Dan Ben-Amos (1969), in his influential article distinguishing "Analytical Categories and Ethnic Genres," does, I think, suggest that attention to ethnic (emic) genres represents both a more enlightened and an ethically superior concern than does attention to genres imposed as supposedly universal categories by the scholar (see as well Harris 1968:568–604). The point is well taken, at least insofar as it makes researchers aware of their own ethnocentrism. Beyond that, however, one must simply admit that genre recognition, and especially genre description, is an analytical activity. The scholar's audience is always the larger academic community, and the analyses offered by "natives" will have to be made meaningful in analytical terms the academic community will understand. For example, Joe Graham has written about the *caso*, an emic genre similar to what I have etically identified as a personal narrative. The designation is culture-specific, as is the particular genre conceptualization itself (i.e., the term refers specifically to "the point" of the story, not the recognized plot). Similarly, Richard Bauman (1972b) has identified an emic genre of personal narrative called the *yarn* among Nova Scotian fishermen.

The discovery of such terms is very valuable, as are the culture-specific studies from which they derive, but most scholars, especially those outside the field of folklore, want as well the cross-cultural advantage of etic terms. The genre they will recognize must present itself in the analytical trappings the academic community has come to expect in the description of a genre—the conventional features of style, content, form, and function. These analytical terms grow out of literary theory and anthropological functionalism. More recently the field of semiotics has developed a more comprehensive but less widely known terminology for a "poetics of folk literature," including rules of presentation, textual patterns, plot structure, and semantic patterns (see Jason 1975; Greimas and Courtés 1979 [1982]). The semiotic and literary critical systems are not directly analogous; however, their similarity is sufficient to warrant choosing the literary-anthropological terminology since it is more widely known.

These four conventional aspects of genre description—style, content, form, and function—are all themselves conceptual constructs, and they inevitably overlap. Bennison Gray (1969) laments the ambiguity of the concept of literary style. For some, style might be what Alan Dundes (1964b) calls the "texture" of the text; Henry Glassie (1968:185) argues that style represents the choice made from among alternative content possibilities. Often style simply implies a characteristic way of manipulating content. On the other hand, content is typically considered either the *Rohstuff* that exists prior to the production or performance (see Weisstein 1968:135-36) or the specific motifs chosen to "fill in" the narrative structure (see Dundes 1962). Structure (or form) is usually recognized as the essential feature identifying any text as an example of a literary genre. Typically, however, prose structure is described in terms so abstract that the genres so defined tend toward large universal categories, even simply the category of narrative itself (see, e.g., Dundes 1963; or among literary critics, Frye 1957 or Kermode 1966). When genre-specific structures *are* identified, they tend to reflect culture-specific functions, as in Dundes's (1971) study of African friendship-breaking tales.[3] And finally, since function is a scholarly interpretation of an item's role in its specific cultural context, the analysis of function brings us back to the discussion of context and its effect upon performance style, especially style as abstracted into such levels as cultural, regional, family-based, generic, or personal.[4]

Defining the Personal Narrative

The features typically used in the description of a genre are inextricably interrelated; their separation or articulation is always arbitrary. Furthermore, a consequence of looking to all four features is an overwhelming inclusiveness—the description of the genre would seem to survey *all* of the "cultural resources" used by a performer (Abrahams 1969a) and audience. Charles T. Scott (1965) has suggested that a solution to this too-encompassing aspect of genre description is to instead *define* the genre by identifying only that combination of features that is distinctive for the specific genre. In this case I would argue that three features combine to define the personal narrative, and these three features draw upon all four conventional aspects of genre description—no one aspect is exclusively essential. The three features are (1) dramatic narrative structure, (2) a consistently implied assertion that the narrative is true, and (3) the self-same identity of the teller and the story's main character (the *Ich-*

Bericht form).[5]

Structure is one feature of narrative that has received considerable attention, especially as an argument for traditionality in oral literary genres. One of the most impressive such arguments I have seen is a study in which Robert Georges (1972) demonstrates the actual transmission of abstract narrative structure in the absence of content transmission in an oral storytelling tradition. In this instance, the narratives are of the genre that would normally be called *Märchen* or fairy tales—except that individual recorded texts *do not* represent indexed (traditional) tale types (plots). Rather, the stories contain traditional motifs in ever-new combinations, but those combinations always maintain the "required" traditional abstract structure of the genre. In that particular culture (Balkan), convention demands that the genre be maintained, while the specific content (the plots created using the generic structure) must vary from one teller to the next. As with personal narratives, the genre is itself the primary traditional aspect of the storytelling.

In rare instances, one can see the obvious power of traditional structure in the personal narrative. The rarity of these instances is tied to the second essential feature of the genre listed above—the implied assertion that the narrative is true. Typically one cannot check on the truthfulness of a storyteller's account of a personal experience. And of course it would be an ungracious listener who would openly challenge any story that seems reasonable. Nevertheless, people will sometimes admit to "making the story better," and in some cases that literary enhancement is not simply a matter of exaggeration or enrichment through fabricated details. Instead it may take the form of actual imposition of a dramatic structure over the otherwise unimpressive sequence of facts. For example, consider the following story told by Larry Scheiber, a native of Huntington, Indiana:[6]

The Christmas Eve Drunk (my title)

Larry: Me and Dudu, anyway, used to go Christmas caroling. And one night I come home—and this was when I was first married, see? My wife still loved me and everything. And I came home so drunk and full of mud and shit from falling down in people's yards. It was one of those drooly winters, you know, not much snow, just shit. And we were covered with mud and everything else. And I smelled like a—oh, Lord—a distillery! You know how rank guys are when they're drunk—.

Carol: I sointainly do!

Larry: I couldn't even stand myself! Aww, God, but I come in there, "Well, hi, lovey-poo!" and it was two o'clock in the morning. And she just said, "Snoot!" [puts nose in air], and went into the back bedroom all by herself with the kids and would not sleep with me.

Carol: Oh, you poor baby!

Larry: Yes! and I was feeling amorous. Here I had about half a hard on. . . . But anyway, I got to laying there in the bed all by myself, and you know, the room starts tilting and all this shit, and you start going ohm-papa, ohm-papa [makes motion of up-and-down ride on merry-go-round with hand]. And I started getting *sick*, you know, and you can feel it coming. And I staggered out of bed—and I had my *combat boots* on in bed—there was *mud* all over the damn sheets and everything! And—at the same time I had to puke, she was laying in there thinking, "It's no time to be mean to Hubby at Christmas time, I'm going back in there and sleep with him."

So she's coming down the hallway in order to make amends, and I'm running down the hallway in order to puke. [Laughter] And I smash into her [smacks fist into hand]—she weighs about a hundred and five soakin' wet—and I knocked her right on her ass and puked all over her. [Laughter] She—honest to God—she didn't speak to me till Easter! She's a witch, boy, when she gets mad, and I ain't shittin' you, that made her mad!

The incident at the base of the story had happened about ten years earlier (from this recorded telling). Some years after the incident, Larry was divorced from his first wife—thus the line "My wife still loved me and everything" in the story. Larry is not suggesting that this incident brought on his divorce, and though in a poignant way the story does reflect a certain self-awareness, it is told primarily for its comic effect. Basically Larry's story is a bemused indictment of his own behavior, and more clearly so when we realize that— except for the fact that Larry once came home very drunk shortly after he was married—the story is almost entirely a fabrication. Larry's ex-wife has consistently maintained that the incident never happened as Larry describes it; rather, she insists that though he spent too much time with "the boys," he very rarely got drunk, and he most certainly did not *ever* throw up all over her (or even in front of her). Though on the surface we simply have a case of conflicting stories, I am willing to accept as accurate the testimony of Larry's ex-wife. One would not forget being "puked on," especially in a situation so dramatic as Larry's story suggests it was. Instead, I think we can assume that Larry did come home drunk from a Christmas celebration. Very likely he was in fact sick at some point during the night, and very likely his amorous attempts were ineffectual ("*about* half a hard on" is probably all too true). He probably surmised his wife's irritation with him accurately enough. To some extent, the story serves to steer attention away from the real source of irritation—his tardiness and neglect of his wife and family—to the more "forgivable" sin of drunkenness. But the amazing *plot* of this short story did not happen; it was created by Larry in part as a response to the demands of the genre of the personal narrative.

Larry is a master of the genre. Whatever his personal motivation for any particular story, his literary or artistic motivation is always to use the genre as a fine instrument, one whose capabilities he knows and utilizes fully. A personal narrative must have a dramatic plot. How can the theme of drunken and inconsiderate behavior be wedded most effectively to a dramatic structure? In this case, Larry chose to build up a dramatic plot by casting his ex-wife as the protagonist and himself as the antagonist in a typical conflict situation. As in Freytag's ideal "pyramid," the rising action, or complication, begins soon after the initial situation leading to conflict is described:[7]

Initial situation
  a) Larry's wife is waiting (until 2:00 A.M.) for him to come home from a night of carousing with the boys (she is home with the children).
  b) Larry comes home late; he is drunk and covered with mud.
Complication (1)
  a) Larry's drunken behavior offends his wife, especially his implied interest in sexual intimacy despite his present unsavory appearance and smell and his understandably reduced capabilities.
  b) Larry's wife responds by refusing to sleep with him; she goes instead to the children's room.
Complication (2)
  a) Larry's wife regrets "being mean" to Larry (i.e., she repents from withholding sexual intimacy as a punishment of her husband).
  b) Larry realizes that he is nauseated and is going to have to vomit. The scene is set, then, for the climax in the structure (and the motivational crisis).
Climax
  a) Larry runs down the hall toward the bathroom.
  b) Larry's wife walks toward the bedroom to join her husband.
  c) Larry runs into his wife, knocks her down, and throws up on her.
Crisis
  a) Larry realizes that he is sick; his actions are "out of control"; he cannot be responsible for his own behavior.
  b) Larry's wife loses her own control over the action of the plot as

Larry's drunkenness and nausea become the directors of the action.

c) Ironically, "drunken Larry," as the antagonist, triumphs over his wife (the protagonist) only in his own mind; his wife's motivations were all, of course, only his own projections (even in the fabricated story); "sober Larry" (the source of these projections and the real protagonist) would welcome his wife's attention and condemns "drunken Larry's" behavior since it shuts him off from his wife's affection.

Finally, the story closes with the wife's bitter response to "her" humiliation—she refused to speak with Larry for three months (till *Easter*—hyperbole, to be sure).

Dénouement
a) Larry's wife refuses to speak to him.
b) Implied: Larry accepts this punishment as just, given the reprehensible behavior of "drunken Larry."

It is appropriate that his wife's response is a refusal to communicate verbally, just as her earlier response was a refusal to communicate sexually. For Larry—who is both exaggerating his behavior and condemning its implications at a symbolic level, since the events did not really happen—the lack of affection from his wife is ultimately seen as something he has brought upon himself. And he asserts this notion dramatically; he creates a personal narrative from the barest of facts. Nothing in the incident itself demands the dramatic structure Larry has given it. Instead Larry has used the genre of the personal narrative as a directing literary strategy.

Though dramatic structure is easily demonstrable in "The Christmas Eve Drunk," it is the inaccuracy of the report itself that allows me to infer some stronger directing power in the genre that encourages such manipulation of the facts toward a literary ideal. Increasingly among literary theorists, there is disagreement and confusion on the issue of fiction as an essential feature of literature. In a larger sense, the argument is moot, since *all* literary products are the result of artistic manipulation. Still, on a relative scale it would seem that a narrative based on a real incident should not be considered fictional in the same sense that narratives obviously created from the imagination of the author are considered fiction. On the other hand, speech-act theorists argue from the other direction that all fiction is referential with respect to real interactions and events and, therefore, that *all* such literature is based on real events. More problematic in folklore studies is the reception of narrative material by the audience. That is, as Tamotsu Shibutani (1966:7) suggests in relation to rumor study, it is necessary to distinguish between the problem of *accuracy* and that of *credibility*. It would seem that even fairly drastic manipulation of the raw material, as in Larry's Christmas Eve story, may positively affect the credibility of the narrative by increasing the pattern and familiarity or universality of the experience for both the teller and the listener.

The personal narrative always involves some manipulation of the truth of the experience. Such manipulation involves a degree of falsification, but generally only so much as to produce appropriate story material. This relatively minor degree of falsification occurs at three levels: (1) in the teller's perception of the experience, (2) in the initial telling of the personal narrative, and (3) in the readaptations of the story to the varying contexts of retelling. Falsification that occurs at the level of perception is reflective of patterns established either through archetypes or universally known structures or through previous personal experience. In the first instance, as C. G. Jung (1958:112–13) suggests, an archetypal or universally shared pattern or theme might create a corresponding vision of the experience in the individual's initial perception, even though in reality the experience does not illustrate the universal theme exactly.[8] And in the second instance, any new experience is comprehended through reference to past personal experience if no collective perceptual pattern presents itself. Thus, the experience is filtered through preexistent patterns even before it is articulated as a story, and these patterns represent both personal and cultural conventions that serve to generalize actions and events into manageable perceptual units (cf. Allport and Postman 1947 and Adams 1971).

With the initial telling of the personal narrative, the teller adapts the perceived experience to the demands of the genre and the specific situation. Many incidents are recognized as "story-worthy" by the teller simply because his perception of the incident and his general sense of the genre fit together easily. Other times a bit more work is involved: the teller *must* negotiate between accuracy and the demands of the genre in order to enhance the credibility or "tellability" of the material (see Shibutani 1966:27, and cf. distortion of initial testimony as discussed by Vansina 1965:76). As Polly Stewart (1975) suggests of the oral legend, personal narratives are "told convincingly rather than fictively." Manipulation of the reality involved is for the sake of rhetoric—to persuade the listener toward an appreciation of the cultural truths *represented* by the story. While it is not important that every detail of the story be accurate or even believed, it is important that the listener know that the story is not intended as a piece of fiction; it is not a first-person joke or a tall tale (or lie), genres which, to be effective, ultimately *require* the listener's recognition of fictionality.[9] For the personal narrative genre to function properly in any storytelling situation, both the teller and the listener must understand that the story—no matter how rhetorically enhanced—is to be accepted as true.

In effect, then, the implied assertion that a personal narrative is true is maintained despite the seemingly contradictory demand that the story exhibit an aesthetically acceptable dramatic structure. Enmeshed in this web of contradictory demands is also the third generic feature—the self-same identity of the teller and the story's main character. The teller's identification with the story character is the primary means of certifying the truth of the incident upon which the story is based. That is, the teller offers the authority of his or her own integrity and personal experience as the basis for the truthfulness of the story. On the other hand, the teller is easily implicated in the "literariness" of the interaction (storytelling) since he or she is the one who has given a piece of reality its dramatic structure and has as well transformed a subjective "self" into a dramatic "character." On a narrative level, the "I" of the story is simply the main character or, structurally in Propp's (1928) terms, the "hero," the person from whose point of view the actions of all other *dramatis personae* are to be defined and evaluated. However, because the teller identifies in actuality with the character, the "I" of the story brings with it a complexity far beyond that defined internally by the actions in the story.

I shall consider the complexity of the teller's identity in some detail later in this chapter. For now, the *Ich-Bericht* form is simply one of the three essential features in the definition of the genre. A fourth feature is equally essential but speaks not to the question of genre but rather to that more problematic query—whether the personal narrative is or is not folklore. I have described the personal narrative as secular in contrast to the memorate—a personal account of a supernatural or psychic experience. However, the modifier *secular* is heuristic, reflecting more upon academic prejudice about the concept of "belief" than upon any real differences between memorates and personal narratives—a point David Hufford (1977) discusses very effectively in considering stories involving "modern" beliefs.

Nevertheless, it is instructive to adopt the distinction between memorate and personal narrative if only for the sake of the methodological aid it provides. Lauri Honko (1964) has suggested that folk beliefs play a significant *generative* role in memorates; that is, the belief usually precedes the experience and thus influences the storyteller's perception of the incident that forms the core of the memorate. If the personal narrative is the secular equivalent of the memorate, then the secular beliefs represented by such academic terms as *values, attitudes,* or Alan Dundes's (1972) term *folk ideas* would form the core of these secular narratives. I would identify such "nonverbalized folklore" as the folkloric content of personal narratives. The folklore, in this case, is neither verbal nor material, nor even customary in the sense of *recognized* behavior patterns. Instead it is the nonverbalized, tacit knowledge that collectively makes up an individual's world view.

Strictly speaking, personal narratives are not folklore, but they are a primary means by which a special kind of folklore is expressed. Nonverbalized folklore—attitudes, values, prejudices, tastes—would be present but "covert" in any kind of folk narrative. As with "unrecognized symbols" in anthropological research, the problem lies in scholarly attempts to identify values the storytellers themselves would not ordinarily verbalize (see Hanson 1975:96-99). The advantage of the personal narrative is that the storyteller chooses the specific situation (plot) that aptly expresses a covertly held value. Milton Rokeach's (1968) comment on the nature of attitudes is useful here: any one attitude, he argues, actually represents two interrelated attitudes—an attitude toward an object or person and an attitude toward that person in a specific situation. By describing a personal experience, a storyteller identifies a specific situation he or she considers a significant showcase for his or her own actions. Why that situation or plot is significant is still a matter for interpretation, but the folklorist can at least be assured that the individual storyteller considers the plot of her story significant—precisely because, to reverse Raymond Firth's (1953) definition, behavior is a way of talking about values. The well-structured plots of personal narratives serve both the teller and listener as vehicles for expressing and learning values.

Describing and Classifying Personal Narratives

Narrative Structure and Function

Structure, then, is an essential feature in our conceptualization of the personal narrative genre. Before structuralism gave way to poststructuralism in critical theory, folkloristics enjoyed a brief day in the sun reminiscent of the earlier influence of the Grimms on philological and comparative literary theory. Both Propp and Lévi-Strauss used folklore materials in their structural schemes, and scholars interested in narrative theory soon gained an incidental familiarity with the structures and content of folk narratives (see Scholes and Kellogg 1966; Scholes 1974; Lévi-Strauss 1963; and Propp 1928). What literary theorists found problematic in structural methodology was the notion of "function." While it was clear that structuralism could explain how a unit of narrative functioned within the literary landscape of the text, it was not so evident how this notion was related to the realities of social life reflected in the text. Alan Dundes's (1962; 1963) substitution of terms derived from linguistics—*motifeme* for the structural slots or functions and *allomotif* for the narrative content that would fill them—removed some of the ambiguity surrounding Propp's *function*. Nevertheless, inherent in Propp's term and methodology and certainly in the "paradigmatic" structuralism of Lévi-Strauss was the tie to anthropological functionalism.[10] More recently, Dundes (1980b) has also reemphasized the connection between the functional substitutes represented in the recognition of allomotifs as interchangeable "symbolic equivalents." To be informative methodologies, most structural schemes have reincorporated the less precise functional units that offer some explanation of how narrative content reflects real social functions in the lives of the people who tell and listen to the stories.

Personal narratives represent a particularly useful case when addressing problems surrounding narrative function, structure, form, and content. By definition, the teller of a personal narrative and the structural "hero" or primary character are one and the same. This fact alone forces a researcher to reconsider the relationships to be analyzed in a structural or functional essay. Typically the object of analysis is a text in folkloristics, but, as Henry Glassie has pointed out, the aim of structural or functional analysis is to relate the object to culture, particularly the culture of the individual presenting or using the folklore item (the object). "A complete statement of an object's functional potential requires a definition of the functional field," says Glassie. The most directly communicative model, he suggests, would be one "which sets the expressing person . . . at the center, and draws in the major lines that relate the person through the object . . . to his context" (Glassie 1973:335). If the "expressing person" is also the main character of the narrative, any structural scheme that focuses upon the relationship between the "hero" and the primary functions in the narrative will inevitably expose certain relationships between the teller and the teller's culture or frames of reference.

Such a structural scheme does not share the subjective paradigm of poststructuralist studies. As Elliott Oring (1976) has suggested in regard to functionalism generally, any function is an abstraction offered as an explanation by the researcher. Even when it is identified as an internal evaluation in the story—as in Labov and Waletzky's (1967) analysis of personal narratives—it still represents the researcher's own abstraction of the unit considered functionally significant. A consistent direction for such functional analysis to take in personal narrative research is one addressing the narrative as a vehicle for personal values or world view. Some researchers follow Labov in suggesting that such values are expressed directly in the text (see especially Robinson 1981). Others move to a psychological analysis which draws an analogy between the literary creation and the personal psychology of the teller, or they "expand" the text (as discussed in chapter 1) to include the teller's biography and/or world view (see Langness 1965; Pentikainen 1977 and 1978; Agar 1980; and Burns 1984). My own contention is that the expression of personal values is indeed the hidden agenda in any such storytelling, and the most effective way to identify those values is to employ a literary folkloristic methodology.

In terms of William Bascom's (1965) classic formulation of the four functions of folklore, the assertion that personal narratives function as vehicles for personal values is too restrictive; it does not speak to functions beyond that of the rhetorical intent of the storyteller. Bascom identified the basic functions of folklore as (1) entertainment, (2) validating culture, (3) education, and (4) maintaining conformity. Oring (1976) telescoped numbers 2 and 4 and claimed that there are but three basic functions, but in either case the explanations (functions) are propounded with regard to the entire group (the culture) rather than the individual storyteller or listener. The overall function under which all functions could be grouped is, according to Bascom, that of "maintaining the stability of culture" (297). In researching the personal narrative, we have moved not only to items that are limited in circulation but also to items that serve primarily to express and maintain the stability of an individual personality rather than an entire culture. The overall function of the personal narrative is to allow for the discovery of the teller's identity (especially in terms of values and character traits) and to maintain the stability of that identity for both the teller and listener.

Stable Content: Character, Values, and Event

To speak of stability is to invoke as well its conceptual opposite—the possibility of change over time. In personal narratives, the "stability of identity" grows out of implications in the teller's use of the pronoun *I*. Time is a factor, as is the notion of identity itself, but whereas time is assumed to be a variable in regard to the speaker's use of *I*, identity is assumed to be a stable entity. Consider, for example, my mother's story of "The Barber Shop." The setting for the incident in this story is Huntington, Indiana, in 1942; my father (Charles Dolby) worked as a barber in a small shop downtown. My mother was thirty-one years old when the incident occurred, but my recording of the story was made when she was in her sixties. Superficially, her use of the pronoun *I* in the story is simply to identify herself as the speaker. In other words, the person who is telling the story is using the word *I* as she normally would in everyday conversation. Typically we give little thought to this casual use of first-person singular; it is simply a part of our grammar. The referentiality involved is assumed to be very straightforward; that is, the speaker refers to herself, and that self is visible before us. Of course, it really is not so simple as that. The complexity in the assumed frame of reference is apparent when we ask who "I" really is, who the listener is, and what is the relationship between them.

In the case of "The Barber Shop," the character "I" is my mother, I am the listener, and our relationship is that of mother and daughter. When my mother uses the pronoun *I* in her story, I "hear" and refer mentally to my current sense of her personality, a sense developed through a long and intimate association. It is, of course, a subjective belief on my part that makes my sense of her personality a real configuration for me. It is amazing how tenuous is the basis for our knowledge of another person. Even in regard to someone I know so well as my own mother, the process by which I come to hold a stable sense of her self as an autonomous personality remains a mystery. Nevertheless, it is that mysterious self that constitutes *one* aspect of the character "I" as I hear the story.

A second aspect of the character "I" involves my mother's personality as I construe it for the period during which the incident in the story took place. In this instance, the event took place before I was born (in fact, before either of my two older brothers was born). For me as listener, the jump to this second aspect of the "I" character is one of the most exciting effects of the intimacy created by the storytelling. It is not simply a matter of going back in time, but rather of going back in *someone else's time*, and back in the evolution of someone else's sense of her own self and the life that has created that self. It is perhaps only infrequently that we indulge our own reminiscences and transport ourselves into our own pasts. Rarer still is the opportunity to experience someone else's past as though it were a present moment. A storyteller gives us a glimpse of someone who *was* but is now changed, a self that shares some consistencies with the person we now see before us, but a self that *could not be known* to us save through a story such as this.

In personal narrative, the character "I" always confronts the listener with the task of integrating at least these two referents into a sense of the personality of the teller. That is, as listener I must combine my current sense of my mother's personality with my understanding of *who she was* as the "I" character in the story. We can appreciate the significance of this referential complexity by considering our response to the character "I" if she were in fact not the storyteller but rather simply the structural "hero," the story's main character. That is, if I were to *read* the transcript of "The Barber Shop" with all the associative cues taken out (e.g., references to Dad, Carol, and Dick, casual reference to downtown, etc.), I would respond to the story and its main character at that static level usually associated with written short stories. I would view "I" as a static character, the story as a revealing sketch, like the chapters in Sherwood Anderson's *Winesburg, Ohio*. There would be no diachronic sense of a "dynamic character" but rather a fixed characterization. I would recognize a personality, but I would not be shocked into a recognition of the author in the character. However, because I know that the teller *is or was* the character "I," my response must integrate at least these two images of the teller, and that integration necessarily creates a dynamic character in my mind. Inevitably, a personal narrative conflates to a *Bildungsroman*, the more so if I have heard other personal narratives from the storyteller or interacted with her in my daily life.

The third aspect of the "I" character is perhaps the most intriguing, for it can seemingly take effect only when—as in the typical telling of personal narratives—the teller and listener share some relationship defined by their common folk groups. In the case of my listening to "The Barber Shop," it is significant that I am the storyteller's daughter. Not only is the storyteller a real person rather than some paper author, but she is a person who is a part of me. As Tennyson says, "I am a part of all that I have met," and in this case certainly a mother can be found in her daughter. Culture and personal behavior no less than biological genes are conveyed through the family. The "I" of the story evokes a natural identification as no fictional narrative character can. We are very much alike—the teller and I—not so much simply because of the genes we share but because so much of what has taught her to define herself has also taught me to define myself. Even when I listen to Larry's first-person narratives, I readily identify with those aspects of his personality that reflect our common enculturation. My response to his experience is not entirely vicarious. Not only does the "I" of his stories share some cultural clay with me, but I consciously acknowledge some sense of identification with the "I" through a recognition of our shared folk groups.

Because the "I" of a personal narrative suggests these various meanings, it would not be surprising if the listener could not identify a stable character or world view for the teller as the functional requirement would have it.

Nevertheless, the personal narrative does elicit just such a response from the listener. Like the riddle, the personal narrative is a dynamic genre. It requires that the listener *discover* the values or character traits the teller expresses through the story. Jan Brunvand (1978:70) describes the traditional "question guessing game," in which an answer is given and the challenge is to formulate a question to which the stated answer would be an appropriate response. Similarly, the personal narrative tells a story which serves as an illustration of a theme, a value, or a character trait. Part of the listener's task is to formulate the question to which the story is an answer, to ask, "What do I know about this person from hearing this story?" And the major clues provided the listener are found in the structure, form, and content of the stories themselves.

At issue in some studies of personal narrative is the nature of the event recounted in the story. What do such stories teach us about historical experience rather than about individuals? My own earlier use of the term *personal narrative* is generally restricted to a teller's own first-person, single-episodic account of a secular experience. I detect in our culture an emic (natural) distinction among personal narratives that are (1) multiepisodic (and thus a form of life history), or again (2) personal narratives (memorates) that recount events generally recognized as supernatural or psychic rather than secular, and finally (3) personal narratives based on an experience the teller or any of his listeners would identify not as supernatural or even "extranormal" but rather as secular. I am referring here not to topical, one-time narratives but rather to the range of personal experience stories that come to be—for a time at least—stable, repeated narratives in the teller's repertoire. This feature of repetition is an essential, though minimal, requirement in the definition of a folkloristic text. A more compelling question, however, is, how does an experience—be it ever so secular—become an event worthy of literary transformation into a personal narrative? Personal perception is the key to the identification of any event. It might be said generally that an individual's personal perception creates an event out of the *Rohstuff* of ongoing life. The telling of a personal narrative merely extends that creative act into the realm of literary expression. The event becomes a story.

What influences the perception of the storyteller such that an experience becomes an event, and that event becomes a story? Scholars of rumor and legend have attributed the creation of memorates to the suggestive power of traditional beliefs or customs. As Lauri Honko (1964) demonstrates, it is the belief in a given supernatural concept (e.g., barn spirits) that allows the storyteller to first perceive a particular coincidence as a supernatural event; it is the tradition of the belief tale that then allows the believer to create a story relating that event. For the secular personal experience story, it is the literary form itself that is primary. The genre of the personal narrative is an established tradition, along with its typical themes. Familiarity with these themes allows the storyteller to perceive an experience both as an event and, more important, as the material for a good story. Much more than the supernatural memorate, the secular personal narrative exists for the sake of its own promotion as a literary form. It reinforces not the traditional beliefs or practices of the teller's culture but rather the themes of literary expression. Themes are the building blocks of secular narrative events. Through personal narratives, life learns to imitate art, history validates experience.

Thematic/Structural Types of the Personal Narrative

The abstraction of literary themes from narratives—oral or written—is an analytical exercise, but the *use* of themes constitutes creative expression. Of course, the use of themes is impossible to pinpoint without the analytical exercise, something a researcher might do in a purposeful manner but an activity that may seem to be an entirely unconscious "competency" underlying the storyteller's performance. In fact, the storyteller is not so innocent of analytical motives as we may suppose. It is, after all, the storyteller himself (herself) who has chosen to create both a story and an event where neither has existed before. There is ample incentive for creating personal narratives, especially in nonauthoritative societies—such as contemporary America— where the individual's value system is increasingly constructed piecemeal and with a certain amount of existential angst rather than adopted intact from a single authorizing source such as the church or an ideologically rigid state. The individual is not only free to choose his own values, he *must* choose. Some choose to affirm the values of various cults or religious groups; others struggle to affirm their own volition, their own power to create exemplary acts—the events of personal narratives. By creating a personal narrative, a storyteller articulates and affirms personal values along three thematic lines: (1) character, (2) behavior, and (3) attitude. The storyteller *chooses* events that illustrate themes of characterization, didactic themes (behavior), and humorous or ironic themes (attitude). The telling *is* the choosing of the theme and the creation of the event.

The personal narrative is—fortunately—a very malleable form. In fact, it adapts itself structurally to the slightly variable needs of these three thematic lines. We shall see in some detail later how this is accomplished, but for now a working generalization might be that the personal narrative closely resembles the *anecdote* when its primary thematic concern is characterization, the *Witz* (or joke) when it is humor or irony, and the *exemplum* when it is ethical elucidation. The nonsecular *memorate*, on the other hand, takes the form of the belief tale or legend. These generalizations about the form of the personal narrative can be useful in identifying just which thematic concern is dominant in any given narrative. Often a story will combine elements of all three primary themes—characterization, humor, mild homiletics—but usually one thematic concern will dominate *and* influence the teller's unconscious choice of form.

Compare, for example, my grandmother's "Spelling Bee" story which introduces the Prologue, with Larry Scheiber's "Tiny Wires and the Chicken Blood" (the text will be presented verbatim in chapter three). Briefly, in the "Chicken Blood" story, Larry and his friend Tiny are two bachelors sharing a trailer. One time, after fishing for catfish with a special bait, chicken blood, they put the bucket of bait under the trailer and forget about it. Weeks later, the bait begins to smell awful. The rest of the story is a humorous account of how they try to get rid of the stinking bucket of chicken blood—with a humorous/disgusting climax in which Larry spills the bucket all over himself. In comparing these two personal narratives, I would contend that my grandmother's "Spelling Bee" story embodies a theme of characterization, while Larry's "Chicken Blood" story involves a humorous theme and illustrates an attitude of mild irony.

There are, of course, elements of both kinds of theme in both stories. There is humor in the "Spelling Bee" story, and the "Chicken Blood" episode does serve to characterize Larry as a basically unruffled, cooperative fellow with a friendly disposition (if questionable housekeeping habits). However, the dominance of the themes of characterization and humor for "Spelling Bee" and "Chicken Blood" respectively can be demonstrated through attention to the structure or form of each story. The theme of characterization generally entails the form of the anecdote. In this case, my grandmother offers a self-characterization through an anecdotal narrative in which her straightforward integrity is highlighted in contrast to the phoniness of the "fine ladies" from the church. There are other traits as well—her competency as a speller, her quiet self-possession, her competitive spirit, even her cleverness in figuring out what the word really was. But it is her integrity—her determination to see that the truth is spoken plainly, that communication between people is as clear as it possibly can be—that is her primary characteristic in this story.

The personal narrative is told for the sake of its literary goal; the event is created to illustrate the chosen theme. In this instance, my grandmother hopes to effectively demonstrate her characteristic personal integrity. This is the literary goal directing her telling of the story. In my own (not necessarily eccentric—I base it on the work of Claude Brémond) view of narrative structure, the directing strategy for the narrator is always a positive or negative fulfillment of a primary thematic infinitive that reflects the narrator's goal vis-à-vis the main character (see Brémond 1970 and Stahl 1973). To illustrate this, think of my grandmother's story as a positive infinitive tied to the primary character trait identified above—i.e., integrity. The "theme," or as Brémond would say, the potentiality that is successfully actualized, can be expressed as "to demonstrate integrity." Thus the basic *function* (Brémond borrows the word from Propp) of the narrative is the three-step sequence:

(1) Integrity to demonstrate (reversed to emphasize the trait)
(2) Procedure for demonstrating integrity (plot of story)
(3) Success (integrity demonstrated)

For now, let me say simply that the anecdotal or theme-of-characterization personal narrative will typically have this structure. A specific character trait—such as those I have enumerated elsewhere (Stahl 1975a) in connection with a similar genre, the local character anecdote—will always constitute the "potentiality" or object of the positive infinitive directing the storyteller's procedure of plot development. And conversely, when we spot such a structure in a narrative, we can readily assume that the teller has actively chosen to affirm this particular trait as part of his or her self-characterization. The teller is perceived as responsible for inserting his or her personal values into the thematic frame of literary characterization.

The theme-of-characterization form of the personal narrative is the strongest form—and by that I mean both the most common and the most impressive, most moving or effective as a form of literary expression. This is certainly not unexpected in light of the pervasive impersonality of contemporary society. No longer is man's very nature handed to him through the church or state or even a pervasive philosophy. He must decide himself who he is, what his most basic traits are, and he must affirm this self-discovered "nature" both to himself and to his audience. My grandmother was a strong woman reared in a sexist society. Born in 1879 into a devout German-American Protestant family in the Midwest, she inherited a culture that characterized women as stereotypes—the bad Jezebel, the good mother, the frail heroine—but rarely recognized genuine and significant character traits in relation to real, individual women. (This sorry tradition continues in American popular culture to a great extent, especially in children's literature and television. I am thinking in particular of the popular "Smurfs" animated cartoons in which the single female—

Smurfette—represents all women, whereas the males all have individualized traits indicated by their names—e.g., Brainy Smurf, Handy Smurf, Lazy Smurf, Poet Smurf, Painter Smurf, Vanity Smurf, etc.) My grandmother found a way to teach herself the value of her own integrity, its value as a significant aspect of her self-characterization, her identity. And she taught me as well. When I remember her story of "The Spelling Bee," I think of her as someone who, even as a young woman, knew that her outstanding personal trait was her integrity. It is her story, not our common genes or a granddaughter's love, that has introduced me to what I can know of her real character.

And now, is Larry Scheiber to be left out in the cold so far as "the strong form" of personal narrative is concerned simply because he is not a woman? Well, no, but in fact he does more often tell stories that are primarily humorous rather than reflective of personal characteristics he hopes to emphasize as part of his identity. I would speculate that this might well be the case simply because Larry does not need to affirm his identity quite so desperately as do many women, minorities, or members of other less socially powerful groups. Despite the overtones of group identity here, the discovery and affirmation of identity is a very personal thing. Ultimately, the choice of which theme to emphasize (and thus which form to use) is tied to individual personality, and of course personalities are complex entities. Larry does occasionally tell a theme-of-characterization narrative, but always laced with humor. In one story about an eventful New Year's Eve—"The Red Velvet Suit" (see Appendix for a complete transcription of the text)—Larry combines three traits into his own positive portrait of manliness. In the first segment of the story, he patiently suffers considerable bodily abuse in an effort to help a stranger who falls into a violent and uncontrollable seizure; in the second segment, he defends the honor of women by challenging (belting in the face) a fellow who insists on using foul language at a party where women are present; and in the third segment, he manfully agrees to fight a much bigger and younger opponent who challenges him to "step outside." Larry obviously hopes to demonstrate the positive trait of "manliness" as he conceives of it and as he identifies with it. The story is told with much humor, but the overriding theme is characterization.

Larry's "Red Velvet Suit," because it involves the theme of characterization, is an anecdotal form of narrative and has a structure similar to that of my grandmother's "Spelling Bee" story above, with—in this case—the positive infinitive of "Manliness to demonstrate."

Let us consider an example of a didactic narrative for comparison, for it would seem that the "exemplary messages" carried by narratives of either the anecdotal form (characterization) or the exemplum form (didactic) might make it difficult to tell the two apart. The following story is one my mother tells relating an incident that occurred during her senior year in high school. The setting in the story is Hastings, Michigan, in 1930.

The First Charge Account

You know about the pair of hose that I charged when I was a senior in high school? I—oh, I wanted a new pair of hose. Well, in fact the ones I'd been wearing were so lacy with being repaired that—you know, sew up the runs? So anyhow, I'd gone into Larson's Dry Goods Store—and they were a real fabulous store there in Hastings. And I wanted a pair of hose and I wanted to know how much they were. Well, they were a dollar and a quarter.

And I—uh—couldn't buy them, and she said, "Well, you could *charge* them." And I didn't know what that meant. But she said, "Well, just take them now and in a week come in and pay on them." So I thought, "Oh, gee, a quarter a week, that wouldn't be too bad. In six, or five weeks, I could have them paid for." So I took the hose and I charged them.

And gosh, the next week came and I didn't have the quarter. And I didn't know what to do about it. Here I worried all week, and finally it came Thursday night and I just *didn't* have any money, so I went to ask my dad for a quarter. Well, what did I want the quarter for? [In hesitant voice] Well, I'd charged a pair of hose. So—he gave me the quarter, but he told me that—I'd have to figure out some way to pay him back. So he finally—we finally arrived at—uh—I could have the eggs that, over so many eggs a week. If the hens laid more eggs than three dozen or whatever it was, I don't remember how many, why I could have those eggs and save up and save them until I got enough money to buy my hose. And that's the way I got them paid back—was with those extra eggs. But geeminee!

As with many exemplum-form narratives, the incident at the base of the story is a "first" for the teller. Freud and Freudian critics attribute a similar significance to first experiences in an individual's life (even if not consciously recalled, as in the story). In this instance, my mother effectively illustrated the negative consequences of buying "on time" when a projected source of income is not available. Typically the purpose of such a cautionary tale is to influence the behavior of the listener, to illustrate the effects of certain personal experiences as a lesson for the listener. The implication is that the teller herself has already benefited from whatever insight the experience affords.

Structurally, the story is built upon the infinitive "economic responsibility to illustrate," and in this case the theme is homiletic—the teller implies that economic irresponsibility is immoral. Again, the basic *function* of the narrative follows a three-step sequence:

(1) Economic responsibility to illustrate
(2) Procedure for illustrating economic responsibility
(3) Failure (economic responsibility not illustrated)

The negative outcome fits the teller's literary strategy as well as a positive outcome would. The teller is able to assume that her attitude toward the incident is clear; the moralistic value, in this case, is assumed to be shared by the audience.

Humorous personal narratives can be categorized as a subtype on the basis of the consistent attitude involved. No matter what the theme, the teller's attitude toward the incident in the story is amusement—usually sparked by a recognition that some embarrassing or incongruent situation caught the teller unawares. Larry's "Chicken Blood" story is typical. It is clear at the beginning of the story that Larry wants nothing to do with the disgusting chicken blood. By the end of the story, we can expect his attempt to avoid being contaminated by the foul bucket to fail. Structurally, the "hero" fails to avoid an ironic reversal; the functional sequence would be as follows:

(1) Contamination to avoid
(2) Procedure for avoiding contamination
(3) Failure (contamination not avoided)

Each of the three forms of personal narrative has its own distinct structure tied to a particular infinitive of potentiality. The anecdotal form involves themes of characterization and typically reflects a structure with a positive closure to the infinitive "X to demonstrate." The exemplum form involves homiletic themes and reflects a structure with either a positive or negative closure to the infinitive "X to illustrate." And the joke form involves humorous themes and a structure with a negative closure to the infinitive "X to avoid."

The variety of themes that fit these subgenres is impressive but perhaps not as infinite as one might suppose. Without suggesting that this is an exhaustive list, I would list the following themes as those most common to the secular, single-episodic personal narrative. Among those reflecting characterization of the teller are (1) honesty, integrity; (2) cleverness, wit; (3) bravery, heroism, fearlessness; (4) practicality, business acuity; (5) charm, seductiveness; (6) loyalty, patriotism; (7) generosity or affection; and (8) manliness or maturity. Humorous themes are generally classifiable as involving (1) embarrassing situations, (2) ironic situations, or (3) incongruent occurrences. Homiletic themes intended to elucidate moral lessons are reflected in stories based upon (1) terrifying situations, war-time experience; (2) horrifying situations, cruel events; (3) unjust situations; (4) poignant situations; or (5) practical problems in managing one's affairs. Such themes are the narrative cores that tie the structural subtypes of the personal narrative to real functional concerns in culture and represent as well identifiable traditions useful in folkloristic classification.

3.
Interpreting Personal Narrative Texts

Constructing Interpretations

For years, emulation of the empirical sciences has inhibited the interpretive study of folklore. Early folklore scholars, in their desire to make folklore a rigorous scientific discipline, readily imposed upon themselves systems of methodological accountability—indexes and archives to serve the "historic-geographic" method, collecting handbooks, and questionnaires for custom and belief mapping. Implicitly, these early folklorists subscribed to the view that folklore research should be "operationalized." In keeping with this positivistic attitude, a modern folklorist, observing and commenting upon a folk narrative performance, is obliged to ask, as Pelto (1979:47) suggests, "If another observer had been at the particular event, and if he used the same techniques, would he have obtained the same results?"[1] Such a nagging concern with accountability leaves little room for creative (and idiosyncratic) interpretation of a folk narrative presentation. On the other hand, it does ensure that the analyses offered with regard to a particular presentation are directly useful in demonstrating the discipline's major theoretical premises or methodologies. It is, as Alan Dundes (1980a:ix) suggests, "safe scholarship."

The interpretation of texts or performances or events—as in literary studies, the arts, or history—has typically been regarded as an intuitive activity. Practitioners usually strive to keep their methodology concealed, just as an artist would seek to draw attention away from the techniques used and direct it instead toward the effects of those techniques in the medium chosen. This purposeful covering of one's tracks is unacceptable in a "scientific" discipline. On the other hand, the interpreter of an item of folklore is hard-pressed to account for his or her interpretation except in personal terms. The specific procedure of interpretation cannot be operationalized; it is too closely tied to the interpreter and his or her own interpretive context.

Gary Alan Fine (1984) has suggested two criteria that would require some accountability in particular among psychoanalytic interpreters of folklore. He suggests that an "adequate" psychoanalytic interpretation must be internally consistent and externally valid. He then applies these two criteria to the work of Alan Dundes, well known for his psychoanalytic interpretations of a range of folklore material. Unfortunately, the application of Fine's evaluative criteria is hampered by insufficient data—in particular, the factors influencing the interpreter's focus, the "tracks" the interpreter usually chooses to leave covered.

It is not enough to say that psychoanalytic theory itself (or any other analytical perspective) accounts for the interpreter's focus and insight. If that were the case, folkloristic interpretation would indeed be operationalized. But there are other aspects of the interpreter's personality and immediate situation, as well as other internalized analytical perspectives, that influence the interpreter's focus and the selection of information to be scrutinized in the interpretation. Needed is a procedure for alerting a reader to an otherwise covert focus directing the interpreter's line of reasoning. With such information available, a reader could evaluate the interpretation as the presentation of a valid response—not a universal response, but one that is valid and consistent within that specific interpretive context.

It is worth noting that the same problem occurs in the initial task of collecting and transcribing a folk narrative text. Elizabeth Fine, in her study of *The Folklore Text*, describes the difficulties a transcriber encounters in moving from the symbolic system of oral performance to that of print. The primary difficulty, she suggests, is in maintaining "the type of perceptual 'focus' employed by a participant engaged in an aesthetic transaction" (1984:107). In other words, the transcriber is challenged by the less obvious task of representing on paper what happens *as the listener observes and hears* the performance. How does the listener hear? The transcriber is in danger of overloading or underloading the text, and readers may be unable to "read" the information supplied about the performance if they are not trained in the transcription symbols used. A focus could not be effectively conveyed unless the transcriber succeeded in supplying just the right information necessary for the readers to "hear the performance" (perceive an "aesthetic transaction") as they read the text. The transcriber must "perform" a transcription (practice the art of transcription with acceptable competence) or at least create an instructional documentary.

A performance-centered text, such as that Fine advocates, or the more common content-centered text found in most folk narrative collections might be considered a *documentary-instructional text*. Both are intended to document a performance. The focus of the content-centered text is the linguistic content;

the purpose of the text is to instruct a reader in the verbal content of the story perceived as central to the performance; the mode of presentation of the text is usually in the form of a play script or short story. The focus of the performance-centered text is the performance; the purpose is to instruct a reader in the aesthetic dimensions of the performance as they relate to the content; the method of presentation varies, as Fine suggests, from linguistic transcription augmented by numerous notational symbols, to multiple texts, to "hybrid art forms" (1984:101-102).

Just as the transcriber of a text chooses a focus in presenting the text, the interpreter constructs an interpretation by choosing points of emphasis according to one or more consistent though often deliberately concealed lines of focus. The easiest line of focus to identify would be the interpreter's analytical methodology. Harder would be the identification of personal information that sparks a given focus, personal associations or situations that encourage the interpreter to interpret the performance or text one way rather than another. This kind of information the interpreter would have to supply. Unfortunately, this is precisely the information the interpreter is reluctant to include or even admit, since it implies that the interpretation offered is not—on its own— intersubjective. The interpreter hopes, ultimately, that the interpretation will be seen as resting on empirical observation, that any researcher encountering this same text and following these same rational lines of argument would obtain the same results. But, of course, the art of interpreting cannot be operationalized in this way. Instead, the *interpretive context* needs to be identified and tied directly to its points of significant contact in the text.[2] Then, the interpreter's response to the text can indeed be accounted for and made accessible to other readers.

Consider, for example, Alan Dundes's interpretation of a joke called "The Wide-Mouth Frog" (1980a:62-68). The plot of the joke revolves around a mother (or father) wide-mouth frog who does not know what to feed her baby. In a brash, wide-mouth manner she asks several larger animals what they feed their babies, finally ending with the same question posed to a potential enemy (e.g., an alligator), who replies that she feeds them wide-mouth frogs. The mother frog answers, "Oh," in a nervous, small-mouth, quiet way. Dundes interprets the joke as a veiled comment on black speech and an indulgence of racist attitudes in a period (the 1970s) when open expression of racism was no longer acceptable.

The interpretation as Dundes develops it is both internally consistent and externally valid, to use Gary Alan Fine's evaluative criteria. However, to be more precise, we might judge the interpretation externally "plausible."

Dundes admits that "it is a legitimate question whether one can effectively 'prove' the validity of one interpretation over another" (1980a:ix). In fact, the very notion of validity is perhaps inappropriate for all such interpretations. It implies that a valid interpretation has revealed, not a unique response to the item or performance but an explanation for the origin and appeal of the stable content or *Rohstuff* of the text. Like all conscientious scientists, folklorists hope to add their piece to the complete explanation of why things are as they are. Without such a goal, interpretation of folklore would probably seem pointless. Nevertheless, most people will admit that interpretations of cultural data are subjective, no matter how convincing, and cannot be regarded as a demonstrably true explanation for the origin of tradition—even a short-lived tradition such as the joke about the wide-mouth frog.[3]

We might return to Dundes's interpretation of the joke about the wide-mouth frog and ask what valid new information one can take away from such an interpretation without slipping into an "origins fallacy" akin to the "intentional fallacy" in literary criticism. Some researchers might find the interpretation convincing enough to seek statistical support for such an explanation; they might, in other words, turn the "theory" into a question for "normal science" (Kuhn 1962) and try to document the prevalence of the joke among people for whom the phenomenon of black speech was indeed an issue. Unfortunately, most American folklore data are not collected using the kind of canvassing system that would be necessary to answer such research questions.

Another alternative, and one I would advocate, is to regard such an interpretation, along with additional information about the interpretive context, as a demonstration of how individuals make everyday folklore a vital part of their understanding of social reality. If we all truly are "the folk," then the folklorist's interpretation is, as Stanley Fish (1980:48-49) suggests, the most "informed," and it is also the most easily accessible as a demonstration, since the professional folklorist is trained to view cultural data as a combination of personal and cultural resources within a specific context. It is a simple step to add sensitivity to the interpretive context to the folklorist's necessary skills in studying folklore. In the case of Dundes's interpretation of the joke about the wide-mouth frog, it might be something so simple as acknowledging a long-standing interest in black American folklore on the part of the interpreter, especially his perspective on other jokes that seem to hide a time-framed concern with blacks in American society (i.e., the elephant joke cycle).[4] Such information would cue the reader, not to disregard the interpretation, because it is obviously biased by personal interest, but rather to abandon any internal resistance against the validity of the interpretation and instead follow it as the author would wish. The reader is invited to decide whether the author has found an effective way to make the folklore meaningful within the context of his own personal/professional reality; the reader is not asked to judge whether the author has proved that his interpretation is objectively and universally valid.

Like other kinds of philosophical relativism, such an approach may be labeled wishy-washy or even subversive; it seems to undermine the scientific enterprise. Actually, a folklorist armed with information about the interpretive context sets out to do exactly what the interpreter of texts (sans interpretive context) tries to do; that is, he or she tries to prove (demonstrate) a hypothesis—in this case, about how interpretations evolve in the minds of interpreters. Belief in the validity of one's approach is necessary in either case, or the project is never begun. Documenting and using the interpretive context simply adds another level to the range of data to be considered in formulating an interpretation.

In my own interpretation of the joke about the wide-mouth frog (formulated casually after hearing the joke in 1978 but before reading Dundes's article), I focused on the frog's incompetence as a parent. In my opinion the joke was about a noisy, incompetent human mother who did not know what to feed her baby. Furthermore, she seemed unabashed at her ignorance of such fundamental knowledge; she demanded in a brash, demeaning tone that some other mother tell her what to do. The ending I heard not as a threat but as a mild put-down and cautionary tale. It implied that feeding a baby—especially breast-feeding a baby—is a very personal thing every mother must learn for herself.

I think I could with some effort transform this sketchy interpretation into a persuasive essay that would meet Gary Alan Fine's criteria for an "adequate" interpretation. However, I feel you as reader would gain greater insight from your reading of my essay if you knew what elements in the interpretive context influenced the selection of this particular focus. For example, it would be helpful if you knew that, while I have never worked with black American folklore as a distinct area in my research as Dundes has, I have done some work with family folklore and women's folklore. It might be helpful to know that I interpreted the wide-mouth frog not as a sign of speech pattern or dialect but as a euphemism for a "big-mouth," someone who talks too much. It would certainly be helpful if you knew that when I first heard the joke, I was a first-time mother-to-be, and one who felt that at thirty-one years of age and with a Ph.D. and several years of college teaching behind me, I should already know how to take care of a baby, how to be a good parent, but was in fact worried over the prospect. It would be easy to see why this personal concern along with the other analytical preferences would influence me toward the interpretation I have suggested. It would be easy to see why I would select and focus on material that would support this thesis. The selectivity apparent in any interpretation is not malicious; it is necessary. Attention to the interpretive context can tell us why—at least in that given context—specific analytical and personal connections developed between the performance or item and the interpretation.

Discovering the Interpretive Context

This important information about the interpretive context can be presented to the reader by contextualizing the narrative text or performance. Contextualizing, within a literary folkloristic methodology, is a self-conscious attempt by an interpreter of a text or performance to make explicit the relationship between the item or performance, the interpretive context, and the interpreter's own response (interpretation).[5] The end product of such a contextualizing process would be an expanded instructional text, one that documents not only the linguistic content of the narrative or aspects of performance but also relevant components of the interpretive context.

What are these relevant components of the interpretive context? As suggested in the Introduction, these components are not so much *in the text* as they are representative of the listener's active response; they are allusions the listener hears or fills in as the story is told. And they are essential to the fundamental act of interpretation. As Seymour Chatman (1978) suggests:

> The drawing of narrative inferences by the reader is a low-level kind of interpretation. Perhaps it doesn't even deserve the name, since "interpretation" is so well established as a synonym for "exegesis" in literary criticism. This narrative filling-in is all too easily forgotten or assumed to be of no interest, a mere reflex action of the reading [listening] mind. But to neglect it is a critical mistake. (31)

Chatman has his own reasons for considering such neglect a critical mistake. My own reason is that this "low-level" process of interpretation is basic, is essential. When expanded to include perceived allusions, it determines what the listener really hears as a story is told. If we can identify the allusions a listener hears, we can know how the interpretive context interacts with the text to influence the listener's response and interpretation. We can posit a theory of folkloristic influence.

Folk Groups and the Formation of Frames of Reference

From birth on, human beings form alliances with other humans and develop frames of reference within those alliances that determine to a great extent their view of the world and often their behavior in it. Psychologist Jay Haley, in studying the often severely restrictive families of schizophrenics, comments: "What confines the members [of the family] so rigidly within their system is the prohibition on intimate alliances of one member with someone outside the family. As a result, the family members are inhibited from learning to relate to people with different behavior and so are confined to their own system of interaction" (1967:264). Sadly, in the larger world, people often extend a similar pattern of behavior into their interactions with groups other than their own; they practice a confining ethnocentrism that influences heavily the frames of reference that define their personal reality.

Arguments for cultural determinism, biological determinism, environmental determinism—and free will as well—are generally overstated for the sake of philosophical rhetoric. As a result, psychological perspectives that consider the "social conditioning" of the individual often seem pessimistically deterministic, while on the other hand even the most sophisticated implications about personal responsibility drawn from "the new physics," when applied to questions of individual behavior and cognition, have a ring of mysticism, or at least the ambiguity of the humanities, rather than the expected "certainty" of the hard sciences.[6] How *do* individuals create their personal reality? How do they manage to convey that reality to anyone else, or understand anyone else's similarly subjective view of reality? Social scientists no less than physicists seek a complete theory that will encompass all aspects of human behavior, but it is still as impossible to explain how one person comes to think and behave as he or she does as it is to explain how human consciousness can make a muscle move.

Nevertheless, one theory that can help explain some aspects of human behavior posits, as did Haley in discussing schizophrenics, the notion of identifiable groups that serve to teach individuals the patterns of interaction peculiar to that group. Whenever the group is stable enough to be viewed as a conservator of shared lore or perceptions, then it is classifiable within the academic concept of "folk groups" and supportive of a special folkloristic brand of sociological theory.[7] Even typically genre-oriented literary folklorists have sought increasingly to integrate the notion of "folk groups" into their own research. Jan Brunvand's (1978) introductory folklore textbook is a genre survey typical of the literary approach, but he includes as well a chapter on "Folk Groups: Bearers of American Folk Tradition." Brunvand discusses four major kinds of folk groups—occupational, age, regional, and ethnic or nationality—but cautions that, while such categories are prominent in folklore research, there are innumerable folk groups that can be identified from the perspective of any specific individual. This flexible concept of "folk group" draws upon the work of such people as Alan Dundes (1965a) and Richard Bauman (1972b), folklorists who have emphasized the individual's full or "part-time" participation in a variety of folk groups.

The significant shift involved here in regard to folk groups is from a view of "the folk" as a homogeneous entity (especially the peasant) to a view that emphasizes the individuality of people in any group and the consequent variety of "social bases" functioning in the formation of reality for any one individual. The groundwork for this shift is found in Alan Dundes's now well established definition of "the folk" as "any group of people whatsoever who share at least one common factor" (1965a:2). A folk group is not a communal undifferentiated unit; rather, the identity shared by any two members of a folk group is not individually pervasive but only sufficient to support a limited corpus of shared folklore. The two individuals are alike—share an identity—only insofar as they share items of folklore significant to their sense of identity.

An individual's sense of identity grows out of a variety of sources and envelops several specific kinds of sensibilities within it (see Bauman 1972a and Dundes 1983). For example, an individual's sense of ethics would typically reflect most strongly the influence of his or her religious upbringing. With respect to personal ethics, a person's religious folk group might be posited as a major (though not exclusive) source of that aspect of his or her identity. Folklore (including nonverbalized folk values) learned either in face-to-face reference groups (a specific church or synagogue congregation) or through more general affiliation (a specific religious denomination) would allow the individual to identify with the religious group while recognizing that this connection represents only a part of his or her personal identity. Similar analytical categories and associated sensibilities could be suggested for other major kinds of folk groups. I have identified eight such categories, but of course the number of possible categories is considerably larger, and the number of actual folk groups is infinite.

On the chart in Figure 3-1, I have represented schematically the connections between the individual and eight significant categories of folk group. The taxonomy is based on general divisions in perceptions of identity: (1) family, (2) ethnic or national background, (3) religion, (4) place, (5) age, (6) sex, (7) social network (socioeconomic class), and (8) occupation. Each of these categories offers to the individual cultural resources of a particular kind—expressive resources that both teach and allow the individual to express the sensibilities that collectively help form his or her identity (see Abrahams 1972b). Such a chart implies a rigid cultural determinism. I should say that my personal philosophy embraces such deterministic explanations as only part of the answer. I cannot give you a "whole truth" even from my own perspective, as "personal consciousness" remains for me a tantalizing mystery.

Briefly, the chart consists of a wheel of folk group categories significant in the formation and expression of individual identity. Indicated as well are sensibilities cultivated most effectively by each category of folk group: the

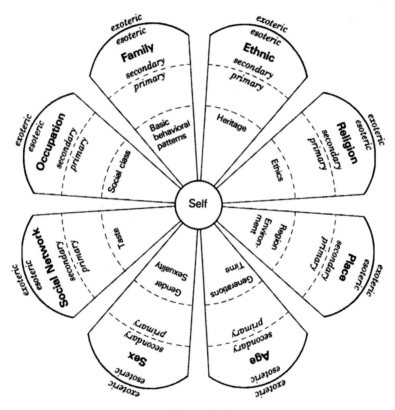

Figure 3.1

family often teaches a sense of personal and local history; the ethnic group offers a sense of heritage and a self-consciously maintained corpus of folklore; religion provides ethical values; locality instills a sense of region and the environment; age groups give a sense of generations and time; sex-based groups (along with the family) create a sense of gender and personal sexuality; social connections are reflected in aesthetic preferences or taste; and occupational group usually determines (in America) one's sense of social class. Each category has a further division into a primary or face-to-face group (e.g., family members with which one interacts often) and a secondary group (e.g., the ancestors and extended family with whom the individual does not interact but whose folklore he or she shares). Finally, the chart divides each category along the esoteric-exoteric axis. Adapted from William Hugh Jansen (1965), the "esoteric-exoteric factor" simply recognizes that the individual perceives his or her own group (of whatever sort) as separate from other groups. Awareness of actual exoteric lore might come through education, but the prejudice in favor of esoteric lore is natural and necessary for the development

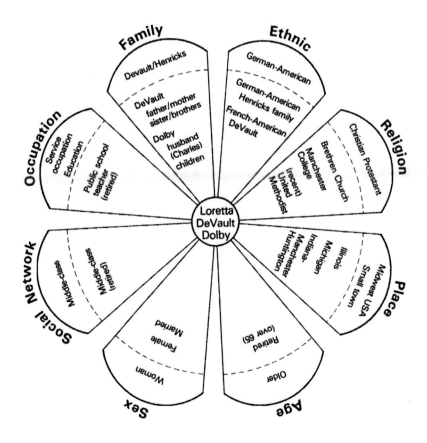

Figure 3.2

of a personal sense of reality.

The usefulness of such a chart is less in clarifying conceptual networks (though that is one aim) than in providing a format for discussing the backgrounds of individual storytellers. Leaving the innermost ring off for now, we can construct a wheel of folk groups for each of the two major storytellers in this study. The first teller is my mother, Loretta Kathryn DeVault Dolby, born in 1911 in Oakley, Illinois. A representation of her folk group background is in Figure 3-2.

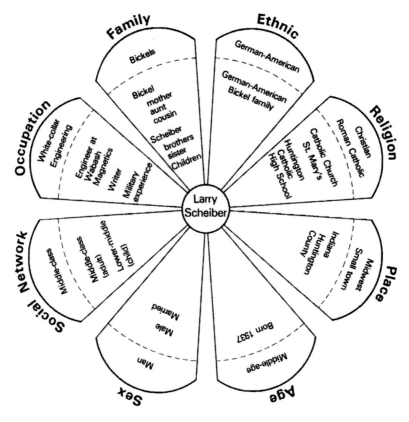

Figure 3.3

The second storyteller is Larry B. Scheiber, born in 1937 in Huntington, Indiana. His chart is represented by Figure 3-3.

In either case, the chart does nothing to indicate which folk group is dominant in the individual's sense of identity or—more important to this study—which folk group or groups might be shared with typical audiences to the stories these individuals tell.

For these more interpretive questions, the chart can serve only as a springboard. The first question is better left in the hands of trained psychologists, whose battery of tests might actually determine which factor is dominant for each individual (see, e.g., Burns 1984). The second question, however, is one that can be addressed more easily than otherwise through a further application of the chart. To identify the primary frames of reference shared by a storyteller and a specific listener, one need only compare the wheel charts of the two individuals and note where there is obvious correspondence. It is this necessary correspondence between at least one folk group on the teller's chart and one on the listener's chart that allows for understanding of a narrative text. The real correspondences in cultural resources shared by the teller and listener are of course much more complex than such a chart would indicate. They are to a high degree responsible for the magic sense of intimacy that accompanies the most effective exchanges of personal narrative.

Personal Narratives and the Creation of Intimacy

What motivates the telling of personal narratives? The question is complex, and any attempt at a comprehensive answer is beyond the scope of this study. However, I can offer one rather simple answer: People tell personal narratives to be listened to. Of course, if it were only that, jokes or legends or songs would do as well, perhaps better. No, when people tell personal narratives, they offer their listeners an invitation to intimacy. They expect their listeners to listen because both they and their listeners know that this is one very effective (and acceptable) way to create and enjoy a sense of intimacy.

Freud found abundant inspiration in a quote from Schiller: "Hunger and love are what move the world." From that quote he devised his "theory of instincts." I am not sure whether I would consider the desire for intimacy an instinct. It certainly is not the same thing as a sexual instinct. Nevertheless, I do think it serves as a motivation in the telling and hearing of personal narratives. This is especially true for people who grow up in our lonely culture. By exchanging personal narratives, people create intimacy where it might not have existed otherwise. Usually we depend upon family ties or shared activities to facilitate intimacy. But our culture is miserly in what it recognizes as appropriate avenues for developing a sense of intimacy. The personal narrative sidesteps this inhibition. Telling and listening to personal narratives is one way people can enjoy intimacy without resorting to the "rights" that are assumed to come with the ties of family or group.

I personally believe that if we each took time to listen to one personal narrative each day, much of the loneliness in the world would disappear. The problem is that the people who most need and want to tell their stories often feel that no one wants to listen. Still, it is one of the most acceptable ways to meet our desire for intimacy. People will tell their stories sometimes, and usually other people will listen. The motivation for both the teller and the listener is a desire for familiarity, a desire to know someone else and be known in return. It requires a certain boldness to tell such stories; it requires human affection to listen. Hunger and love are large words and can be construed in many ways, but these may indeed motivate the telling of personal narratives. At the very least, a person tells a personal narrative because he wants to be listened to.

The details of a personal narrative are both known and unknown. That is, the listener will already be familiar with some of the information stated or alluded to in the narrative, while some of the information (for example, the event itself) will be new. It is the interplay of this shared culture and the unique event that allows intimacy to grow. The narrative itself creates a literary world in which shared culture draws attention to itself and to the intimacy it represents. In the remainder of this chapter, we shall explore why the personal narrative is so effective in meeting this need for intimacy.

Larry Scheiber grew up in the small northern Indiana town of Huntington during the years of World War II, when the Erie Railroad was still a major factor in the community and the Catholic church supported both a friary and a convent on the rolling hills outside of town. I grew up, about ten years later, in the same home town. Larry and I both remember Sutter's Ice Cream, Wolf and Dessauer's, the Spot, the Tivoli Theater, the Idle-Hour Quarry, the Hotel LaFontaine, Moon and Moon's Laundry, Repp's Grocery, the Hawley house, Township School, the soda fountain of McKean's drugstore, the Erie depot, and many other places that have since been razed, burned, or otherwise removed from the landscape. Larry and I share the frame of this bygone era and the ongoing history of this Indiana community. The inexhaustible store of allusions just within this one frame is impressive. There is little in an individual's personal history and sense of reality that does not touch upon such shared cultural resources and thus link us to our fellows. In the personal narrative, such allusions are abundant and essential; their richness keys the performance of this inescapably self-referential genre.

Consider, for example, the following transcription of the "Chicken Blood" story (mentioned in the previous chapter) as told by Larry Scheiber.[8]

Tiny Wires and the Chicken Blood

Larry: OK, when I got out of the service, Tiny decided that he was going to be my—
my—parental instructor as to hunting and fishing and all this stuff—little
knowing that I'd lived practically underground for three years. I probably
knew more about the outdoors than he ever dreamed. But anyway he was
going to show me how to catch catfish. So he said he had a secret bait. I said,
"Well, put it on me—what is it?" He said, "Never mind, we'll just go get it."
I says, "Is it expensive?" He says, "Two dollars a bucket!" Says, "Bucket!
—You don't pay for a bucket. . . ." He says, "Just keep cool." So we got in his
big Oldsmobile, and we whiz over here to Scarborough's—you know, where
they got all the chickies—brack, brack—[Laughter].

Carol (my sister): Oh, yeah—

Larry: Yeah, yeah—Wires comes out about ten minutes later with this damned
bucket of BLOOD CLOTS, man. There was feathers in it and chicken shit.
[Groans]

Carol: Oh, gag!

Larry: He said, "You hold this." And I said, "Your ass!" He said, "Hold it, damn
it—you know I can't drive with it." So I'm holdin' this thing. And it, oh,
Lord, you know how you, your forehead gets cold? [Laughter] And stuff?
And you feel dizzy? And I'm holding this quivering mass of blood clots in
my lap. [Laughter]

And we go out behind Township School, see. Wires said, "Bring the
bucket!" I said, "You take this fuckin' bucket; I'll carry the poles." So I drag
the poles down the hill and everything. And here comes Wires boppin' down
there with the bucket. And I said, "What do ya do now?" He said, "Just take
a big handful. . . ." [Groans] I said, "Wrong-o, YOU take a big handful!" So
he baited my hook. This stuff had all congealed, and it looked sorta like liver.
I didn't know chicken blood would do that, but... but it hangs right on your
ol' hook, ya know? You get a great big glob of that crap and ya cast out, and
it hits the water, kafush! [makes arching motion with hand]—skawat!—and
it just sinks 'cause ya put weight on it. And ya just set there and set there and
pretty soon—tug, tug, tug—and ya reel in a catfish. And ya open its mouth
and there's all this—blechh—ya have to dehook 'em, ya know, oh, God!
I couldn't stand it. I finally set up on the bank and drank beer. Wires was
having a ball—[In a high voice imitating Wires] "Oh, look at the cat— . . ." I
said, "Come on Wires, let's go. God, I'm not having any fun." Said, "Let's go
back and get some broads or something and drink beer and tell lies."

So we went back to his house, and naturally I got to carry the bucket again.
And I stuck it under his trailer. And this was, oh, I don't know, about June.
Long about July [pause]—[Laughter] . . . the neighbors started complaining
that we'd killed an animal or something. But we were sorta getting used to it
a little bit at a time, ya know. We'd built up a tolerance and we didn't smell

anything. God! Everyone that drove by there'd roll up their windows and gag. [Laughter]

One day I stayed out of town about two days—think I was shacked up with some broad or something. I came back to the trailer and about passed out. Said, "My God, Wires, there is something!" So we got to lookin' around under the, under the boards under there. We thought a rat crawled up there and died or an old cat. The Wall's Trailer Court's full of vermin. But anyway, I see this five-gallon bucket and I thought, "Oh, my God, that's that bucket with that blood in it." [Groans] God!—So I crawl under there and I clear the rim. And that thing's just heavin' with maggots. [Up-and-down motion with hands] Brrr-room, brrr-room—[Laughter].

Oh, God, what happened—the maggots'd get in there and eat the blood, ya know, and then more flies'd come and lay maggots on top of them. And the ones on the bottom'd suffocate and die. And then more maggots'd make more flies. It was an endless circle, ya know?! That thing smelled so . . . God! But anyway, I told Wires to get that thing outa there. He says, "Oh, no. . . ." He says, "I'll give ya a case of Mickey's Malt if ya get it out of there." I says, "Tiny, I'd like to 'cause I like it, but, ya know, there's certain things I can't be bought on." And he says, "Two cases of Mickey's!" I says, "Oh, hell, I'll do it for one." I'm hairy, ya know—so I got under there and drug that thing out, and it—oh, God! I just wish you could have seen it!

Carol: No!

Larry: He says, "What'll we do with it?" He wanted to bury it, see, and I said, "God, no, those maggots'll all hatch, and there'll be six billion flies, and we'll be responsible for wiping out the world!" [Laughter] Plagues!—So we decided we couldn't bury it and if we burnt it, it'd stink, the goddamn stuff. I said, "I've got it, man, I got it. Let's throw it in the river and let the fish eat 'em. That way we'll be doing our bit, you know." He said, "Good idea!" So, naturally I got elected again to hold it on my lap while he drove. [Laughter]

There's a bridge out there, one bridge past Broadway, just a little stoney job, about three-foot-high railing. I said, "You drive across that and go *real slow*." I said, "I'll just heave the whole goddamn mess over the railing, and we'll take off like a big-ass bird." So he's driving real slow and I'm hangin' out the window—this thing's *heavy,* man! My ol' biceps isn't all that big, ya know. I'm holdin' onto that damn bucket. Wires says, "OK, give 'er hell!" So I get my arm underneath it [motions accompanying actions described]—so I [throwing motion]—uhh!—I threw it as hard as I could. Hell, it must've weighed sixty pounds! It made it right to the railing and jumped back. [Motion with hand straight up, and noise—apparent from motions that the contents of the bucket came down all over him] [Laughter and groans] Did you ever just drop a glass of water—see how it shoots up? Hell, I was hangin' out the window or the whole car woulda been full. I'm not kiddin' ya, it just buried me in maggots.

Uh, so naturally—I heaved the contents of my tummy—which added to the mess. That goddamn car reeked, and I reeked, and Wires was laughin' his ass off. [Laughter] He said, "Get out—get out!" Hell, he wanted me to walk home, man! I was hangin' out the window 'cause he wouldn't let me back in. He rolled the window up on me, powered the window—whrrr—. There I am hangin' out by my waist, ya know. "Let me in, Wires, ya son-of-a-bitch," I says, "I'm getting crusted!" [Laughter] You know, the wind was dryin' me off and those things were cakin' on me. Then he drives up to the car wash. Still won't roll down the goddamn window. I says [in strained voice], "What are ya gonna do?!" And he puts in the quarter and [Makes noise of water jetting from hose]. He uses the high-pressure water bit. Maggots flyin' all over the place. The whole bottom of the car was full of maggots. 'Cept they wouldn't come off of the car. That was the *goodest* part. He had to go home and get 'em off with a putty knife. [Laughter] I laid there in the yard just laughin'.

Carol: Oh, that's beautiful!

Larry: Oh, God—it was hell! Every time I think of Tiny, I think of that goddamn bucket of maggots.

Scholars who have made use of the notion of "cultural resources" in discussing narrative texts have usually attended to the genre itself as a resource used in performance (Abrahams 1968; 1969a; Burke 1950) or identified "culture-specific ways to key the performance frame" (Goffman 1974; Bauman 1977; Hymes 1975). Nevertheless, it is clear that allusive frames tied to the content of the narrative are also shared resources that influence significantly the effectiveness of the performance. Melville Jacobs in his insightful study of Clackamas Chinook myths and tales commented upon the esoteric allusive frames that often frustrated his attempts to collect oral performances: "Narrators usually delivered relatively bare bones of their stories, while the native audience immediately filled in with many associations and feelings which a non-member of the group could not possibly have" (1959:1). These "associations and feelings" are drawn from the abundant store of knowledge and experiences held in common by the teller and audience. The allusions are brief and suggestive rather than elaborate and explicit because they are presented in what Edward T. Hall describes as a "high-context" situation: "A high-context (HC) communication or message is one in which most of the information is either in the physical context or internalized in the person, while very little is in the coded, explicit, transmitted part of the message. A low-context (LC) communication is just the opposite; i.e., the mass of the information is vested in the explicit code" (1977:91).

In telling "Tiny Wires and the Chicken Blood," Larry is able to refer to local resident Kenny (Tiny) Wires, the old Township School, Broadway, Wall's Trailer

Court, and "the car wash" without further explanation because he can assume these local allusions are shared. However, he does elaborate on the reference to Scarborough's, saying, "you know, where they got all the chickies—brack, brack." He assumes, rightly, that the high-context frame of the community does not necessarily ensure that an allusion to Scarborough's will be understood, and of course it is important to the plot of the story that Scarborough's be identified as a place Wires could buy chicken blood. Folklorists interested in the performance of narratives have stressed the "emergent quality" of a storytelling such as this. That is, performance is a use of cultural resources that emerges within a specific context. Richard Bauman suggests that "we consider as resources all those aspects of the communication system available to the members of a community for the conduct of performance" (1977:38). I would simply expand the sociolinguistic perspective on what constitutes available "aspects of the communicative system" to include such allusive frames as these—what Roland Barthes (1974:18-20) designates as "cultural codes" in his scheme of five major codes under which the "signifiers" of any text can be grouped. Without borrowing further either the jargon or more intricate theoretical concepts of semiotics, I think we can address Larry's story using this reformulated notion of the literary allusion. In addition to the emic concept of genre or the tacitly shared routines for framing a performance, the body of knowledge shared by members of a group constitutes a vast potential source of high-context references to be used by the teller and in turn recognized by the listener.

Larry draws attention to this referential code by elaborating his allusion to Scarborough's. He knows that a good storyteller does not casually allude to knowledge not shared by his audience, and in this specific context (with this specific audience) he allows a reflexive comment on the convention of high-context or esoteric allusion to emerge within the storytelling itself. Larry manages this with good humor and little disruption of the story. Part of the reason Larry is able to do this is quite simply that he is a master storyteller, but there are more specific analytical reasons as well. To return to Roger Abrahams's "rhetorical" approach to folklore, we can agree with him that the genre itself is a primary cultural resource available to the teller (see Abrahams 1968 and 1972b). In this case there is indeed an emic sense of the conventions associated with the personal narrative, including the convention of "high-contexting" information about the storyteller, and the frame he shares with the audience. This convention of esoteric reference is intentionally foregrounded in the personal narrative, in contrast to such *fictional* forms as the tall tale or joke, on one hand, or such *impersonal* forms as the legend or anecdote, on the other. The effect of this tacit comparison of genres (literary reflexivity) is to force an awareness of the convention of esoteric allusion in personal narratives and that body of cultural information that must be shared personally by teller and audience in this specific context.

By making the convention of esoteric reference explicit through the metanarrational device of explaining an allusion (Scarborough's), Larry draws attention to the fact that he and his audience share certain cultural codes. The personal narrative, unlike the tall tale or legend, forces an awareness of shared cultural codes. Teller and audience are made self-conscious through such contexting as that involved in Larry's explanation of Scarborough's. And what they become conscious of is the rarity of such low-context material in personal narratives. People whose primary storytelling genre is the personal narrative often presume upon a pervasive high-context or esoteric frame even when it does not exist or is at least not so high as they suppose. We all know people who jump into a story involving relations, friends, and places unknown to us; often they leave these casual references unelaborated, and, as listeners, we typically *do not* draw attention to our outsider status in regard to this frame. Why? The personal narrative, through its typical abundance of esoteric allusions, maintains the illusion, if not the reality, of intimacy between teller and listener.

The basis of good storytelling or effective communication generally is shared cultural resources, and the basis of intimacy is an *awareness* that certain cultural resources have been shared *and* certain personal facts or ideas have been expressed. I would see four steps in a movement from culture to intimacy, at least as intimacy is realized in regard to a literary activity such as storytelling. The first "step" is simply the assertion that people do share cultural resources. The scholar's job is to identify these shared resources; most folkloristic and anthropological research is devoted to this task—i.e., the identification and description of genres, tale types, motifs, storytelling situations, patterns of behavior, performance styles, customs, beliefs, stereotypes, world views, conceptualizations of time and space, kinship patterns, even bodily features that are recognizable as shared aspects of the culture studied. The second step beyond this assertion is a recognition of the *use* of these cultural resources by the storyteller in an effort to persuade or influence the audience. This use may or may not be intentional; we must assume that a performer could not possibly be aware of consciously choosing *all* of the cultural resources he or she uses. Rather, it is the *scholar* who analyzes the performance as a creative use of cultural resources. Furthermore, it is the audience (or more accurately, each individual listener in the audience) who must respond to the teller's use of cultural resources. The third step, then, is the listener's referential use of his or her own store of cultural resources in understanding and appreciating the teller's storytelling. We can assume that many of the cultural resources used by the teller are shared by the listener; others will be of the "mistakenly assumed" variety mentioned above. The fourth step is a recognition that certain esoteric or localized or even presumably private resources are in fact shared; intimacy comes as the teller and listener each indulge that delightful sensation of recognizing or perhaps projecting one's own personal knowledge into someone else's performance or response.

How people are able to convince themselves that a shared frame of reference is really shared is the question behind much research in the social sciences. Usually, the question is left unarticulated behind the stronger, analytic inquiry into the frames of reference shared generally rather than intimately, and the function of these widely shared resources. On the other hand, when the focus shifts from the general to the personal, to idiosyncracies and deviations, the larger patterns the scholar outlines cannot accommodate these more personal and intimate frames of reference. Part of the reason for the scholar's dilemma is a philosophical shift. The individual's awareness or identification of a frame of reference shared with his listener represents to some extent a personal belief. On faith, the individual indulges his sense of intimacy; he *believes* that the relationship between himself and his audience is sufficiently intimate to allow for the typical proliferation of esoteric allusions in his storytelling. One clear incentive for telling and listening to personal narratives is the desire to experience this socially acceptable form of intimacy.

Personal Presence and the Power of Performance

Intimacy, *performance*, and *response* are terms charged with specific meanings when used in the context of sexual rather than verbal interactions. Nevertheless, there is certainly something similarly compelling in the exchange of personal narratives that is unfortunately belied if one views performance as simply a rhetorical manipulation of shared cultural resources. There is an important animation and vitality at play in the telling of a story and in the listening. Much of the power of performance is in its immediacy and demonstration of personal presence. Roger Abrahams (1972b) recognizes a similar concept in identifying the "esthetic emotion" at the center of any performance of expressive folklore. In the telling of a personal narrative, this "power of performance" is augmented by the obvious originality of the story's content. Performing a personal narrative is a gesture toward intimacy; it combines the animation of performance with the intimacy of esoteric references and personal life history.

According to Edward T. Hall (1977:92), intimacy fosters the most efficient form of communication. Very little time, energy, or words need be spent contexting a listener in an intimate relationship. On the other hand, the power of performance is not diminished in a high-context situation. For reasons quite apart from the appropriateness of performance so important in rhetorical theory, the power of performance enhances any storytelling, but especially one that offers to share some aspect of the teller's inner life. To return to the metaphorical link between verbal and sexual performance, there is something in the telling of personal narratives that convinces both the teller and the listener that they have shared a significant emotional experience. This feeling is created out of the intimacy of personal narratives and the emotional effects of performance—the power of performance itself.

Power of performance is a term I would suggest to identify mutual recognition by teller and audience of the animated state of performance. This state is best explained through reference to information from experimental psychology. A storyteller such as Larry Scheiber obviously performs with great animation, but the meaning here is much more specific. The animated state of performance is always a physiological and psychological reality. Several years ago, psychologist Stanley Schachter (1964) proposed a frame for understanding human emotional response. According to his theory, two factors must coexist for a person to experience a "true emotion": (1) the individual must experience a change in physiological state (usually from nonarousal to arousal), and (2) it must seem appropriate to interpret this new state in emotional terms. The power of performance is just such a conventional interpretation of an altered physiological state; people (both performers and audiences) interpret the physiological effects of performance as an emotional event.

In light of the overtly intimate nature of personal narratives, it is not surprising that the power of performance produces a particularly satisfying emotional effect upon both teller and listener. Recent medical research (Lynch 1985a and 1985b) has demonstrated that the very act of speaking (no matter what is said) raises the speaker's blood pressure, rapidly and appreciably. On the other hand, the act of listening lowers blood pressure through what is called the "orienting reflex," again an equally marked change in the individual's physiological state. If we bring together Schachter's two-component theory with the information on the physiological changes caused by telling and listening to stories, it is easy to see why the power of performance is interpreted (consciously or not) as an intimate emotional exchange by the teller and audience.

The teller is aroused by his own telling, not so much in the manner Robert Georges (1979) has documented—i.e., as a direct result of the teller's response to his own story content—but rather simply as a physiological response that is *interpreted* as an intimate sharing. The teller attributes his enjoyment of his performance to the reasonable belief that he has actively enhanced the personal relationship between himself and his audience. The listener experiences a sense of relaxation brought on by the activity of listening; the change in physiological state is immediate and noticeable. The listener attributes the change to the activity of listening to someone's personal narrative; the listener experiences an emotion that is, in this instance, perceived as both intimate and pleasurable.

The cultural resources necessary for the performance of personal narratives include esoteric allusions that in turn create a sense of intimacy between the teller and his audience. The power of performance combines with this sense of intimacy to make the exchange of personal narratives an emotionally satisfying experience for both the teller and audience. Even a raucous and mildly masochistic story such as Larry's "Tiny Wires and the Chicken Blood" endears the teller to the listener and vice versa, simply through the positive psychological effect of the storytelling itself.

Creating Instructional Texts

This intimacy is more marked in the exchange of personal narratives than in other kinds of storytelling. Nevertheless, the allusions that make up a large part of the interpretive context are present in any storytelling and can be identified and treated in an instructional text. The first step in constructing such an instructional text would be to represent the interpreter's response in segments relative to the documented content of the text. A second step would involve identifying both the communal and private folklore significant in the interpreter's response to the text or performance. And a final step would involve identifying and demonstrating the interpreter's analytical perspective. In chapters 4 and 5, these three steps will be demonstrated through the construction of two contextualized interpretive texts. Chapter 4, interpreting Larry Scheiber's telling of "Koo-Nar, King of the Rats," employs only steps one and two, the segmentation of the text and the identification of private and communal folklore.

Private and Communal Folklore

The contrast between private and communal folklore indicated in step two is similar to Raymond Firth's (1973) distinction between private and public symbols. However, as I am using the terms, communal folklore might be widely shared and corroborated through research but not necessarily acknowledged as public or even traditional by the people involved; they may well believe that it is exclusive to their small group. In contrast, private folklore is in fact exclusively shared (and cannot be corroborated outside of the group), *and* it is privately or even personally generated through group interaction or personal experience. Thus, while communal folklore is often mistakenly assumed to be culture-specific and exclusive, comparative research demonstrates that it is not. Private folklore, on the other hand, is universal only in the largest sense, at a structural level. Its traditionality is limited by the context of personal or private history which spawned it.

Communal folklore includes representative texts of traditional tale types or motifs as well as the identifiable themes and allusions embedded in the texts of personal narratives. Private folklore would include those private traditions effective in creating meaning for a text but usually excluded from surveys of communal folklore, namely, (1) the narrowly culture-specific lore that constitutes part of an "idioculture,"[9] (2) the individual's impressionistic store of traditions that attach to either his own or another individual's life history—those subjectively significant items I would call *personalore*, and (3) the listener's interpretation of the teller's identity, personal values, and beliefs as reflected in the story. These three kinds of private folklore are not exclusive to personal narratives. However, because personal narratives are dependent upon such private folklore both functionally (to create a sense of intimacy) and by definition (the stories are idiosyncratic rather than traditional), the personal narrative is an ideal genre for exploring the role of private folklore in the interpretation of folklore texts.

Identifying the Interpreter

A corollary to the segregation of communal and private folklore is the identification of the audience and the transformation of audience members into interpreters of the text. A potential interpreter must first of all be competent as an audience member, but how can we assess the competence of an audience? In the early 1970s literary critics found themselves groping toward the audience familiar to folklorists while folklorists were busy expanding the notion of oral performance to include the literary interest in rhetoric. At the same time, cultural anthropologists were discovering "ethnosemantics," the "actor's definition" or "insider's view" of behavior. Most of these new perspectives involved a shift from the earlier authoritarian stance of the critic to an exploration of the individual or collective interpretive authority of the audience or culture group itself. Dundes's notion of "oral literary criticism" drew upon emerging theoretical developments in all three disciplines and clearly called for scholarly attention to the role and competence of the audience in the interpretation of oral texts.

Chapter 5, interpreting my mother's telling of "The Canary, or The Yellow Dress," represents a contextualized interpretive text involving all three steps mentioned above: (1) a segmented presentation, (2) identification of communal lore and personalore, and (3) an abstraction of the interpreter's analytical perspective. Together, the second and third steps require that the interpreter be specified, that the interpreter be a real individual offering his or her own oral literary criticism of the personal narratives. The concept of oral literary criticism assumes a traditional text—an item whose basic content is known in the community. Can oral literary criticism be useful in the study of personal narratives? One certainly can elicit commentary about personal narratives from the teller or audience, but such commentary might well be offered in an effort to obscure the real effect of the storytelling. The purpose of oral literary criticism (or of the kind of directed negotiation toward a consensus on "What is the point?" suggested in Livia Polanyi's sociolinguistic study, for example) is clearly to support a collectively shared or accepted interpretation (Polanyi 1979). The aim of the personal narrative, on the other hand, is the creation—even the foregrounding—of personal identity and the sense of intimacy between the teller and the audience, or in fact, each individual listener.

This does not mean that a personal narrative cannot be interpreted in terms meaningful to a community larger than that of teller and listener. However, a literary exegesis in this case should first address the two questions most clearly tied to the unique qualities of the genre and its presentation in context rather than moving immediately to the larger critical question of how this story can be made more universally accessible, more collectively meaningful. Efforts to understand a personal narrative involve asking how the story reveals aspects of the teller's identity to the listener, and how the listener's critical response was evoked through the presentation of the story. To effectively address these questions, I would propose a methodology purposefully restricted by certain prerequisites. These are (1) an acknowledged "documentary" frame, (2) clear allowance for the *individual* response of the listener, (3) commentary by an audience-interpreter whose relevant folk group is the same as the storyteller's,

(4) identification of an audience-interpreter who knows the conventions of literary criticism and could thus translate emic commentary into etic terms for purposes of (as Pertti Pelto suggests) "cross-cultural study of behavioral systems," and (5) an audience-interpreter willing to accept full responsibility for the act of interpretation.[10]

The first three of these prerequisites could be met through the oral literary criticism of perceptive listeners as Dundes envisions or by the articulation of "covert culture" through the methods of the "New Ethnography." Even the fourth could be met by the necessary critical competence of what Stanley Fish calls "the informed reader" (Fish 1980:48-49). However, as Fish graciously admits, "my reader is a construct, an ideal, or idealized reader." More specifically, Fish reveals that "the reader of whose responses I speak, then, is this informed reader, neither an abstraction nor an actual living reader, but a hybrid—a real reader (me) who does everything within his power to make himself informed." Fish would guarantee the critical competence of the reader by playing the role himself. Fish is himself the reader of *Lycidas* or *Paradise Lost*, and though others have read the texts and though he and these other readers share the frame of an "interpretive community," it is his own response alone that he can know and present as the response of the reader.

Literary critic David Bleich is much less apologetic about this inevitable subjectivity of the reader (Bleich 1975; 1978). He dispenses with the abstract hybrid and identifies the reader as himself or as another specific and real individual (by name) if that person has articulated a response. By recognizing other people's stated interpretations as valid responses, he affirms unequivocally the second prerequisite outlined above. But, unlike Fish, he cannot guarantee the fourth except when someone with established critical competence is the reader. When Bleich is himself the reader, then because of his critical training, his interpretation of a work of literature has an ideal "negotiative presence" among literary critics. To make the commentary of an "untrained" respondent (e.g., an undergraduate student) useful to his own academic audience, Bleich must add his own explanatory comments to these solicited responses—and indeed the resulting expanded criticism is quite impressive. Nevertheless, both Bleich and Fish are able to communicate with the larger scholarly community because they use etic units, conventions of the discipline that facilitate the "cross-cultural study of behavioral systems." But behind the conventions and accepted patterns of analysis is the unique web of responses and perceptions that is each man's interpretive signature. Robert M. Adams concludes much the same thing: "Given the way things are, it is only the pattern that one *personally* makes out of the patterns that yields any effectual command of a subject. Criticism, like history, is thus a *private* art one of whose conventions is that the critic shall *seem* to use evidence in accordance with a public code" (Adams 1971:213-14). The reader-response critic, conscious of his subjectivity, struggles not so much with the fact of his subjectivity but rather with the inescapable demand that he translate his personal response into the conventions of his own most influential interpretive community.[11]

.To return, then, to the question of the audience's critical competence, it would seem that my best recourse is to follow the lead of Bleich and Fish and accept my own response as listener in a natural context as the critical commentary I can most reliably articulate in terms meaningful to my colleagues. Other listeners *could* articulate their responses, and those responses, as Dundes suggests, would be quite valuable, especially if the listeners were clearly immersed in the culture of the teller. Nevertheless, an articulation of my response is at least potentially more valuable. Not only am I an insider in many of the folk groups important in my informants' identities, but I also am the informed listener of requirement number four, and I am willing to accept full responsibility for translating my hearing of the story into understanding, of deconstructing my personal response. The basic assumption underlying this methodology is that anyone's response to a personal narrative told in its natural context is to regard the story as a reflection of the teller's personal philosophy and stable identity. What is important is not so much whether the listener succeeds in *accurately* assessing the teller's values and personality but instead whether we can see *how* the listener came to hold the interpretation he or she offers, how the listener's response evolved.

Freud found the analysis of his own dreams a useful device for a number of reasons. A folklorist interested in personal narratives can take a cue from Freud and demonstrate a sensitivity to the privacy of informants and a commitment to a rigorous method of analysis by reconstructing his or her own strategies of response to the intimacy of content and context in personal narratives. Such a methodology focuses on a *literary text* created by an individual rather than spotlighting the individual directly; that is, it represents a literary rather than a purely psychological approach. And the folklorist-interpreter assumes responsibility for the interpretation offered by tacitly agreeing beforehand that any potentially embarrassing psychological "evidence" in the interpretation can be used to indict the interpreter alone, not the storyteller. Through these two procedural safeguards, researchers can claim a reliable methodology without compromising an ethical concern for their informants' psychological privacy when those informants agree to tell their personal narratives to shape-shifter friends who with little warning become folklorists. The basic directive in this methodology is toward an analysis of the generic conventions, themes, folkloric allusions, and personal frames of reference that are significant in the trained folklore scholar's own response as natural audience to the personal narratives of informants.

The Focusing Power of Analytical Schemes

The interpreter's analytical scheme, then, is a significant agent for focusing the response to or interpretation of a personal narrative. And if the interpreter is also the folklorist, then this analytical scheme will reflect the influence of folklore and literature's research paradigm. It will in fact reflect the individual's *cumulative* experience in devising an analytical focus, the myriad of analytical schemes considered, tried, pondered, rejected, or adapted through the years of scholarly training and practice. Individual interpreters will use their analytical schemes in idiosyncratic ways; this is why such schemes can be considered a part of the variable interpretive context.

In this study, I try to provide some information about this cumulative analytical influence by labeling my analytical practice in summary code glosses throughout chapter 5. Nevertheless, in keeping with the naturalistic paradigm adopted at the beginning of this study, I am content to allow this information to emerge as part of the instructional text. My use of the terminology (*discourse, type, style, theme, rhetoric, culture*, etc.) is, in fact, not very precise. Rather than impose some false sense of rigor, I must admit that in actual usage this imprecision is typical. However, the concepts, for all their imprecision and idiosyncratic application, are powerful and real influences upon my interpretation of these or any other literary text.

The third step in creating an interpretive instructional text requires the inclusion of this analytical scheme. It is beyond the scope of this study to analyze my analytical scheme and reconstruct its evolution. Gene Wise (1980:363-69) would have us do this unto others but not, thank goodness, unto ourselves. I can, however, offer the following signposts if anyone else cares to undertake the task. Three works undeniably implicated in my research are Roland Barthes's *S/Z: An Essay* (1974), Seymour Chatman's *Story and Discourse* (1978), and Alan Dundes's *Interpreting Folklore* (1980a). In addition, a chart which emerged as I created the analytical gloss is as follows:

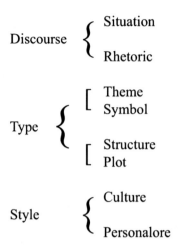

This analytical "strategy" is only implicit in chapter 4 but explicit in chapter 5. The tripartite scheme draws upon Dundes's essay (in *Interpreting Folklore)* titled "Texture, Text, and Context." In my adaptation, texture becomes style (linguistic content detail embodying cultural or private allusions), text becomes type (the translatable content or plot), and context becomes discourse (the context perceived by the interpreter within the interpretive context). As a category, style includes both communal folklore (culture) and private folklore (usually personalore), examples that are selected by the interpreter as significant reflections of stylistic choice in the narrative. Type includes themes and structure as would story outlines in a type index of personal narratives if such a compendium existed, as well as the common literary analytical concepts of plot and symbol. And discourse is used to designate examples of rhetoric or aspects of situation that either move the story along or frame it. The interpreter attends to discourse as a kind of metanarrative that influences interpretation but is not part of the content of the story. These three levels of analysis will be included as a running gloss to the instructional text in chapter 5.

The objective in presenting these expanded texts is to make the practice of interpreting folklore a more acceptable one in the discipline. Not all interpretations need document the interpretive context so fully. Having made the point at such length, I hope that the more general claim will be acknowledged—that the interpreter's task is to be true to his or her personal insight into the folklore and that the reader's responsibility lies in respecting that choice of focus.

4.

Koo-Nar, King of the Rats

Larry Scheiber was born on January 10, 1937, in Huntington, Indiana, and he grew up there, never leaving home until he joined the paratroopers for a three-year stint in 1957. At age twenty-three he returned to Huntington and his former job at Wabash Magnetics, an electronics plant on the east side of town. Larry decided to "bach it" rather than stay with his mother, who still lived in Huntington. His first bachelor flat was an unimproved garage behind the house of his friend Jim Brown. This garage is the setting for Larry's story of his encounter with an unusually large rat.

Very briefly, the story begins with Larry's description of his austere living quarters and his emphasis on the winter season and the obvious hardship of living in an unheated garage during a northern Indiana winter. One consequence of his living in a garage is the presence of a large rat, whom Larry dubs Koo-Nar. The rat expects to be fed. One night Larry forgets to feed Koo-Nar, and later he dreams that Koo-Nar attacks him in bed. In his dream he kills Koo-Nar by strangling him. Only in the spring when he moves out of the garage does Larry discover that he really had killed Koo-Nar. It was not a dream. Koo-Nar's corpse lay just below the bed, preserved by the cold.

My interpretation of this personal narrative views the ordeal of staying in the garage as a self-imposed initiation ritual, a rite of passage into manhood, and the rat is the primary symbolic adversary. The purpose of the initiation is twofold: first, to devise and successfully pass a test of endurance, and second, to discover a personally significant symbol that will serve in a personal evaluation of manhood. From my perspective, the lengthy stay in the old garage is a classic endurance test, and the rat is a symbol for the negative masculine sex-role stereotypes Larry hopes to replace with the more positive norms he has learned to value—namely, the positive traits of courage, physical toughness, and independence.

To present this interpretation more effectively, I would like to create a tutor text of "Koo-Nar, King of the Rats." A tutor text, as explained in chapter

3, is not simply a carefully documented performance text, such as that which closes Elizabeth Fine's study of *The Folklore Text* (1984). A tutor text is an instructional text that allows the interpreter to document contextuality, or the interpretive context. It is rather more like the analytical text Roland Barthes offers in *S/Z*, his interpretation of Balzac's *Sarrasine*. And, like Barthes's *S/Z*, the tutor text will be presented in analytical segments. An unsegmented documentary presentation of the text (version #1) can be found in the Appendix.

KN-1: [Setting] Koo-Nar, King of the Rats

The setting for the presentation of this story is a typical one for Larry. The situation is a late afternoon (after work) social hour at a local bar. Anthropologist Susan Ervin-Tripp suggests a useful distinction that breaks down the setting into its two referents: "that of *locale,* or time and place, and that of *situation*" (1964:86). The locale in this case is the Do-Drop-Inn, located in Huntington across the Wabash tracks on South Jefferson Street (doesn't every town have a Do-Drop-Inn?). This particular version of "Koo-Nar" was recorded on October 17,1974, a Thursday. The Do-Drop—or Terry's, as Larry usually called it—was one of Larry's favorite spots. The owner (and frequent bartender) was Terry Pastenbaugh, and because Larry was a regular, Terry tolerated a fair number of signs that identified this as Larry's "home territory bar."[1] Some of these signs include a Wabash Magnetics bumper sticker on the back entrance (several other regulars also work at Wabash), a few of Larry's "Campfire Corner" articles from the *Huntington Herald-Press* tacked to the bulletin board on the south wall near the bar, and a wall mounting of a "quarrow" donated by Larry. Unless one asked about the "quarrow's" origin, the small stuffed bird could go unnoticed or perhaps even scorned by those who fancy impressive wall trophies such as deer, bear, wildcat, or maybe an owl or hawk. There is, in fact, no such creature as a "quarrow," though it might now qualify as one of the mythological creatures, like the hoop snake, so popular in early American folklore. The "quarrow" was actually created through Larry's skillful taxidermy—a combination of a quail and a sparrow. Quite in character, Larry created as well a myth to explain the origin and habits of the strange fowl. According to Larry, the creature was a freak of nature that appeared suddenly at Larry's favorite mushroom spot. Because the bird stole the best mushrooms, Larry had no choice but to do it in. I might add that though the Do-Drop-Inn has changed hands, names, and decor since 1974, the "quarrow" survives in another bar across town on East Market, Larry's new "home territory bar."

Terry's in 1974 was a long, narrow building, approximately twenty feet by seventy feet including the small back room where supplies were stored. Like most of the "buildings on the bridge"—for which Huntington was once recognized in the National Almanac—Terry's had an upper floor that had once served as an apartment but was now condemned. Though the building was of simple wood frame construction, it had not suffered the considerable deterioration so obvious in the structures actually over the waters of the Little River (a branch of the Wabash that runs through town). The front of the building was plain; a single high window let some daylight into the long, dark interior. A handpainted sign advertised the name of the bar, while a commercial electric sign announced that Miller beer might be consumed within. Red plastic-covered booth benches were set all along the north wall of the room. The bar ran along the south wall and was about twenty feet long. Typically, the hard liquors were displayed behind it on a tiered platform. A microwave oven (for heating "Jet-wiches," a sandwich of cheese and dried beef) and racks of potato chips, pretzels, and beer nuts were at the far end of the countertop. Stools lined the bar, and a jukebox was flanked by two booths on the north wall. Just beyond the end of the bar and the row of booths was a single pool table with the usual low-swinging metal-shaded light casting shadows over the players.

The locale itself adds much to the situation in this case. Not only is there a typical "bar situation," but there is also a typical situation for Terry's on a Thursday afternoon after the major industries in town have closed down for the day. Many of Larry's friends or coworkers stop in for a few beers and maybe a game of pool before going home for the evening. I should mention that most of the patrons are men. The few women that do come in always sit at one of the tables and wait for Terry to come and ask for their order (unless they are with a man—who goes to the bar and orders for them). Needless to say, the context is not one in which I am a natural participant. I had never been to Terry's before my first interview there with Larry. On the other hand, though I am not a habitué of the Do-Drop-Inn, the "bar situation" itself is flexible enough to accommodate me and the various role characteristics the bar patrons (including Larry) might assign to me—even that of fieldworker intent on recording oral stories. For Larry, then, the situation is typical in all respects except for my expectations that he will (1) sit at a table with me and my sister, Carol, and (2) allow me to record his stories. Normally, Larry would sit at the bar, swapping stories with friends and greeting customers as they come in. Though Larry makes a point of speaking with any women who do come into Terry's, he usually does not join them for any length of time at their table, but rather wanders back to the bar or to other groups.

My presence and expectations do alter the typical context, then, but the usual situation is for the most part intact. The audience for Larry's story includes me and my sister, Carol, as well as other bar customers who occasionally turn their ear in our direction. Most of the regulars have heard Larry's stories before, but a number of them seem to enjoy the obvious notoriety Larry has earned and the fact that someone actually wants to record his "lies." My sister is, as will become obvious, an appropriately responsive audience member. She has known Larry longer than I have, and because she is closer to him in age, she shares many more acquaintances and cultural references with him than I do. (In 1974, Larry was thirty-eight years old, Carol was thirty-three, and I was twenty-seven. I had not lived in Huntington since 1970; Carol and Larry both lived in Huntington and worked at Wabash Magnetics.) On this Thursday afternoon we were seated in a booth, and Larry had ordered a round of drinks. I soon learned that one of the "rules" of bar behavior—at least at this bar, but also generally, according to Cavan's study (1966:117)—was the understanding that women do not offer to buy drinks in a mixed-sex group. Even my fieldworker role was no match for a long-standing sex-role dictate.[2] If Larry ever buys into women's lib, I owe him at least a dozen rounds of beer.

KN-2:   Carol: I must hear about Queue-Nar the Frog.
        Larry: Koo-Nar, not Queue-Nar.

This first exchange between Carol and Larry alludes indirectly to one of Larry's "Campfire Corner" articles. During the period of this recording, Larry regularly wrote a local nature-and-humor column for the hometown newpaper. Recently, Larry had written up a report on "The Koo-Nar Saga" in which he detailed a frog-hunting adventure that closed with the capture of the "biggest and most elusive" bullfrog of all—Koo-Nar. The huge bullfrog was dubbed "king of the frogs" when first sighted. After several unsuccessful chases, Larry finally caught the frog in the beam of his light and threw his No. 2 frog gig, and "Koo-Nar was dethroned unceremoniously." Not only did Larry get to eat the large legs of Koo-Nar at the Labor Day frogleg feast, but he also tanned the skin of one leg and stretched it over his knife sheath, webbed foot still intact. I suppose the magical implications of eating the flesh of the conquered king are obvious enough, as is the symbolic transferral of potency represented by his covering the knife with the skin of Koo-Nar's leg.

Larry does not explain why the frog is called Koo-Nar, only that he was "king of the frogs," that is, "the biggest and most elusive." Even though Larry does not say where the name Koo-Nar came from, he does make a point of correcting Carol's pronunciation of the name (the spelling in the first line represents my approximation of Carol's pronunciation; Larry's pronunciation of Koo-Nar is as it is spelled). Larry's attention to the pronunciation grows in part from the narrowly spread tradition surrounding the name: only he and his buddies had used the name before its appearance in the "Campfire Corner" article. Larry was still in a position to dictate how the name should be pronounced, since as far as he was concerned he had made the name up himself.

The name does seem to be entirely Larry's own creation. Unlike the "new comparative mythologists," I shall not attempt any real or possible reconstruction of unconscious linguistic sources that may have influenced Larry's creation (or recombination/selection) of the word *Koo-Nar*.[3] However, an association that appears meaningful to me is the similarity between Koo-Nar and Kohinoor, the name given to the very large (106 or 109 carat) diamond from India that became one of the crown jewels of England in 1849. This famous gem was very likely in the news during the coronation of Elizabeth II (1952), when Larry was in his teens; he could have been taken with the name and unconsciously retained the association with great size and the crown (or kingship). Whether or not Larry really made such associations between the two names, to me as listener the regality and size associated with the name Kohinoor (pronounced [ko-a-noor]) enhances my appreciation of the name Koo-Nar. It connotes more fully the sense of power, great size, uniqueness, and regality of the creature identified by the name.

Beyond the introduction of the name Koo-Nar, an interesting game of implicature is represented by the brief exchange in segment KN-2. The ethnography of bar talk is fairly complicated, as Spradley and Mann (1975) have shown, but a cardinal rule is that women are never to be overtly aggressive in exchanges with men. Carol's opening statement is easily heard as a mildly veiled command; she says, "I *must* hear about Queue-Nar the Frog." If she *must* hear the story, then Larry *must* tell it. Larry's response to the mock order is to correct Carol's pronunciation—a mild and appropriate put-down, but a put-down just the same (he could have ignored the pronunciation). The rhetoric of the statement is perceived by Larry as inappropriately aggressive. Inadvertently, Carol has placed Larry in the position of having to defend his manhood, at least as defined in the bar context. Acceptable bar bantering must ultimately support the cardinal rule of male aggressiveness and female passivity. And Larry feels the pressure of this rule even if Carol has missed it (or perhaps purposefully flouted it).

KN-3: Carol: OK, who named him Koo-Nar? In the first place?
      Larry: Well, we named him after the king of the rats who used to

live—
Sandy: King of what rats?!
Larry: You never heard about Koo-Nar—the king of the rats?!
Carol: Nooo, you never told me about Koo-Nar [laughs], the king of
         the rats.

Following the awkward opening, the dialogue takes an unexpected turn and sets the scene for the story that follows. Carol briefly acknowledges Larry's correction *and* implied message by answering, "OK." Because "OK" enjoys so many context-based meanings in our culture, Larry is free to assume that in saying "OK" Carol recognizes his "authority" both in regard to the pronunciation of *Koo-Nar* and in regard to his role as a male and a regular at Terry's. Carol then uses a more acceptable tone but again, more subtly this time, challenges Larry to defend, not his authority as a male but rather his "authority" for dubbing the frog "king" and giving him the name Koo-Nar. Larry responds to this with his usual unnerving straight-faced seriousness, introducing in an offhand manner the "king of the rats" as his "obvious" source. This is our first clue that Larry is a consummate tall-tale artist (even when not telling "tall tales"). As Henningsen says of the tall-tale teller, "He does not expect to be believed, but he wants not to be interrupted as long as he lies consistently" (1965:213).

Larry is not literally lying in this instance—he did borrow the notion of Koo-Nar, king of the frogs, from his earlier notion of Koo-Nar, king of the rats. The "lying" technique is rather in his seemingly straightforward assumption that "king of the rats" is an acceptable cultural allusion. In fact, as we shall see, the allusion is shared or collective only in the narrowest sense—that is, among Larry's close friends. Through the story that follows, the allusion becomes an element of idioculture or private folklore for Carol and me, as it was for Larry's usual audience of regulars at Terry's. Larry uses this bit of personalore as a source in this offhand allusion just as an accomplished liar would make a most matter-of-fact reference to an entirely fictional frame he imposes upon his listeners as acceptable and true. In typical lying contest form, Larry answers the challenge to one lie with another lie. In this instance, my response to Larry's second lie reflects my familiarity with the genre of the tall tale and my sensitivity to motifs of folk literature. The eagerness of my question—"King of what rats?!"—is all too obviously that of an overzealous folklorist who has caught what she hopes is a real live (indexed even) folkloric allusion in the midst of the mundane.

Actually, the immediate association I had—the one that prompted my question, I am sure—was not motif B241.2.4, King of Rats (there is indeed such a motif), but rather the better-known traditional tale that turns on the death of the King of the Cats, Aarne-Thompson type 113A, The King of the Cats Is Dead. In this enigmatic tale, usually a man comes home, where his wife and house cat are waiting for him, and announces that he has seen a cat funeral or someone has told him that X (some name) is dead, whereupon the house cat leaps up and says, "Now I am king of the cats," and disappears (usually up the chimney). I have always been intrigued by the tale, perhaps because the man finds himself unwittingly playing a role in a "cultural system"—the kingdom of the cats—which has all along existed before his very eyes without his once suspecting it. Whatever the reason, my response to Larry was much as I would have put into the mouths of the man and wife in AT 113A: "King of what cats?!"—or more precisely, "Where is there a kingdom of cats? I have never heard of it!" Larry responds to exactly this implication in my question when he says, "You never heard about Koo-Nar, the king of the rats?!"

Larry's response is also a play on a personal allusion shared only by Larry, me, my husband, and Carol. The allusion involves only the first part of the question and an exaggeration of the tone of disbelief that usually accompanies it. The personalore involved is an earlier incident, not long after I had first met Larry, in which I had commented on Larry's use of a famous quotation in one of his "Campfire Corner" articles. He responded that he didn't know who had said it, so I suggested Bartlett's *Familiar Quotations.* He replied something like, "Hmm, what's that?" And I, in sincere disbelief, countered, "You've never heard of Bartlett's *Familiar Quotations*?!" Thereupon, I was startled and amused by an odd gesture. Grasping his upper lip between his thumb and forefinger, with his chin slightly extended, Larry pulled his lip toward me in repeated tugs while exclaiming, "No, I've never heard of Bartlett's *Familiar Quotations*!" Thus mildly chastised, I acknowledged the possible insult of my incredulous tone and dropped the subject of Bartlett's *Familiar Quotations.*[4] Nevertheless, I always now associate the gesture with the phrase "You never heard of . . . ?" and especially when Larry brings it to mind, as in the pointed use of the phrase here in his comment on the king of the rats.

Finally, it should be noted that Carol's response brings the "lying" frame full circle by dispelling any lingering possibility that "king of the rats" is indeed a cultural (in the large sense) allusion. She says, "Nooo [picking up Larry's mocking tone], you never told me about Koo-Nar [laughs] the king of the rats." In other words, it is clear that Carol knows there is no real, or even a traditional, "king of the rats" to which Larry is referring; rather, the only way she would ever know about this alleged "king of the rats" is if Larry were to tell her, since it is obviously his own creation—the fictitious frame for the lie he is going to tell. So, of course, Larry then proceeds to tell his story.

KN-4:   Larry: OK—when I first got out of the service . . .

This introductory clause is part of the orientation, as Labov and Waletzky (1967:32) identify it; in this instance, it is an indication of the approximate date and place of the incident to follow. Getting out of the service usually means going home, especially if one is so young as Larry was when he finished his three-year stint as a paratrooper (he was barely twenty-three). The incident, then, takes place in Huntington, and the date is midwinter, early 1960. An important bit of personalore is assumed in Larry's casual reference to the service. In fact, Larry was very proud of having served as a paratrooper—not so much out of patriotic fervor (though he is quite patriotic) but rather because parachuting is such an adventurous and hazardous activity. Even in this allusion to his three years as a paratrooper, Larry already introduces the dominant theme of the story—his determined efforts to "prove his manhood." Twenty years later, Larry still wears his "Screaming Eagles" paratrooper jacket. As we shall see, the parachute itself is symbolically retained and used (in a new capacity) even after his return to civilian life.

KN-5:   Larry: . . . I was poverty-stricken. I went through my—my, what-do-you-call-it, separation money like flies on shit, you know? Buying drinks for the whole crew. I'd go into bars and just say, "Give everybody a drink," and throw in a wad of money and go into the next bar and say, "Buy a round for the house," and lay it out. I was really cool!

Carol: You were so glad to be home—

Larry: No, I wanted to make friends—'cause—I'd been out of circulation for so long.

With the completion of the sentence, Larry introduces the important secondary theme of poverty, or surviving economic hard times. The implication is that the hard times are temporary. The theme of *surviving* hard times is effective only if it can be perceived as a test that can be passed at some point in the future. "Poverty-stricken" in Larry's case is to be seen from a middle-class perspective: it is a blow that can be remedied in time. In fact, in version #2 of "Koo-Nar," Larry identifies very specifically the time period that must pass before he successfully survives economic hard times. He says: "And for the first two weeks, you know, I didn't have a paycheck or anything. See, I was workin' at Wabash Magnetics, and when you work there, you don't get paid at the end of your first week. You don't get paid until the second week.

And I did not have shit—I mean literally nil, and I wouldn't accept anything from anybody 'cause I was too damn proud." Larry can well afford to be "too damn proud" to accept anyone's help because he knows that he will be paid at the end of two weeks; he is not caught in the trap of hopeless poverty. His self-description as "too damn proud" is in fact so overstated as to be tongue-in-cheek from the perspective of several years later. A similar ambiguity lightens the tone of some of Larry's best "Campfire" articles, in which Larry's family is depicted as "poor but proud." With nostalgic humor, he writes about the mixed virtue of such poor but hopeful beginnings.

To return to version #1, we might well be intrigued with Larry's explanation of *why* he was "poverty-stricken" (in version #2 he offers no reason except that he had not yet received a paycheck). In version #1 he actually seems to be awkwardly flouting the Maxim of Quantity, as Grice and Pratt identify it: "Do not make your contribution more informative than is required" (Pratt 1977:130). That is, rather than letting his listeners assume that he simply was broke because he had not yet received his first paycheck (as in version #2), he confesses that he has blown his military separation money in an obvious effort to buy some new friends, to "get back into circulation." Like most intimate exposures of a more serious nature, this disclosure was not expected or required by his audience. Neither Carol nor I (having never served in the military) would have thought to ask, "Yes, but what about your separation money?" Instead, the revelation is entirely of Larry's own choosing. Perhaps he feels safe in doing so because we are women, or maybe he even intentionally does so because we are women and would welcome some sign that he is a vulnerable and sensitive individual who recognizes his need for social relationships. As one male journalist has said, "Suddenly, to be male and vulnerable is to be utterly acceptable—but only to women" (Engel 1982:13). Not only is a vulnerable male acceptable to women, he is in fact appealing *if* he can manage to impress the woman who witnesses his vulnerability that his confession is exclusive—a sign that she in particular is worthy of his trust. Having been reared by two women (his mother and aunt), Larry likely has learned that confession to women more often produces a bond of intimacy rather than judgment. Whether he *prefers* the intimacy over the judgment is not necessarily implied, but I think he has discerned a subtle sex-based rhetorical rule: women rather like to be the recipients of intimate (*verbal*) exposures by men. In this case, it is significant that in version #2, where two males—John Fisher (a friend of Larry's) and Mark (my husband)—are present, reference to the squandered separation money is entirely absent.

It is interesting that Larry's direct articulation of his desire to make friends and get back into circulation comes after Carol's suggestion that his extravagance is in fact exuberance at being home. Larry denies this more "respectable" motive—there is nothing shameful about joyful (if thriftless) celebration at being home again, after all. This is our first clear indication that Carol will consistently try to determine Larry's evaluation of the story content (the incident) and express it verbally herself, thereby inviting his agreement or further elaboration (or disagreement, as in this case). Whereas Labov and Waletzky (and Robinson in reassessing their study) suggest that the teller himself offers the necessary evaluation of a personal narrative, I would argue that this feature of the story is always individualized among the listeners and teller and may even be articulated separately as in this case, through short dialogue among the participants while the story is being told, or, as is often the case with my mother's stories, not articulated at all but rather silently evolved within the teller's or listener's own understanding. (This would put the form of the personal narrative more in line with the oral legend as Dégh has described it, rather than the typical folktale—even when the audience does not verbally interrupt (see respectively Labov and Waletzky 1967; Robinson 1981; and Dégh 1965b). Larry's own evaluation of his behavior was actually expressed somewhat sardonically just before Carol's comment. He says simply, "I was really cool!" By thus labeling his own behavior, Larry implies that he was actively striving to be "cool," something a really cool person does not do. And of course in the 1970s the word *cool* used in this way is slightly anachronistic.

Finally, we hear within this segment our first colorful hint that Larry exhibits an inexhaustible supply of traditional expressions or expressions modeled on traditional ones. Some are simply standard examples of folk speech—"a wad of money," "a round for the house," "out of circulation." Others—for instance, the proverbial simile "like flies on shit"—are obvious reminders that he is not inhibited by whatever social, religious, or personal pressures might discourage the use of "dirty words." In fact, the only real inhibition I have ever noticed in Larry's oral storytelling is his conscientious avoidance of the word *fuck* when speaking to women. In his story of "The Red Velvet Suit" (see the Appendix), we can see his self-imposed censorship at work in his substitution of the sound *eff* [*F*] for "fuck" and the sound *emm eff urs* [*M-fers*] for *motherfuckers*. In fact, he is complaining about someone else using the terms (a striking example of unsolicited oral literary criticism)! Larry says, "We'd been there about five minutes and here comes some little punk in, goin 'F-this, F-that,' calling people M-fers." He then comments, "I asked him three times, I said, 'Hey, man, people have got their wives here and stuff. Now cool it or I'm gonna break your jaw!'" When a fight ensues, the hostess of the party calls Larry a "son-of-a-bitch troublemaker" and tells him to leave. Larry responds with disbelief and asks, "Didn't you hear what he was sayin'?" When the hostess replies that, yes, she heard and, no, she didn't mind, Larry says, "Well, then you're a damned hog!" Obviously, Larry feels no decent woman would (or should) tolerate this particular "dirty word" in her presence.[5] In fact, Larry complained when I showed him the transcript of his story "Tiny Wires and the Chicken Blood" (see chapter 3) that he would *never* have said "fuckin' bucket" in front of a woman. I assured him that his writer's love for assonance was obviously just too compelling in this instance.

I should point out that Larry is well aware of the variety of contexts in which euphemisms or simple avoidance of "dirty words" is appropriate. On the other hand, he is also aware that for a man to use a euphemism in place of a "dirty word" is, as Larry would say, a "sissy-assed thing to do." It is interesting to see how he gets around this dilemma in his "Campfire Corner" articles, in which, of course, he is expected to keep his language "clean." Rather than resort to traditional euphemisms (though he sometimes does use them tongue-in-cheek), Larry translates the dirty slang into its most literal (and least recognizable) expression. For example, in "The Koo-Nar Saga" he writes: "From across the pond out of the darkness there issued a stream of comments questioning the legality of my family tree, the reputations of my ancestors. . . ." Easily, we can see that Larry has been called a bastard and a son-of-a-bitch, but he wouldn't dare print that. On the other hand, he does want his readers to know that *in the proper context* he does indeed "talk like a man," and so do his friends. Terry's is a man's world. Women in "the bar situation" are expected to tolerate (perhaps share) the use of dirty words, at least up to a point dictated by current taste (or the values of the bar regulars).

Before leaving this segment (or more accurately, its counterpart in version #2), I should clarify one item of reference generally restricted to residents of Huntington—Larry's place of employment, Wabash Magnetics (now Kearney Wabash). Wabash, as it is usually called by its employees, is a manufacturing firm that produces electric coil windings and high-voltage power supplies. Most of the production lines are "manned" by women who wind, glue, solder, magnetize, assemble, and pack the factory's products. Inspectors on the lines are also women (Carol was an inspector at Wabash in 1974). Except for the office secretaries, nearly all the nonproduction employees and upper-level production supervisors are men. Larry works as a technical engineer at Wabash. Much of his day-to-day social interaction with women (at least in 1974) grew out of the asymmetrical employment arrangement at Wabash, and this pattern was reinforced by the typical male-dominant bar culture at Terry's.

KN-6:   Larry: Well, anyway, to compensate for this [pause] obvious lack of
                   thrift, I moved in a guy's—it was supposedly a garage, but it
                   sorta leaned at a forty-five-degree angle and had about an inch
                   slits in the boards—between the sides. And I hung a parachute
                   up for a ceiling, you know, and I parked my MG under there.
                   And I had a *bed*—three innersprings and three mattresses!
                   And—and that's all I had in there for furniture—and then an
                   ironing board, and then I had a vise on the ironing board—and
                   that was my kitchen.

This description of the spartan living quarters in Jim Brown's garage completes
the orientation section. Each of the five items Larry mentions in the orientation
section feeds into the theme of masculinity. That is, aside from the overall
rugged existence suggested by the description of Larry's living quarters, Larry's
description invokes a series of minor symbolic items that also serve the theme
of masculinity. The first of these is the garage itself. Initially, the garage would
seem a poor image; Larry describes it, in version #2, as "an old shabby-assed,
fallen-down thing that had a pile of bricks down at one end holdin' it up. And
it had half-inch cracks you could see between the boards. I mean it was really
sad—leaned at a forty-five-degree angle." No man would want to identify with
such a building; it is definitely not properly erect but seems to be instead well
on its way toward going flat. Larry proceeds to remove the bricks from the
corner (as he explains in version #2), "which made it lose another ten degrees."
He looks at the sagging structure and says, "Hell, I'll lift it," and he does. The
garage is now properly erect, and its erection is both symbolically and more
mundanely a tribute to Larry's masculinity. It is, after all, a manly virtue to be
competent in the engineering and performance of tasks of construction and
building repair.

The second item Larry mentions is his parachute. Telling the story in
1974, Larry seems very aware of the symbolism with which he surrounds the
parachute and its use as insulator and wall covering in his rough abode. He
says in version #2: "I had this big parachute; I'd stretched it across the ceiling
hoping it would hold in the heat, my body heat, ya know. And I had another
parachute halfway through the garage, and I had my MG pulled in it, on the
other side of the parachute. 'Cause I was still living this old paratrooper role,
ya know. Had the strings a-hangin' down, and I'd built a little fireplace and
had a big fire cracklin' there. I was really cool. And I had gourds all hollowed
out with candles in them." Larry knows that he was still clinging to the ready-

made macho image he had earned as a paratrooper, and he knows that he was probably overplaying the role, bringing in the romantic Robinson Crusoe imagery (hollowed-out gourds, hand-built fireplace, insulating draperies). He was, as he says, "really cool." But, self-conscious or not, the symbolism of the parachute certainly adds to the theme of masculinity in the orientation section. Along with the parachute, Larry's MG is a third symbol of machismo. *MG* is the accepted acronym for a small sports car from Morris Garages. As Priscilla Denby (1981) has pointed out, in American culture vehicles of this sort are an acknowledged male symbol. Men who own MGs readily identify with them, keeping them shiny and in top running order, and Larry seems to follow the convention.

The fourth item Larry describes in some detail is his bed: "And I had a *bed*—three innersprings and three mattresses!" In version #2, he reduces the number of springs and mattresses to two each: "I got two bed springs and put 'em in there and two innerspring mattresses, put those on top of the bed springs. And it was 'broing, broing'—[makes up-and-down motion with hand]—better than a waterbed!" The seemingly innocent word *bed*—and especially the more recent waterbed—bring immediately to mind the notion of "going to bed"—not alone, of course. Larry accentuates the obvious by including hand gestures and onomatopoeia that suggest someone (ones) bouncing on the bed (reminiscent of the perennial newlyweds' car slogan: "Hot Springs Tonight"). In addition to the meaning in the story, the word *bed* picks up some extra charge from its use in the specific storytelling context. *Bed* is always an awkward word in mixed company, or rather it is one usually avoided unless the speaker actually wants to (in a seemingly innocent manner) insert some slight sexual innuendo into the conversation. Edward Sagarin quotes Randolph and Wilson on the subject of Ozark word usage: "Even *bed* is not a term to be used by 'nice' girls before male strangers" (Sagarin 1962:100). Larry, of course, *has* to mention bed at some point since it figures in the plot of his story; nevertheless, it serves well early in the story as a sign of his constant readiness to engage in sexual activity and thus as a symbol of his masculinity.

Finally, Larry mentions his kitchen table—an ironing board with a vise on it. The ironing board itself is certainly in keeping with the Robinson Crusoe image already established. Superficially, it is simply an old piece of junk relegated to the storage shed (garage). Larry, being resourceful, puts it to use as a table—since, as he says, he has no other furniture. However, no man's man would ever be caught with an ironing board sitting around in his house—unless, of course, he could in some way make it obvious that the board is never used for ironing but only as a makeshift table. Larry accomplishes this by attaching a vise—an obvious sign that the ironing board is in fact a work bench (an acceptably male piece of furniture) that also serves as a "kitchen table." Thus, the otherwise feminine piece of furniture is transformed functionally and symbolically into a masculine one.

KN-7:   Larry: Really, I lived in this shack, and I'd wake up with snow drifts on my bed.

         Carol: Think how it toughened you, Larry! You're a better person for it!

         Larry: Did you ever take a bath in Lake Clare in February?! [High-pitched] Oh, hoho—God! It makes my goodies blue just to think about it. Oh, Lord!

In a summary sentence, Larry capsulizes the rigors of life in a garage through a most effective exaggeration: "I'd wake up with snow drifts on my bed." The thematic impetus behind Larry's decision to stay in the garage—snow drifts and all—is more clearly expressed in version #2. There he says: "I really didn't have anywhere to live, you know. And I didn't want to move into Mom's 'cause that seemed like such a sissy-assed thing to do. So my buddy Brown, he was living with his mom—he had no shame—[Laughter], he said, 'You can live in our garage!' Well, I actually asked him. (You guys got me tellin' the truth.) I actually asked him if I could live in his garage. And he said, 'You're out of your mind!' ya know. And I said, 'Well, can I live in there?' And he said, 'Hell, yes!—if you can hack it.'" Larry bluntly states that he did not want to move back into his mother's house. There are subtle clues, however, that from the perspective of fifteen years later, Larry is somewhat amused by this obvious posturing and overemphasis on a macho image. He says moving into Mom's *seemed* like "such a sissy-assed thing to do." He humorously accused Jim Brown of having "no shame," though it is clear that Larry is stereotyping himself for us (listeners) through his use of this melodramatic convention. Nevertheless, he makes it clear that it was *his* decision to live in the garage, not because he had to but because he wanted to prove that he could "hack it." Later in version #2, his mother says, "You've proved your point, you're a big outdoorsman." He even lets the storytelling situation itself lend support (insidiously) to the theme of proving his masculinity. He corrects his statement that Jim Brown had suggested his staying in the garage. Instead, he asserts that he has been caught in a lie, that the truth is he *asked* if he could stay in the garage. His confession makes it hard for us to entertain any notion but that he had asked to stay in the garage, that he sought out his own test to prove his manhood. ("You guys," by the way, can in midwestern usage include females, as it does here, just as "y'all" in the South is inclusive.)

Carol responds to Larry's capsule statement with an evaluative comment that, superficially anyway, reinforces Larry's he-man image. She implies that his stoic endurance has bolstered his manly character: "You're a better person for it!" But again, as with Larry's own tongue-in-cheek comment about Jim Brown, Carol's tone is not without a tinge of sarcasm—as though she recognizes the overstatement or stereotyping invoked through Larry's exaggerated description of his wintry testing ground. Larry is not about to let Carol's mild sarcasm pass unnoticed. He immediately poses a rhetorical question: "Did you ever take a bath in Lake Clare in February?!" Neither Carol nor I bother to answer, of course, since it is obvious that Larry is actually implying that he *did* bathe in Lake Clare in February—clearly the ultimate test of his manly stoicism. He then rather dramatically recreates an illusionary midwinter plunge and its effect; that is, he raises the pitch of his voice and utters a startled response cry (Goffman [1981:101] would call it a "transition display") as though he had just entered the icy waters before our very eyes. As if the falsetto cry were not enough—Legman (1975:465) describes the sudden use of falsetto as an example of metonymy in which the understood referent is castration—Larry explicitly reminds us that he has thus willingly tested his most vulnerable parts.[6] Even the memory of the icy bath is enough to "turn his goodies blue"—which, I suppose, is an obvious reminder that he indeed still has them. Though *goodies* is not conventional slang (or rather its usual meaning is something edible, such as party appetizers—mountain oysters?), it is clear in this context that Larry is rather nicely avoiding any traditional terms that refer to the testicles while yet invoking sufficient associations for clarity. Though even in mixed company the term *balls* is frequently used, generally as a synonym for *guts* or *nerve,* still it is a bit awkward for a man to publicly use the term *balls* in front of a woman when referring specifically to his own body. To me at least it seemed that Larry was purposefully avoiding the word that would mentally (linguistically) invite a personal exposure while at the same time flirtatiously invoking the kind of "catch-tale" word play that embarrasses the audience rather than the teller for hearing the taboo implication.

A locally restricted cultural referent is Lake Clare. Some additional humor attends this allusion for those who live around Huntington, in that even in summer Lake Clare is very cold. The lake was originally a limestone quarry; the spring that feeds it keeps the water cold, as do the depth, the straight, clifflike banks, and the general paucity of aquatic vegetation. The lake is on the northeast periphery of Huntington, not far from the Wabash Magnetics plant. The whole notion of anyone bathing in Lake Clare in the wintertime is ludicrous, but the image effectively conveys the secondary theme of enduring severe winter conditions, all part of the symbolic testing of the "great outdoorsman." And of course beneath the imagery is the primary structural function of the test, specifically in this case "Manhood to prove."

KN-8:   Larry: So anyhow, where in the hell was I anyhow—?
        Carol: King of the rats!
        Larry: OK, OK, Koo-Nar, king of the rats—. [Everyone: Right!]

This brief exchange—which would make absolutely no sense out of context—is an example of what William O. Hendricks, and Barbara A. Babcock soon after, have called "metanarration" (see Babcock 1977:62). That is, the dialogue is a reflexive dimension of the storytelling. Larry's question— "Where in the hell was I anyhow?"—refers to the ongoing story itself; he is in effect telling his audience that he has temporarily lost his place in the narrative. In light of the raucous dramatics preceding this segment, I would suspect that Larry has lost himself in a moment of self-consciousness, perhaps embarrassment. Whatever the reason, Larry has temporarily lost his train of thought, and he asks our aid in returning him to the narrative. It is interesting that Carol simply invokes the tacitly recognized title of the story ("Koo-Nar, King of the Rats") rather than picking up some catchwords from the immediately preceding narrative content—something like "bathing in Lake Clare" or "the garage." Carol does not in fact answer Larry's question at all. Since, as Grice and Pratt suggest, coherence in any conversation depends on implicatures, we might ask what is implicated by Carol's comment (see Pratt 1977:154). As is typical throughout the text, Carol's statement is evaluative, and in this case, it is metanarrationally evaluative. That is, she suggests indirectly that it is time to move away from the orientation section of the story and get on to the complicating action, the plot itself. (As suggested earlier, unlike Labov and Waletzky, I view the evaluation as a scattered or evolved phenomenon shared by the participants rather than a separable segment in the teller's text.) Larry's response to Carol's implied suggestion is a slightly nettled "OK, OK." After all, it is his story. But I concur with Carol, Larry agrees, and we move on.

KN-9:   Larry: OK, when I first moved in there I didn't have money zero.
                 And—and all I had was three pieces of celery that a guy gave
                 me from work.
        Carol: Oh, you poor baby!
        Larry: —So I made soup out of it in a tin can. [Laughter] I really and
                 truly did, honest to God, that's all I had for all week. And as

things got better I bought a loaf of bread and—but listen, let
me tell you, before I moved out of there I had money stashed in
nail cans, and . . .

Carol: You were a miser!

Larry: Yeah, you could say that! Really!

Larry backtracks briefly with a reiteration of his "poverty-stricken" state on moving into the garage. By way of illustration, he begins what I think would have been a fairly detailed embedded story of his soup-making experience (the experience *is* reported in detail in version #2). Carol interrupts Larry with some bantering mock sympathy, and Larry then compresses the incident into a single sentence and goes on to defend the truth of his statement. Though Carol's statement may seem intrusive in light of the fuller detail I am assuming Larry *might* have included, it is more accurately simply a response to her own interpretation of Larry's line about the celery. Unlike Larry, who likely intended to present the lie about the soup in accepted tall-tale fashion (remember, Henningsen suggested that a good liar expects not to be interrupted so long as he is consistent), Carol seems to hear Larry's sentence as a *fait accompli,* a kind of close-ended imagery that sums up his economic situation. (Carol also contends that she was a bit inebriated, but I don't think our various "ethnographies of speaking" accommodate such an explanation.) In any event, Larry resorts to a simple bare-faced assertion of the truth of his statement—"I really and truly did, honest to God, that's all I had for all week"—rather than seducing his listeners into believing him through the time-honored tradition of the well-told lie. For the beauty of it, here is his development of the incident from version #2: "And good old Louis Shoenauer was eating his lunch one day and he says, 'Larry, you want any of this?' He had celery sticks and carrot sticks there. And I said, 'No, I'm not hungry.' He said, 'Come on down and eat 'em, I'm awful full.' So I said, 'Well, maybe I'll eat them later.' So he said, 'OK,' and he handed them to me, and I put 'em in my pocket. And I got home that night, and I got a big old coffee can that was in there and I dumped the nails out—it was full of rust. And I filled it with water, and I got it boiling; Brown gave me a little hot plate. And I got this water boiling, and I gingerly and carefully [pause] chopped this celery and carrots into this coffee can and boiled it for two hours. And Brown brought me out some salt, and I put that in there. This had to last me two weeks, ya know." Like most tall-tale tellers (and Larry does tell some traditional tales), Larry skillfully accumulates detail after detail until the punchline is just a breath short of being unassailable.[7]

There is something about this wonderfully patient and minutely detailed description that evokes both a nostalgic and a pleasantly sensuous response, at least from my perspective. Like the celebrated luxuriousness of Keats's verbal imagery in "The Eve of St. Agnes," where Porphyro "with glowing hand" but a strangely restrained deliberateness brings to the bedside bowls "of candied apple, quince, and plum, and gourd; with jellies soother than the creamy curd, And lucent syrups, tinct with cinnamon," so Larry in his plain but clear prose creates a brief interlude that delights in the natural sensuousness of quietly restrained verbal detail. He "gingerly and carefully" chops the celery and carrots into the can of boiling water. In version #2 at least, he is in no hurry to skim over the details of his adventure. As in so many children's adventure stories, every mundane action is infused with great significance through attention to minute detail, as though the actor stood back and watched himself performing the most interesting of rituals in a world made real only through his own wonderfully rich verbal detail.

Larry returns the focus to the theme of poverty and contrasts his economic problems at the beginning of his ordeal with the wealth he has accumulated by the time he is ready to leave the garage. In what is now a fairly consistent pattern, Carol restates or label Larry's behavior ("You were a miser!"), and thus offers an evaluative survey of this brief segment. In this instance, Larry concurs with Carol's evaluation—"Yeah, you could say that! Really!"

KN-10:   Larry: Anyway, this rat lived in there with me, you see? Not by invitation! And, every night I'd hear him in the garbage bag, and I'd flash a light over there, and he'd run like hell. And he was a *big dude*! Well, he got so when I'd flash the light over there, he'd just go [puts thumbs in ears and wiggles fingers while making noise and sticking out tongue], blll-bll-bl. [Laughter] I'm not kidding you, this was a BIG RAT!—looked like a raccoon! [Laughter] And as long as I fed the dude we were on peaceful terms.

In American culture, rats are rarely viewed in a positive light. My own view of the symbolic aspects of Koo-Nar is cumulative from three analytic perspectives. They are, briefly, (1) collective symbolism, or the perspective of the "informed reader," (2) personal symbolism, or my subjective perspective, and (3) intranarrative symbolism, or story-specific (restrictive) symbolism, symbolism that evolves through the specific actions of the (nontraditional) plot. The first two perspectives represent again related but slightly conflicting views within the field of reader-response criticism represented by Stanley Fish (1980) and David Bleich (1978) respectively. They do not reflect exactly the distinction made by Raymond Firth (1973) between public and private symbolism, although these terms may seem roughly synonymous; the difference is (as in Bleich's "subjective paradigm") that the second perspective does not represent ethnographic insight into private symbols but rather the interpreter's subjective response to public and/or private symbols. The third perspective can be discussed more effectively in the next segment of the tutor text, since essential plot material (on which this symbolism depends) is presented there.

At the first level, as an "informed" listener, I can research some of the collective symbolism attached to rats generally. Much of the "totemistic" symbolism is culture-specific and for the most part tied to non-Western sacred systems. Certainly within some cultures there have been some positive associations with rats. In Chinese tradition, for example, the rat accompanies the god of riches and should not be killed at the New Year festival lest the riches it symbolizes be lost (see Eberhard 1970:213). Typically in Western tradition, however, the rat is associated only with disease and death. In medieval symbolism it was associated with the devil. And, according to Cirlot, "a phallic implication has been superimposed upon it [the rat], but only in so far as it is dangerous or repugnant" (Cirlot 1962:259-60). Though this "phallic implication" is only associative, it is this particular association of the rat with the usual focus of male sexuality that is, I think, a prominent symbolic connection in the story of Koo-Nar. The adversary in this ritualistic testing is a male and an embodiment of the negative traits associated with maleness.

The rat may be seen as a symbol of the wickedness, vileness, or danger so often associated with sex generally (especially in the strongly conditioned world view of American children or adolescents). In a provocative comparison of other educational systems with our own, Ruth Benedict illustrates the unfortunate disregard for conditioning attitudes in American sex education: "The adult in our culture has often failed to unlearn the wickedness or the dangerousness of sex, a lesson which was impressed upon him strongly in his most formative years" (1968:430). Especially for men (boys), the rat may serve as a symbol for the evil they are taught to associate with their own sexuality. Not only are American boys taught that sex is "bad," they are taught that male sexuality represents a particularly evil compulsion, the blight that keeps them lower than the angels. There is nothing heroic in this view of male sexuality, no virtue to strive for. The rat cannot deny its aggressive, vicious nature, and, by implication, neither can a young American male easily deny the aggressive sexuality his culture says is his by birthright.

A second level of symbolism—personal symbolism—simply reinforces the negative association with the rat. J. D. A. Widdowson, in an article on "Animals as Threatening Figures in Systems of Traditional Social Control," comments that rats are often "associated with a dark cellar in which the naughty or annoying child is threatened to be put, where [rats] will eat them" (1978:37). Whether rats are ever specifically mentioned or not, I think all children (and many adults) simply assume that rats live in all dark cellars. At least I can remember believing this as a child. Unfortunately, I was one of those "annoying" children given to temper tantrums (long since outgrown, of course!). Whenever the various strategies my parents employed in trying to distract me from such outbursts failed (and they never resorted to anything more violent than a glass of cold water in the face, which always made more of a mess than it was worth), they would remove me to the "coal bin" downstairs and leave me there to scream it out on my own. I *knew* there had to be rats down there, but fortunately I never had a chance to dwell on the possible terror of it all—my sister and brothers always managed to distract me by heckling through the heat vents. Actually, I have always been a little disappointed that I have no phobia (of rats, cellars, the dark . . . heckling, maybe) to show for my experience. On the other hand, I do harbor an uneasy suspicion that if you yell too long or too loudly about anything, the rats might get you. Just ask my sister or brothers; that's what they always told me.

The third level of symbolism—the restrictive symbol, the symbol within the story and reflective of the story—can be assessed only with a closer look at the ongoing plot. This story-specific symbolism evolves most dramatically in the next segment with the unfolding of Koo-Nar's actions after Larry fails to feed him.

KN-11: Carol: One night you forgot—
        Larry: One night I forgot to feed him, and I heard him under the bed. You could hear him running around in the bed springs. Anyway Koo-Nar got in bed. And I had this terrible nightmare, and I dreamed Koo-Nar was, was chewing on my leg. And you know how you move in slow motion in your dreams? And I dreamed I grabbed him and choked him and choked him, and the harder I choked him the harder he'd bite, you know, and he wouldn't let go. And finally—he just succumbed—as rats do when one shuts off their air. And I dreamed I just *threw* him [makes motion with arm] just as hard as I could, but it was all slow motion in the dream. (Course, when you got seventeen blankets and a snow drift on top of you, it slows you down, too.) But I never really woke up!

Carol picks up on Larry's implication for the ongoing plot in the previous segment. Larry had said, "And as long as I fed the dude we were on peaceful terms." Carol anticipates the next sequence as a typical interdiction/violation pair (functions II and III in Propp's [1928:26-28] scheme; the second pair of medial motifemes in Dundes's [1964a:63]). That is, she hears Larry's closing statement as a self-imposed interdiction: Thou shalt not forget to feed Koo-Nar. And she anticipates his violation of that interdiction: "One night you forgot [to feed Koo-Nar]." Larry repeats Carol's structural cue exactly and moves on into an expansion of the "complicating action," as Labov and Waletzky (1967:32-33) would name it. In terms of plot, this segment simply outlines how Larry "finally got rid of the noxious bastard," as he says in version #2. However, to return to the symbolism of the rat and its particular evolution *within* the story, we can see that this segment is much more complicated than its structural role would suggest.

There are three significant aspects in the intranarrative symbolism of the rat: (1) the rat in the experience itself, (2) the rat in the narrative (the rat as projection), and (3) the rat in the dream. The rat in reality (the experience itself) is quite simply a pest. The barn rat, as it is more commonly known, averages in length about sixteen inches (half of which is its long, hairless tail). Raccoons (as in Larry's comparison) are typically twice this size, so Koo-Nar must have been a rare specimen indeed (or maybe a case of motif number X1227, Lies about rats) (see Thompson 1955:v.5; see also motif X1227a [Big Rat] in Baughman 1966). Farmers are particularly antagonistic toward rats, since they consume and contaminate grain and other foodstuffs as well as annoying, sometimes biting, livestock and poultry. And in the city rats are a nuisance as well. The title of Richard Dorson's collection of folklore from Indiana's Calumet Region, *Land of the Millrats,* is a clear indication of the symbolic significance of rats even in an urban culture. Dorson reports that aggressive rats constitute one of the recurrent "mill themes," and he presents several "rat stories" told by the "millrats" (steelworkers). There are several tales of rats biting workers while they sleep or in retribution for not feeding them part of their lunch. One particularly crafty and aggressive rat was named "Vito the Rat." One worker complains, "These damn rats, they'll walk up to you like a fucking dog and look at you like, 'Hey, buddy, you better give me some food or I'm going to bite your ass off'" (Dorson 1981:88, 94-100).

The experience Larry relates is not entirely unrealistic, then; rats are aggressive, are very bold about taking food, and do often grow to a fairly large size. Symbolically, at the level of the experience itself, the rat is an obnoxious pest known to bite people seemingly without provocation. The rat as presented in the story draws to it not only this cultural notion of the rat as a proven molester, but also the more individualized projection of the storyteller's own anxieties about himself. In psychology, as Alan Dundes suggests, projection refers to the tendency to attribute to another person or to the environment what is actually within oneself. What is attributed is usually some internal impulse or feeling which is painful, unacceptable, or taboo. The ascription of feelings and qualities of one's own to a source in the external world is accomplished without the individual's being consciously aware of the fact. The individual perceives the external object as possessing the taboo tendencies without recognizing their source in himself. (1980a:37)

You will recall that within the collective symbolism of the rat, there is an association between the rat and the phallus as a dangerous or repugnant object. Though Cirlot does not mention who (or more specifically, which sex) is perceiving the phallus as dangerous or repugnant, I am suggesting that in this case the internal symbolism is from the male viewpoint. Symbolically, Koo-Nar is a projective animation of male sexuality—which the storyteller has been taught from childhood is dangerous, evil, aggressive, and repugnant. *By creating a narrative* out of the experience of staying in the wintry shack and encountering the rat, the storyteller exploits the potential of the personal narrative to its fullest. He chooses a symbol and a plot and uses them to display and evaluate ideas he would find too disturbing to deal with directly. In this case, it would seem that before his self-imposed period of separation and initiation in the garage, he had not yet faced up to what his own sexuality meant to him or how it was to be integrated into his sense of himself as a person, and especially as a man.

The experience of staying in the garage is obviously a significant part of his effort to determine what it means to be a man. His story of the experience is a major part of this effort at definition. Koo-Nar symbolizes all of those negative aspects of sexuality typically learned in childhood and adolescence. It is contingent upon members of either sex to contemplate their own sexuality at some point, usually when it becomes an increasingly important part of their social relationships. This is why other cultures have formalized periods of initiation. Western culture relegates such learning to an informal and personal level, where it often remains unexamined and psychologically forbidding. American culture teaches a young person that sex is dangerous and repugnant. Because an orgasmic-level response (in either sex) is finally compelling and uncontrolled, eventually a young man perceives his own sexual experience as a response that escapes his rational control and instead moves him to its own demands. With these two forces in juxtaposition, a young adult can hardly learn (as have the poets, so they say) that sexuality is the surest path to ecstasy. He will learn instead that his body betrays him by tying him to an evil power he can neither control nor escape. As Benedict warns, many American adults fail to "unlearn" the wickedness and dangerousness of sex. If sex is wicked, an orgasmic-level response is uncontrolled wickedness. The menacing rat with its unprovoked aggression easily embodies all that is repugnant in that view of male sexuality our culture teaches its children.

The rat in the story is a projection, a "noxious bastard" charged with all the nastiness the storyteller had been taught to associate with his own sexuality. Briefly, he creates a sense of the terror the rat inspires in his image of Koo-Nar frantically running through the maze of open-coil bed springs, on up through the innersprings to the top mattress, where Larry lay listening: (from version #2) "And I heard that son-of-a-bitch runnin' around down there in my bed springs, and he was going berserk 'cause he was hungry!" Sexual desire is often described as a "hunger."[8] Koo-Nar's hunger has in it a desperate, demanding quality. The sexuality Koo-Nar represents *is* dangerous because it seeks to inflict injury and pain; it *is* repugnant because it exhibits the unthinking coarseness and desperateness of animals in heat. If Koo-Nar symbolizes male sexuality, what intelligent and sensitive man *would* willingly embrace such an image of himself? It is the storyteller's culture that has taught him to see his own sexuality negatively, that has taught him to project only a negative image onto whatever appropriate symbol his environment provides. The image he projects—the stereotype he accepts—is not true, is not "natural" or at least need not be. The storytelling is one way this value, this image, can be scrutinized and perhaps rejected or changed.

In an interesting reversal, the storyteller becomes the victim of his own projected stereotype of male sexuality. He casts himself empathically in the role of those most often subject to such animalistic attacks. Koo-Nar's attack is not that of a lover, it is simply the brutal aggression that stereotypically characterizes male sexuality—all male sexuality, rats or men. And yet Koo-Nar is not entirely unappreciated. Larry admires his boldness, his great size, his insistent animal energy. Stereotypical male sexuality is not without its own attraction. Our culture tells us over and over again that what a woman really wants is a powerful, aggressive male who in his uncontrollable desire will ravish her and force her submission. Koo-Nar is a worthy adversary, but he is not a lover. Koo-Nar's biting is in earnest. Male sexuality—as Koo-Nar symbolizes it—is a fighter's skill and cunning, and the object of a sexual encounter is to defeat the partner. But a more positive and human sexuality that differs from this stereotype is what the storyteller intuitively comes to recognize as an attribute characteristic of a man who is confident of his manhood for other reasons. If a man can devise and pass his own test for what is truly important (to him) about being a man, then the necessity to behave as a rat does is gone.

Koo-Nar is a symbol for the negative stereotype of masculinity. In choosing his own test of hardy endurance, Larry incidentally ensures that the rat will not control things. Instead it dies.

And Koo-Nar does die—both in Larry's dream and, as he learns later, in actuality (and, of course, as we are presently aware, in the story). The wonderfully complex embedding of the death of Koo-Nar is one of the strokes of artistic genius in Larry's story. We are told that Koo-Nar's attack and demise take place in a dream, a "weird" dream, as Larry says: (from version #2) "I dreamed that Koo-Nar was in my bed and chewing on my leg 'cause he was hungry. And I dreamed that it hurt so bad right on the calf of my leg where he was chewing that I reached down and tried to strangle him. And the tighter I'd squeeze, the tighter he'd bite, ya know? And I thought, my God, I could never last and I would just pass out, but I thought I was *not* dreamin'. But anyhoo, I dreamed that he finally died and relaxed his grip. And the curious part of it is, when you dream, everything's in slow motion. And I dreamed that it just took a gargantuan effort to throw him out of the bed. But I finally got rid of the noxious bastard." Like the medieval "dream vision," Larry's dream is presented as a narrative to be analyzed and evaluated—an allegory. Larry is conscious of this displacement himself, and he conveys his awareness to his listeners through metanarrational cues: some direct—"I thought I was *not* dreamin' "; some more subtle—the intentional mispronunciation of *anyhow* as a sign of his exasperation with his own efforts to describe his sensations in the twilight world of a "lucid" dream.

The dream provides a fruitful arena for Larry's own analytic turn of mind. Larry knows that dreams are symbolic expressions. Folkloric awareness of the significance of dreams is in evidence from antiquity up to the present. "Freudian significance" of dreams is a popular allusion even among people who have never seen any of Freud's works. People relate their dreams to others with an awareness of the depth of hidden meaning they carry. The most shocking motives and behaviors can be recognized and related in dreams because, after all, we all know that is what dreams are for. Dreams are puzzles. As Legman says of dirty jokes, tellers laugh hardest through jokes both they and their audience know are most autobiographical or most revealing (1975:22). But that is what jokes are for. Dreams are for interpretation; that is why we tell them. We expect dreams to be projective and symbolic. As Freud suggests, the more offensive or forbidden a notion is to the dreamer, the more likely it will be buried (censored) by layers of symbolism or distortion (1963:122-32). Like the medieval allegorist, people who tell their dreams recognize the dream as an acceptable frame for the analysis of behavior and ideas. This is the ancient tradition Larry draws upon in his embedded dream-tale of Koo-Nar's attack and death.

Larry's dream is interesting in part because it is a lucid dream, a dream in which the dreamer knows that he is dreaming. If he so chooses, Larry has every reason to believe that his dream is in fact a vivid and clearly remembered dream, a significant dream. It may even be as significant (at a symbolic level) as the dream-tale Andrew Lang reports from Chinese tradition as supporting his interpretation of Apollo as "Lord of Mice." He cites a myth in which "the king of the rats" appears to a besieged monarch in his dream and assures him that he will have victory the next day. Rats gnaw the bowstrings of his enemies (motif K632), and the king triumphs in the battle (Lang [1970]:112). In Larry's case, the absence of evidence (no dead rat to be found) makes it difficult for Larry to decide whether his experience is real or simply a vivid dream suggested by Koo-Nar's frantic noises in the springs below. William C. Dement reports that "because the dreams of REM sleep are 'real' to the dreamer, and because the human memory must sort and process an incredible amount of information, it is not unusual for a person who is presumably sane to 'remember' some dream detail as if it were a fact" (1976:85). At the time of the incident (or perhaps we should say, at the time of the dreaming), Larry is not at all sure whether the Koo-Nar of his dream is the real Koo-Nar simply being a vicious pest, or a necessarily symbolic Koo-Nar that behaves in symbolically significant ways in his dream.

It is clear, I think, that so long as Larry interprets the incident as a dream, he is willing to scrutinize the experience for symbolic significance as he would any other dream. In fact, in both versions he includes commentary on the nature of dreaming experiences (metadreamology?). He seems very aware of the proverbial slow motion phenomenon of dreams; in both versions, he ties the phenomenon to the difficulty in finally getting rid of the dead rat, or (symbolically) of ridding himself of his inhibiting stereotype. The embedding allows his symbolic use of even this traditional mental kinesics of dreams. And, in the manner of a tall tale, he offers a realistic explanation—the many blankets and snow—for the difficulty he has getting rid of the rat. Either explanation is plausible; he may be dreaming or he may be awake. Koo-Nar may really be chewing on Larry's leg, or he may be a symbol in Larry's dream, an embodiment of animalistic sexuality threatening to destroy him (or at least overpower him). The dream-story format allows Larry to focus on the rat as symbol—a symbol that lives in two worlds, one real (the garage) and the other imaginary (his dream).

Because the dream format allows Larry to admit (recognize) that Koo-

Nar is a symbol, it provides a viewing screen on which he can project the many attributes of the symbol and thence sort out those that are acceptable or "true" to his rational mind from those that are not. In this embedded frame he can see the negative and false stereotype that Koo-Nar represents; he can see it at a further remove. Koo-Nar of the dream is only a mentifact, a stereotyped representation. He can be killed unceremoniously. The real Koo-Nar is symbolic as well, but he "personifies" the overall sense of personal sexuality. Surely this cannot be sacrificed; that would constitute psychological castration. The dream frame allows the negative stereotype of male sexuality to be thrown away. But, psychologically at least, the better parts of the complex symbol remain. The positive aspects in Larry's understanding of his own sexuality are not sacrificed. Some of the "wicked" aspects of sexuality have been "unlearned," and yet the essential positive force of sexuality has not been lost. If the rat symbolizes the phallus, then, in this complex narrative at least, it is the stereotype (the ghost image, the dream image) of the phallus that must be sacrificed, not the symbol itself—and certainly not the referent of the symbol.

So this is my interpretation of the symbol in the story, in the dream. When people recount dreams, they may take offense at the interpretation offered by the listener-interpreters who happen to veer too close to the truths that have been distorted by "dream-censorship," or at least this is Freud's explanation for the resistance he observed in his patients. Any interpretation of "symbols" in personal narratives will likely be viewed even more readily as offensive or wrong since the conscious mind and real behavior create the story, not the mysterious unconscious mind. But, I am not a psychologist. The interpretation I have presented is my responsibility and may very well say more (to you) about my concerns with male sexuality than Larry's. The demands of the subjective paradigm can be onerous at times if accepted conscientiously. Still, I feel the foregoing lengthy discussion of the symbol is a necessary representation of how meaning evolves for the listener when a potentially symbolic object or action is perceived in the story. If you want to know what Koo-Nar really symbolizes, you will have to ask—not Larry (though I am sure he has an interpretation as well), but rather, yourself.

KN-12: Larry: And I didn't find out that dude was for real till spring!

This one line abruptly closes the structural sequence. The remaining narrative material is in fact a series of combined flashbacks and evaluative commentary—very unusual in oral narratives (unless the story is told by

Larry Scheiber, a most extraordinary teller). The internal evaluation in the material that follows this summary line is more in keeping with the evaluation segments Labov and Waletzky recognize in their study. And the flashbacks are reminiscent of the reverse unfolding that typically closes Arthur Conan Doyle's famous detective stories. In this case, Larry expands the rest of his story into a detailed account of *how* he found out "that dude was for real." However, the basic structure of the story as a whole can be seen as coming to a close in this very brief assertion that the real rat had indeed been killed. The implication—even before Larry's elaboration—is that Koo-Nar had actually died from Larry's stranglehold. Larry just did not know about it until spring. With the proof that he had killed Koo-Nar, Larry completes the procedural chain emanating from the initial structural function "Manhood to prove." Using an adaptation of Claude Brémond's structural methodology, I might chart the structure of the narrative as a series of internal functions that cumulatively serve the theme of proving masculinity (see Brémond 1970 and see my adaptation of his model in Stahl 1973).

When placed in juxtaposition, the story structure and the symbol of the

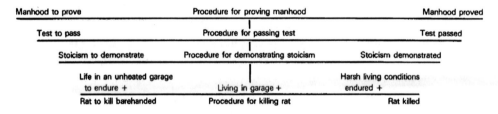

Figure 4.1

rat seem to be parallel influences on Larry's definition of masculinity (there are, of course, many other influences as well, but they are not apparent in this story). The structure (when completed) supports the attribute of "toughness" as an essential part of that definition. The symbol of the rat, on the other hand, would imply a repugnant, animallike sexuality if that symbol were allowed to "feed" the definition. However, when it is proved that Larry has killed Koo-Nar, this death allows Larry to claim toughness as his personal attribute and as an acceptable part of his definition, and it allows his denial of an animallike sexuality either in himself or in the definition of manliness he now chooses to accept.

It is not until spring and the discovery that Koo-Nar had in fact been killed that Larry can claim to have proven his toughness, and only then, it seems, is he ready to affirm toughness and deny animallike sexuality as parts of the definition he chooses for this important sex-role norm in his self-concept. Through the structure of the tale and the symbol of the rat, he has analyzed the stereotype of masculinity and decided (at least in respect to these two characteristics) what *he accepts* as part of his definition. The corpse of Koo-Nar is a visible sign that he has devised and met his own definition of manhood.

KN-13: Larry: I was gonna move into Momsy's, see? Mom all this time had
                 just been having a heart attack.
        Carol: Poor Mom!
        Larry: Yeah, poor Mom, one day she said, "Scheib, for God's sake,
                 you've proved you can live through the winter and all that
                 crap in a shack. Now come home!" I says, "OK, just for
                 laughs."

Larry begins his explanation of how he discovered that Koo-Nar's attack was "for real" by citing a consequence of the first of the last two structural functions. That is, he indicates that because he is satisfied that he has successfully endured the harsh living conditions for the duration of the winter season, he is ready to end the test and return to a more comfortable situation. Even so, he implies that part of his reason for ending the test is his sensitivity to the distress it causes his mother. "Momsy's" heart attack is metaphoric, thank goodness; nevertheless, Larry effectively conveys the message that he would have stayed in the shack had not his mother been so concerned. Carol's interjection—"Poor Mom!"—would seem to be a simple recognition and reinforcement of Larry's filial concern. But in fact, the tone and the parallel modifier in Carol's usual

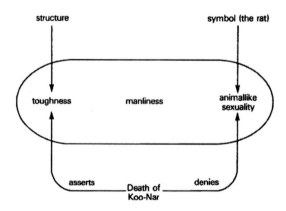

Figure 4.2

words of mock sympathy—"poor baby"—suggest that Carol knows that Larry is simply playing with a stereotypical notion, that he is using the traditional value of filial devotion as the basis for a metafolkloric game. Accomplished player that he is, Larry picks up on Carol's bid (repeats her words as a meta-narrational cue) and expands his use of the "devotion to mother" motif into an obviously projective dialogue in which his mother not only expresses her concern ("Now come home!") but also articulates the primary theme of the story, the test to prove manhood.

In most folkloric or psychologically traditional narrations, it would be the father figure who pronounces judgment or rewards the hero when he passes the test. In the absence of a father, Larry's mother must recognize that the test has been passed—but her pronouncement must not seem to carry the authority of judge (father) but rather the pride and concern of a mother. Larry accomplishes all of this through the dialogue he reports as the actual words of his mother. I would attribute the words to the text, the demands of the discourse. As Mary Louise Pratt suggests, textual criticism is built on the assumption "that in literary works, the range of deviations which will be construed as intentional is much larger" than in other speech contexts (1977:170). For me, Momsy's dialogue is an artistic manipulation (intentional deviation) that effectively displays Larry's own evaluation and articulation of the theme. Though the dialogue is not true to traditional expectations, it is a rhetorically effective projection of the theme out of the mouth of the hero and into the mouth of his mother.

This complicated rhetorical maneuvering moves the theme of manliness rapidly through all four possible levels of textuality—from metafictional ("Yeah, poor Mom, one day she said . . ."), to realistic (what his mother really said), to mythic (the combination of the mother/father motifs), and finally to ironic ("live through the winter and all that crap in a shack").[9] Larry (as *dramatis persona*) is free then to accept the intentionally misplaced commendation of his absent father (the only one who can really certify his manliness) and at the same time, free to superficially respond to his mother's (stereotypical) maternal need to have him safely back home with her. With masculine pride obviously intact and duly recognized, Larry agrees to go home for Momsy's sake—"just for laughs." But, literary trickster that he is, Larry puts the words of the stereotypical tough guy into his own mouth and laughs at his own posturing along with us.

KN-14: Larry: So I'm packing up all my stuff out of the old shack, see? And
I pull all my blankets off the bed, which hadn't been changed
all winter [groans and laughter]. And when I got down to the

         bottom sheet—[lowers voice] there's all this rat shit. And I
         thought, "Oh, my God!"
Carol: Koo-Nar'd been living in your bed.
Larry: All that time I'd been wondering what happened to Koo-Nar.
         Then I remembered that dream I had that night and I thought,
         "By God, I got him!" And I saw in a flash: he shit his drawers
         when I choked him to death. [Laughter]

Two important literary strategies are set in motion with this segment of the storytelling: (1) the "Koo-Nar episode," as Larry calls it in version #2 (prime intertextuality), is confirmed as a real event rather than a dream, and (2) the first segment of the tripartite evidence of Larry's theory explaining the episode is presented. With regard to the first strategy, we must remember that Larry "didn't find out that dude was for real till spring." For nearly four months Larry has carried around in his head both the memory of the dream about Koo-Nar and a vague awareness that Koo-Nar had at some point stopped bothering him. He says, "All that time I'd been wondering what happened to Koo-Nar." But apparently he does not make the connection between these two notions in his own mind. Instead the connection comes as a kind of revelation when he discovers the rat shit in his bed and questions how it could possibly have gotten there. In version #2, he details his thinking that brings about the revelation: "And I says, 'Now wait a goddamn minute. This is too weird 'cause I know there's no rats in here.' After the Koo-Nar episode and I had that bad dream, I bought rat poison and stuff 'cause I'd been paid. And no one ever ate it, so I knew there were no rats. Well, anyway, here's all these rat turds in the bottom of my bed, and I thought, 'Goddamn, that's really strange—except— maybe Koo-Nar really did get in bed with me that night, and maybe I really did choke him.'"

In this burst of insight, the erstwhile dream is transformed into reality (for the *dramatis persona* anyway). The episode is no longer reversible; it is confirmed. As Susan Stewart contends, the distinction between reversible and nonreversible structures is "symptomatic of a more basic division between fictive and nonfictive events in social life. Nonfictive events are those that happen in social time, that 'really did occur' and cannot be 'taken back.' In contrast, fictive events are framed as reversible events. They can be taken back" (Stewart 1978:64). What had previously been perceived as occurring in "dream time" is now seen as happening in "social time." Larry's memory of slow-motion movements notwithstanding, the experience is confirmed as a real event, something concrete.

This revelation is of course an important part of Larry's proof in his case for "Larry Scheiber's manliness." It is also significant (to me) as an indication of our dependence on physical evidence as proof of the reality we accept as true. If Larry's dream had been only a dream, would its effect in the real world have been the same? Well, certainly there would not have been any four-month-old rat shit, a dried corpse, or a scar on Larry's leg. Very likely he would not have told his dream; he might even have forgotten it entirely. In such an instance, the dream would have been, as David Bleich argues, "functionally nonexistent," The dream would lack "negotiative presence." It would mean (affect) nothing in the real world. Bleich compares an unexpressed interpretation of a piece of literature to an unremembered dream: "If it is forgotten, it might as well not have taken place; if it subsequently emerges in unexpected contexts, it has acquired a negotiative value" (1978:296). But how will we know when and if it "emerges" in a later context? It can emerge later only if it has already affected reality in the mind (subconscious if you wish) of the person who dreamed or interpreted but did not earlier articulate that mentifact. Unfortunately, however, Bleich is right: we will never know and subsequently use the reality of the dream or unvoiced interpretation until it gains negotiative presence through interaction with the physical world (the sad truth of Donne's "Exstasie"). Larry must seek proof that the symbolic message he may in fact have already assimilated from his supposed dream is not idealism but reality. He does not feel free to accept his response to the dream as real or significant until he has proof that the incident was not merely a dream but rather an actual incident.

Once convinced that his dream experience was real, Larry considers it "tellable."[10] By implication at least, he pinpoints for us the moment in "real time" when he came to perceive the sequence of events *as a story*—that is, the day he moved out of Brown's garage, in April, 1960. Much of the rest of his story is in fact metanarrational: he reconstructs how the story grew in his mind as he contemplated the significance of his dream-qua-actuality. Like the good mathematician that he is, Larry presents his thought process just as one would write out the proof in a mathematical exercise. His first theorem is: "he [Koo-Nar] shit his drawers when I choked him to death." As Edward Sagarin tells us, "uncontrolled defecation is synonymous with fright," and the expressions "shitting his pants" and "scared shitless" are proverbial images for this occasionally literal sign of extreme fright (Sagarin 1962:64). Larry skillfully plays on this traditional literal/figurative confusion and, incidentally it would seem, introduces a humorous personification through the imagery of a rat wearing "drawers" in the first place.

Though Larry would seem to be using the expression innocently enough, there is some significance in the fact that he has adopted an archaic form rather than the more typical "shit his pants." "Pants" in American colloquial speech usually means "trousers" or "slacks." Rarely is it used to indicate an undergarment worn by an adult male. So in the typical expression "pants" refers to the outside pants or trousers and is actually more a figurative than a literal referent (one hopes). In Larry's expression, on the other hand, the "drawers" in question are definitely underwear, the garment that would in the literal representation of the expression receive the fright-inspired deposit. Since Koo-Nar did not really wear "drawers," the shit is deposited instead in Larry's sheets. And this is only fitting; the sheet is a kind of undergarment, especially as Larry describes it in the bed-stripping scene (version #2): "And I get down to where there's nothing left in the room but the bed. And I pull all my big warm winter quilts off, [pause] and I get down to where it's nothing but sheets. And I take off my top sheet, and down at the foot of the bed is—rat shit!" Short of personifying the bed, we can still appreciate the ludicrousness of a verbal striptease that ends with a bottom sheet full of rat shit.

The sheet is significant in other ways as well. Normally a reference to bedsheets would carry connotations of sexual play, as in Hamlet's lament over his mother's marriage to Claudius: "Oh most wicked speed to post with such dexterity to incestuous sheets," or as in the typical American version of Child #81 (Matty Groves or Little Musgrave) in which Lord Arlen asks of little Matty, who is in bed with the lord's wife, "And how do you like my sheets?" The sheets on Larry's bed, however, are not likely to inspire visions of "nights in white satin." Carol and I both groan at his disclosure that the bed has not been changed all winter. Soiled sheets are, however, often assumed to be an aftermath of sexual activity (as in the feminist slogan "If you're really liberated, you'll make *him* sleep in the wet spot"). In fact, in many cultures a "bloodied" bedsheet is proudly displayed by the newlywed husband as a sign that his wife was a virgin (see, e.g., Brandes 1980:182). On the other hand, a grimy bedsheet with rat shit on it can suggest only the most uninviting scene for a sexual encounter, or perhaps more significantly the absence of sexual relations altogether (of course there is always "her" place). I would guess that the only "significant other" to have shared Larry's bed in the garage is Koo-Nar, and it is Koo-Nar's interaction with Larry that has soiled the sheet.

In keeping with Koo-Nar's function as a symbol, the dirtiness of the sheet and especially the rat shit suggest the "dirt," the sordidness, associated with sexuality. A symbolic corollary to Larry's first theorem, then, would be that the vilest dirt of all is to be found in bed. Sex is repugnant and animalistic, or at least the accepted explanation of male sexuality defines a man as animalistic, an uncontrolled defiler in regard to sex. A definition of masculinity that includes a vicious sexuality is like a bed with rat shit in it. The bed should remain the suggestive but positive symbol it has always been, but the dirty sheets should be ritually removed.

KN-15: Larry: And I got to looking around, and I pulled these mattresses. And between these mattresses and the parachute—which served as a wall between my MG and my bed—there lay KOO-NAR preserved by the cold!

Carol: Poor baby, with your throttle marks on his very throat.

Larry: Well, he was scrawny—and decimated—and he looked as though—he'd *dried* there.

Larry's second theorem is: "there lay KOO-NAR preserved by the cold!" The second step in his proof of the reality of the dream event is the discovery of the corpse of Koo-Nar. This is a triumphant recognition that he has, indeed, "kilt the dirty bastard." In version #2, Larry actually reenacts the dream activity in his efforts to find the corpse: "And I thought, 'Well, now where would he be?' So I flop down on the mattress and I reconstruct the whole dream, see? And I think, 'Ooh, Koo-Nar's hurting my leg,' so I reach down and I grab him, and I throw him out of the bed—in slow motion. And I think, 'Aha! He would be over by the parachute which separated me from my MG!' And by God, I pulled the old mattress back, and I looked down there, and there's Koo-Nar! Ta-da! Stiffer'n a goddamn board!" As an engineer, Larry delights in solving problems, and his literary allusions or parodies are usually suggestive of the mystery genre. In this instance, he verbally (and at the time of the incident, physically) reconstructed the activities leading to the "crime" just as Sherlock Holmes would bring together the significant pieces of the mystery in an elucidating summary of the crimes he investigates.

Larry is careful to point out (in both versions) that Koo-Nar has been preserved by the cold. Not only is this a subtle reminder of the harsh conditions Larry has had to endure, but it is another clue in the mystery game—an explanation for the absence of any notable stench usually associated with decaying flesh. (Of course, if the rat shit didn't bother him, olfactory sensitivity may not be one of Larry's strong points.) Few things smell worse than a dead rat. The expression "to smell a rat"—meaning to suspect that something is wrong or that there is danger—implies that the rat is still alive and lurking about portending danger. It also implies that the rat has a characteristic bad odor, which we can assume is rendered insufferably rank through the rat's demise. In the case of Koo-Nar, only the freezing temperature has inhibited the natural decay and telltale odor that would have alerted Larry to the presence of a dead rat in his near vicinity (beside his bed!). In version #2, Larry states clearly that the corpse is frozen: "This was like in April, but it was still colder'n a bitch out. And there he was, froze solid, and not a *mark* on him. I checked that dude over and over and over, and not a mark on him."

Frozen or not, the notion of turning a dead rat over and over *and over* (three times!) in one's hands for the sake of discovering any "marks" on it is pretty disgusting. Ostensibly Larry includes this comment as another minor bit of evidence that he did indeed kill the rat by strangling it—as opposed to hitting it or catching it in a trap, methods that would have left marks on the corpse. (Poison, the other "markless" possibility, is ruled out by the uneaten poison bait and the synchronicity of the corpse being just where Larry thought it would be from his reconstruction of the action.) It is interesting that in version #1, Carol suggests that the manner of death *would* result in marks on the corpse—"with your throttle marks on his very throat." Some might question just what "throttle marks" might look like or perhaps even what implications the word *throttle* (as a noun) might suggest. My own response is a strong suspicion that Carol simply does not know what a dead rat would look like (nor does she probably want to know) and that she is instead offering an intertextual response tied to the personification of Koo-Nar ("poor baby") in the story rather than a realistic response to some notion of the appearance of dead rats. On the other hand, Larry, the great outdoorsman, is used to handling dead animals. In version #2, with two males in his audience, Larry readily assumes that they will understand the significance of no marks on Koo-Nar. And John Fisher does in fact pick up on the implication right away; he says, "You killed him in your sleep"—obviously, otherwise he would have had marks on him. In Larry's definition of masculinity, men are supposed to know the "lore of the woods." Women, on the other hand, must have such things patiently described for them.

Larry does then describe for Carol and me the appearance of the dead rat: "Well, he was scrawny—and decimated—and he looked as though—he'd *dried* there." At no point does Larry interject an aesthetic or personal judgment on the appearance of the dead rat. Instead the careful description conveys the symbolic implications of the rat's appearance most effectively (the dashes indicate the deliberateness of his speech and the selective precision of his thought). Certainly, the description is realistic enough. In one sense, the description is an example of rhetorical naturalism, an imagery that evokes a deterministic world view, a sense of the inescapable animalism of the real world. Even now I feel a twinge of the sudden overwhelming sense of angst I experienced on hearing the description. The sensation was fleeting, thank goodness, but in retrospect it gives me pause. I sincerely believe that I would have experienced disgust rather than terror had I actually seen the dead rat. But in Larry's description—the attributes of the corpse he has selected and oh so carefully matched to the increasingly charged words he speaks—there is the specter of terror. There is no sign of violence on the corpse; rather (as Larry describes it), there is evidence of a gradual wasting away, of shrinkage, of irreversible dehydration. Like the "thoroughly small and dry" atmosphere of T. S. Eliot's poetry, Larry's description bears a message of despair. The death of a rat would be of little consequence, but the corpse should bloat or be consumed by the vermin or scavengers we depend upon to save us from the terror of watching the life force—vital to us all—evaporate into the waste of dry air. One of the "folk ideas" Alan Dundes cites as fundamental in the web of ideas surrounding belief in the evil eye is the opposition of wet and dry: "Life depends upon liquid. . . . The consistent principle is that liquid means life while loss of liquid means death. 'Wet and Dry' as an oppositional pair means life and death. Liquids are living; drying is dying!" (1980a:101). Larry's choice of words captures this notion perfectly. Koo-Nar, who had been "king of the rats," the biggest, a worthy adversary, now lies a dried corpse. We despair of knowing where the life force has gone.

Within the story itself, however, the corpse of Koo-Nar is not so much a general symbol for unthinkable annihilation but rather a more restricted image of impotence. As in the haunting ballad "The Unquiet Grave," death brings the "withered stalk," and the lovers can no longer unite in love and life. But a healthy twenty-three-year-old man is not likely to be consumed with fears of death or impotence, nor, I think, would these be the concerns of the man in question even at age thirty-seven when he told the story. Rather, the fear, if there is one, is that a sexuality which is only self-centered and aggressive like the hunger of the rat will lead to a symbolic impotency, an absence of love. If liquid is the physical life force, its equivalent in the world of symbols is love. Both liquids and love are in the control of the living; *they* decide when either will be given or withheld. The animalistic aggression that cannot give but only destroys has no place among the symbols of the living. Koo-Nar must be found and recognized for what he is—the false lover who would have us believe that the stereotype of a hateful, competitive sexuality is to be tolerated in any definition of what it is to be a man.

KN-16: Larry: But there that son-of-a-bitch was. And I thought, you know, "One plus one equals two." And I looked down at my leg and there was a scar, a big hole. I'd never bothered to look at my leg before. Guys don't look at their legs, you know. But that

little son-of-a-bitch had *gnawed me!* And I *got him,* even in my
sleep, which proves what a great hunter I really am!

Theorem number three is: "I looked down at my leg and there was a scar,
a big hole." After pronouncing this third theorem, Larry summarizes the proof
in reverse order: [3] "that little son-of-a bitch had *gnawed me!* [2] And I *got
him,* [1] even in my sleep." This summary very neatly brings the three-part
explanatory or evaluative section of the story to a close. Larry then most
obligingly metacomments on the theme of masculinity and the way in which
these three theorems support the theme: he says, all of this "proves what a
great hunter I really am!" The structure of the story has been summarized (by
Larry) and its content evaluated. The primary function of the structure has
been closed (earlier, when it was noted *in the story* that Koo-Nar had been
killed), and the theme of that primary function has been reaffirmed through
the evaluative expansion. Larry has proved his manhood; he is indeed a great
hunter. Or more accurately, he is a great "outdoorsman," the term Larry more
often uses to describe himself. The hunting imagery is actually very limited in
the story, and Larry knows this. Killing a rat by choking it to death is hardly
a typical exploit of the "great hunter." Larry calls himself a "great hunter"
with clear irony; he intends that we see in contrast that he is indeed a rugged
outdoorsman who has demonstrated his ability to endure the harshest of living
conditions. The story of Koo-Nar is not a direct brag but rather a brag by
implicature. And Larry, as usual, has managed to brag with a poet's skill.

I dare not leave this final explanatory segment without comment on some
of the details of this short section. One thing noticeable early in the discourse
is Larry's use of the proverbial "One plus one equals two" (see Taylor and
Whiting 1958:270). This is a traditional proverb, and Larry, with his usual
penchant for reflexivity, indicates through the discourse a metafolkloric
comment on proverb usage. That is, by embedding the proverb in his statement
as *dramatis persona,* he implies (as does any literary artist when he or she
intentionally uses folklore) that this is a proper or typical context for the
proverb. Larry in effect consciously points to a "law of use," as Alan Dundes
would name it, in regard to this particular proverb (1966:506). The proverb
is a catch phrase for synchronicity; it is a sentence to be used when some
meaningful information might be attained by bringing two otherwise separate
facts together. Jung defines synchronicity as "a meaningful coincidence of
two or more events, where something other than the probability of chance
is involved" (1971:505). Larry recognizes the "meaningful coincidence" of
his dream, the rat shit in his bed, and the corpse of Koo-Nar, and he draws a
conclusion from these facts: the conviction that his leg must have been bitten

by the rat. Even before he checks, he *knows* that "one plus one equals two." He expects to find the scar, and he does.

And what about the scar? Larry claims that not only did he fail to notice the wound on his leg when it was freshly gnawed, but over the course of the four months after, he had not had occasion to notice the scar that replaced it. The reason for this inattention, he suggests, is that "guys don't look at their legs, you know." The "you know" suggests that Larry sees the involved characteristic as a generally acknowledged part of a standard masculine stereotype. Whether it is true or not that "guys don't look at their legs," some of the implications of his saying so are interesting to contemplate. For example, are there certain parts of their body men do spend a good bit of time looking at? Or is he implying instead that women, in contrast, do spend an inordinate amount of time looking at their own legs? Actually, the significance of his statement is in its representative role as a verbalization of sex-role stereotyping. As Stanley Brandes noted of the men of Andalusia, "Men are preoccupied with behaving in a masculine manner and with determining in whatever new situation might arise how their reactions *should* vary from women's" (my emphasis) (1980:6). While it is likely true that women might more often look at their own legs, the point of Larry's comment seems to be a clear assertion that he has behaved as a man *should* behave (according to the stereotype) and has not looked at his own legs (something women do and, therefore, something men must not do).

It is probably just as well that he did not look at his leg and discover the scar before. He might not have made the connection between the scar and Koo-Nar; rather, he might have devised some other likely explanation that would not carry the symbolic weight of the wound inflicted through Koo-Nar's unprovoked and aggressive attack. Larry might do well once the mystery has been solved, however, to seriously look at the scar on his leg and contemplate its meaning. He does this in part by telling the story at all and by inviting his listeners to hear whatever resonances emanate from the story through their associative and interpretive understanding. The scar is a clear sign of Koo-Nar's aggression. The symbolism of the attack is more complicated than it may initially appear. The symbol is not introduced to conflict with the theme of masculinity but rather to support it, and yet it is male sexuality that is being scrutinized through the symbol. Much of the seeming conflict stems from Koo-Nar's role as a symbol for the culturally instilled notion of male sexuality. According to this notion, male sexuality is aggressive, competitive, domineering, chaotic, and animalistic; when frustrated or perverted, it becomes cruel and sadistic. The sad truth is, however, that the stereotype is accepted as reality, and it seems an impossible task to expose the layers of cultural dross for what they are and discover beneath them some sense of an essential and true personal sexuality. "Townsmen," Stanley Brandes tells us, "vastly emphasize the differences between the sexes and believe that these differences are fundamentally biological rather than social in origin" (1980:6). Similarly, Sydney L. W. Mellen, in his provocative study *The Evolution of Love* (1981), discounts the intelligence and self-determinism of people generally and simply assumes that all "problematic" human behaviors are evolutionary survivals that have attained the status of biological determinants. He leaves little room for human self-enlightenment.

A symbol, such as Koo-Nar, presented in the context of a personal narrative is indicative of the storyteller's and listener's efforts to enlighten themselves. Larry could not easily tell (and I for one could not comfortably listen to) a confession of the fears and concerns symbolized by Koo-Nar's attack. Instead the symbolism muffles these concerns that are unspeakable or unhearable. Koo-Nar's attack is a brutal, unthinking, and self-serving rape provoked only by the rat's own hunger. In the world of symbols, Koo-Nar acts as man fears he acts; culture has taught us that male sexuality is *by nature* aggressive and brutal and self-serving. In his story and in his dream, the storyteller is the victim of Koo-Nar's attack; he is the woman or the passive homosexual partner that suffers the aggression of the stereotypical male. Through the symbolization he gains empathy with the victims of such attacks. When he *gets* Koo-Nar, he "kills" the stereotype, or at least that part of the stereotype the rat symbolizes. This does not mean that Larry is now willingly a victim or that he has learned to enjoy the status of a victim. He has indeed been momentarily "feminized" (the "hole" in his leg is too obvious a symbol) or perhaps forced into the role of an unwilling fellator (the choking scene and the later-discovered emission) or perhaps fellatrice (after all, it is his leg the rat is "gnawing"). Basic to any of these interpretations is the notion of victimization. He has learned that the subject of a stereotypical male attack is always victimized, overpowered, and "put down" (made to appear and feel inferior).

There is still a dilemma in the symbol, however. Empathy with the victims of aggression can easily turn to a defensive fear or dread of that aggression *if* the aggression is seen as unavoidable, as biologically determined. Brandes says of the men in his study: "[They] are unafraid to joke about playing the phallic, 'male' part in homosexual intercourse. This role, at least, is consistent with masculine notions of genital assertion and aggression. It is, rather, the dread of assuming a feminine posture—of being the victim of sexual attack, instead of the perpetrator—that preoccupies the men of our town" (1980:6). In the typical closed cultural view, one may be either a victim or a perpetrator of sexual attack; there are no alternatives. No one *wants* to be "the woman"—even women don't *want* the stereotypical role they have been handed. But, because women have for so long accepted their stereotype, as men have accepted theirs, the woman becomes a symbol herself—the perennial victim.

"Feminine" behaviors have no place in a definition of masculinity; they are immediately and obviously symbolic. Larry's story of Koo-Nar does very little to tear down the stereotype of femininity. This is not the storyteller's concern. Masculine and feminine are still polar opposites. As Alan Dundes's study of the "crowing hen" reveals, our culture still teaches us that male is good (or at least powerful) and female is inferior (1980a:160-75). But Larry does symbolically reassess the belief that men are inherently victimizers. He at least faces the specter of brutality in his own definition of manhood and decides that a man can be "tough"—a real outdoorsman—without being brutal. With some relief, I think, he "unlearns" the wickedness of male sexuality his culture has taught him. He no longer holds an exaggerated sense of his own aggression.

KN-17: Carol: Right! However, it doesn't prove where the name Koo-Nar came from.

Larry: OK, all the time I lived with Koo-Nar before [pause] his demise, for some reason I just knew his name was Koo-Nar. Because he was the king of the rats, the biggest of all, and it just seemed fitting that I name him Koo-Nar.

This last segment is what Labov and Waletzky would call the "coda"— "a functional device for returning the verbal perspective to the present moment" (1967:39). This particular coda demonstrates very nicely Carol's complementary sense of intertextuality. In this case, she is the one who makes the metanarrational leap from Larry's closing line—"which proves what a great hunter I really am"—back to the initial dialogue that introduced the subject of the story in the first place. She says, "However, it doesn't prove where the name Koo-Nar came from." With only mock seriousness, Carol charges Larry with having failed to do what he implied he would do by telling the story. Her comment is, I think, only a thinly veiled metafolklore; she is in fact ironically underlining our tacit awareness that the genre of the personal narrative has as its primary function the articulation and evaluation of fundamental values, themes, and symbols, rather than the superficial recounting of mundane information. Larry's response, then, continues this double-entendre by saying, in effect, that he named the rat Koo-Nar because the rat became symbolic, because Larry came to see him as the king of the rats. Anything that significant must have a name, and one that Larry invests with meaning—Koo-

Nar, the king of the rats. It is no small thing to conquer a king, especially one that has ruled so long (symbolically) in the minds of men. For Larry, at least, he rules no more.

Koo-Nar, King of the Rats: A Review

The foregoing analytic presentation or tutor text represents my attempt to describe how meaning evolves as the story is heard, or more precisely, how meaning evolves for me within "performance time." Obviously a review is possible only after performance time has elapsed, only after the mind is no longer engaged in the complex task of grouping a vast range of associations into what Goffman calls "primary frameworks" (1974:21-39). A review is a kind of reflexivity not normally a part of (occurring within) performance time; rather, it is a critical activity enjoyed only after the performance is over—or the text read. The conventional concerns of literary or folkloristic analysis—style, form, theme, traditionality, symbolism, characterization, function, or effect—typically take into account the whole text or the completed performance. This review, then, will focus on such whole-text concerns as they help me organize my reflections on the story.

An outstanding feature of Larry's story is its style. Usually something is said to have style whenever the implied evaluation is a positive one. That is, its style is good rather than bad. Beyond this simple usage-based definition, the question of what constitutes style is a philosophical one turning on speculations about artistic intent, authorial choice, or cultural taste. Bennison Gray (1969) suggests that as an analytic tool the notion of "style" is so ambiguous as to be useless. But he also recognizes with a sigh that critics go right on using the term anyway as though there were some sort of consensus on its meaning. The use of *style* to mean "good style" has popular backing at least. To say that Larry has style, then, is simply to suggest that his use of the language is both effective and entertaining or impressive. From this popular perspective, a storyteller who did not delight or impress his audience through his use of the language would be seen as lacking in style though his storytelling might be quite effective nonetheless. I think it is safe to say that Larry's story (or Larry) has style. Certainly his frequent use of traditional or original metaphors is something we can appreciate in the style of the story. Traditional expressions—"out of circulation," "run like hell," "on peaceful terms," "having a heart attack," "One plus one equals two"—are probably still aesthetically effective at a subconscious level; it is their effectiveness that has made them traditional, yet they delight us precisely because Larry makes the extra effort to recall and use them, to linguistically connect with our store of shared culture. His original metaphors are even more effective because we must simultaneously recognize the figurative implications and visualize the literal referent without the aid of tradition. Such participation by the listener makes the expressions all the more enlightening and amusing.

As with his use of "One plus one equals two," Larry's use of traditional metaphor is sometimes quite complex and indicative of one overall characteristic feature that gives his style its literary (i.e., aesthetically pleasing) quality. Larry's style is reflexive; often reflexivity takes the form of metafolkloric framing, as in the proverb above. Sometimes reflexivity is entirely rhetorical even with this supposed *true* story, as, for example, is the case with the finger-wiggling gesture and nonsense sounds Larry uses to convey a sense of the rat's brazenness as he calmly eats his food in the glare of Larry's flashlight. Larry often uses pauses and pitch and volume variations self-consciously. For example, it is usually apparent when Larry pauses in his narrative that what follows the pause is to be understood as one choice made from among a number of variously significant words and accompanying story-specific connotations. In the last segment of the text, Larry says, "All the time I lived with Koo-Nar before [pause] his demise. . . ." What follows the pause is very significant, and Larry wants his listeners to know that it is significant, i.e., that he has purposefully selected this word (*demise*) in an effort to counterbalance the violence of the attack, the violence of the strangulation, even the terror of death. Larry intends the restrained meaning of *demise* as an ironic contrast to the violence of the actual death itself.

We have seen many examples of what literary theorists call "intertextuality" in the story—from the irony in anachronistic word choice ("I was really cool!") to obvious metanarrational cues ("Where in the hell was I anyhow?"). The plot of the narrative exhibits this intertextuality as well. In fact, the story's form is clearly internally balanced in the same way that the classic detective story is a mirror-image presentation of action and ratiocination. This story, at least, fits very closely the formula John Cawelti abstracts from the classic detective texts. In those texts, as in the story of Koo-Nar, "the balance between inquiry and action is the most immediate expression of a larger and more general problem of proportion in the classical formula that derives from a fundamental tension in the structure of the story" (Cawelti 1976:108). On one hand, the order of actions and the order of "proofs" are internally balanced. On the other hand, the violence and disturbing symbolism associated with the rat seem uncontrolled and must be "contained" within the story through appropriate reflexive cues, as when Larry is about to discover the corpse of Koo-Nar but pauses to explain that the parachute served as a wall between his MG and his bed, or as in the light irony of his comment just after relating the death of Koo-Nar—"he just succumbed—as rats do when one shuts off their air."

Normally, style and form or structure would be the only superficial features to receive much attention in the discussion of a narrative text. Setting, for example, is usually perceived as significant only in regional literature or foreign texts. In Larry's story, it is not the cultural setting that is primarily significant but rather the symbolic dwelling itself. The old garage Larry chooses as his residence is symbolic not simply in its physical properties (as suggested earlier) but also in its function as a place of isolation. As in many cultures, young adults in America find that late adolescence is a time of separation from the family of their childhood. They go to college, join the service, take a job, or get married. Whereas other cultures often have recognized rituals that make this kind of transition tolerable, our culture has very little beyond the celebration of marriage, and that is only a short rite, symbolic rather than preparatory. For Larry, the transition from hometown boy to paratrooper was a sudden change, aided perhaps by the severe discipline of military boot camp. When he returned to Huntington, he needed a period of transition and some symbolic activity that would help him assess his three-year experience and determine what his new role should he. This liminal or transition period was not demanded or even encouraged by his culture; rather, he chose to separate himself awhile longer from the community he would eventually rejoin.[11] He chose the old garage both for its symbolism as a place of isolation and for its functional role as a place for testing, a proving ground for manly toughness.

The primary theme of the story is this drive to demonstrate *to himself* his manhood. Sexual identification is necessarily a part of anyone's self-image, but for Larry, sexual identity and self-identity seem almost synonymous. Possibly this is astonishing only to a woman—as Simone de Beauvoir said, "The truth is that man today represents the positive and the neutral—that is to say, the male and the human being—whereas woman is only the negative, the female. Whenever she behaves as a human being, she is declared to be identifying herself with the male" (1961:383). For Larry, the major premise of this syllogism is taken at face value, and in this story that is all that really matters. To prove himself an acceptable person—to formulate a positive self-image— he must prove himself a man. The need to prove his masculinity was perhaps to some extent a carry-over from his days in the service. Paratroopers, like the Marines, are reputed to be daring and proudly virile. I would suppose that three years among such men would seal the equation between selfhood and manhood. And it would likely keep every man in constant dread of appearing anything but absolutely masculine. To Larry's credit, his initial decision to stay in the shack, though growing out of a desire to prove his manhood, represents as well his willingness and determination to test not just himself but also his own definition of masculinity.

When Larry moved into the garage, his definition of masculinity was drawn from his culture and perhaps exaggerated by special indoctrination in the military. His experience in the garage allowed him to examine on one level the attitude of toughness and its place in his definition, and on another level—the symbolic—the animalistic trait of aggression, especially as it is traditionally associated with male sexuality. By telling the story of Koo-Nar, Larry reevaluates these attributes and slowly builds his own foundation for a personal ethic—one that accepts toughness as necessary in the definition of masculinity but one that questions the place of vicious aggression in the definition, and more particularly in actual social relationships. Koo-Nar teaches him what it is like to be a victim of unthinking aggression. Though he pointedly does not identify with women, he does come to empathize with what he feels must be their response to the animalistic sexuality he had assumed was his by nature. He seems to recognize the stereotype for what it is and to straight away dispatch it—as he does the rat—as something unsuitable in the definition of a man. In Larry's world view, fuck *should* be a most objectionable word to a woman. It is only among other men that he need maintain the illusion that masculinity necessarily implies an animalistic sexual appetite. The stereotype is still there in the real world—it is a powerful "folk fallacy," as Alan Dundes would name it—but there is no need to accept it as part of his personal self-image.[12] Instead, toughness—which comes only through proving himself to himself—is the attribute he chooses to wear as his badge of manliness.

Traditionally, literary criticism would ask what the "effect" of a piece of literature was. Like the function of an item of folklore, the effect of an item of literature was perceived as discoverable, as something that could be detected and articulated after careful observation. David Bleich, more forcefully than any other reader-response critic, has argued that the reader must not suppress his or her own *personal* response, as that is the only effect the reader can really know. My interpretation of Larry's story is unavoidably my own. Symbols, especially, evoke a "multivalency of meanings." The meanings I hear in the story I have already expressed. The effects of the story on me would, in another era, have been presented as "latent functions" perhaps, rather than as my personal responses (see Merton 1949:73-139). The first effect is relief (literary critics would say "catharsis," but that might too readily bring to mind the rat's unfortunate indisposition). It is a great relief to discover that the rat has died, especially given the interpretation of the symbol I have suggested. In the complex web of projection that must attend any such interpretation, it is likely that at least one strand is traceable to my own ambivalence relative to the stereotype of male sexuality. It is, after all, women who are traditionally depicted as afraid of mice and rats. As listener, I may be the one who projects onto Koo-Nar the negative stereotype of animalistic aggression. But that is something for you, the critics of this critique, to ponder.

A second effect of the story (and this *would* translate into a latent function) is sincere admiration for Larry. It is not so much that I myself would define as masculine, or even "tough," someone who endured the wintry conditions Larry did. And I certainly would not expect anyone who considers himself a man to pass such a test, or any test, to prove his masculinity. But, the question of masculinity aside, I do admire someone who seeks out meaningful adventures—someone who, like Thoreau, experiments with his own living and evaluates his experience in an effort to learn what is most fundamental and essential to the human condition. In short, I admire Larry's more serious mask as the natural philosopher. Even more, however, I admire and am moved by his talent as a storyteller. Freud claims that in our modern culture, only the artist retains the "omnipotence of thought" that yields magic (1950:90). For the brief time that Larry tells his story, all his abundant energy and zest for the outdoors enter into the play of his literary artistry, and he creates the world of the story before my eyes, almost in my mind—like the shaman.

5.

The Canary, or The Yellow Dress

Loretta Kathryn DeVault Dolby was born on October 10, 1911, in Oakley, Illinois. She moved to Michigan while still a young girl and taught in a one-room school in Altoft after finishing high school and county normal. In 1935 she enrolled at Manchester College in North Manchester, Indiana. She was graduated from Manchester in 1938 and worked for a year in Fort Wayne, Indiana. In 1940 she married Charles Dolby of Huntington, Indiana, who at that time worked as a barber and carpenter. He later served as a city fireman in Huntington, and she resumed her teaching career at Clear Creek School in Huntington County. They had five children: Carol, Richard, Steven, Sandra, and Thomas. I am the fourth of these children. The story that is presented as an instructional text below is one I have heard many times. Like Larry's story, it relates an incident that occurred during that transitional period just before the primary responsibilities and perspectives of adulthood are fully accepted. In this case, Mom was a college student enrolled in summer school for her very last class before graduation.

The instructional text will be segmented as was the text in chapter 4. In this text, however, a summary list of analytical codes will close each segment. These codes were discussed briefly in chapter 3. The three primary codes are discourse, type, and style. A second and third version of the story are included in the Appendix.

TC-l: [Setting] The Canary, or The Yellow Dress

The setting here refers to the actual situation in which the story was told. It was a Saturday morning, October 13, 1973. The locale was my parents' home on Vine Street in Huntington, Indiana. The kitchen is large. My father expanded both stories of the wood frame house toward the west in 1948. The kitchen is twelve feet by eighteen feet, with cupboards all along the west wall except for the two single-sash, counterbalanced windows above the counter. Yellow texture-painted walls make this the cheeriest room in the house. A chrome-

and-formica table sits in the center of the kitchen with six tubular-frame yellow chairs spaced around it. Today one extra table leaf has been inserted, since my brother Steve's family and my husband and I will be here for the noon meal. The two fluorescent lights are burning though it is nearly midday. From the circular light fixture hang Mom's yellow ceramic lovebirds on their tarnished copper swing. There they have swung since 1960, when one of Mom's fourth-graders gave them to her as a Christmas present. Above the alcove leading to the basement and back door are two ceramic fruit arrangements that have flanked the kitchen clock for as long as I can remember. My brother Steve, Dad, and my husband (Mark) are in the garage (connected north of the house by an enclosed back porch). Dad included a small workshop when he built the double garage. It serves as a social locale for the men in the family. Steve's children—Michelle and Kyle—are in and out of the kitchen while the story is told. My mother, Steve's wife (Bobbie), and I are sitting around the table. I had asked Mom to tell Bobbie about the time she and her roommate ate twelve hot dogs between them. The verbal context suggests that Mom cues the story of "The Canary, or The Yellow Dress" herself by picking up on the topic of inflationary prices initially voiced at the close of the "Hot Dog" story.

> Mom: . . . and right around the corner was this Coney Island hot dog place, and we could get three hot dogs for a quarter. And my roommate usually was waiting up for me. So this particular night I went down and got twelve hot dogs for a dollar and took them home. And the two of us sat there in bed—a little after midnight—eating twelve Coney Island hot dogs. [Laughs] —But, now you can't get *one* for a quarter let alone *three*!

Analytical codes (Segment TC-1):
Discourse/Situation: Setting
Discourse/Situation: Verbal context

TC-2:   Mom: When I was at Manchester that last summer. . . .

The verbal context is atypical in this instance. Mom knows that I am trying to get some of her stories on tape, so she obligingly provides and accepts her own cue. And, of course, neither Bobbie nor I am inclined to take the floor, as might otherwise be natural even in a family interaction where grown children are expected to show respect by not breaking in when their parents are speaking. This particular interaction rule is fairly well established in our family. Because the behavior pattern is tacitly shared, newer members of the family (in-laws) must gradually learn it. That is, one learns to listen when Dad reads a newspaper article aloud or to not interrupt or compete when Mom tells one of her stories. The text in this instance is not verbally interrupted, an example of family convention influencing the strategy of discourse.

The date implied in this segment can be approximated from a general notion of when Mom attended college. She was graduated from Manchester in 1938 with a B.S. in Elementary Education. Her last year closed with one more course yet to be taken. She taught a course in tests and measurements during the summer of 1938 in order to pay tuition for her own last requirement. So, the date of the story is "that last summer"—1938. In a version of the story recorded a year later (October 3, 1974), she responds directly to my question "What summer was that?" with the answer, "The summer of thirty-eight." (See "The Yellow Dress"—version #2, in the Appendix.) Furthermore, it is apparent in the second version that I am incorporating an unspoken allusion to the waning years of the Great Depression—the 1930s in the United States—when I ask, "How could they afford to be giving away a hundred dollars?" The theme of surviving economic hard times is sounded early in the story and is emphasized throughout the text. It is also a common theme in a number of other stories in my mother's repertoire of personal narratives.

Another important allusion in this segment is in the offhand reference to Manchester. Manchester is both a town in the state of Indiana and a college; the North in North Manchester (the name of the town in which Manchester College is located) is usually dropped in daily conversation. Actually, there is no other Manchester around except for the small settlement in Dearborn County, Indiana, which is, to be sure, south of North Manchester. The town of North Manchester was formerly called simply Manchester, presumably after the city in England (though I would suspect its counterpart in York County, Pennsylvania, given the Brethren and Mennonite background of many people in and around Manchester); its name was changed to North Manchester when the postal service reported the earlier existence of the Dearborn County village.[1]

The town of North Manchester is in Wabash County, just twenty miles northwest of Huntington. It is a small town with a typical store-fronted Main Street (State Road 114). The campus of Manchester College is located on the north edge of town along the Eel River. Immediately prominent in the town are the large oak and sycamore trees that line the wide common ground between residential lots and the major north-south streets. A few of the streets still proudly exhibit their original red-orange Indiana brickwork, and there are a few remaining ceramic herringbone sidewalks that were so common when

Mom went to school there. Large oak trees and red brick buildings dominate the campus of Manchester College as well. Oldest of the college buildings are the three-story Administration Building with its central chime tower, a smaller brick building that used to house the library and now serves as a classroom building, and two dormitories—Oakwood Hall for women and Ikenberry Hall for men. These and a few other buildings that have since been razed or remodeled were the physical confines of the college when my mother was in school. The trees, the river, and the Pacific Central tracks that run behind the campus are as they were then, except for rust on the sad old tracks that feel the wheels no more.

Manchester alludes to much more than the physical environment of the town and campus—idyllic as that environment is. *Manchester* is also a catchword for a kind of experience—the "Manchester experience," as it is usually touted in the public-relations bulletins. In this segment of Mom's story, it is understood that Mom and I share this experience by virtue of our both having attended Manchester College—granted that our sojourns there were some thirty years apart. In mentioning Manchester, she can assume a resonance that I will hear but that Bobbie—who is also listening—will miss. Like most northern Indiana residents, Bobbie knows that Manchester is a small, church-related college, and she knows that Mom went there to earn her teaching license. And though Bobbie attended college herself and therefore knows some of the general stock of student lore (see Toelken 1978), she is not able to participate as fully in this more specific allusion to college life at Manchester.

Analytical codes (Segment TC-2):
    Discourse/Situation: Verbal context
                    (Speaker cues her own story)
    Style/Culture: Noninterruption as sign of respect
    Style/Personalore: Dates Mom attended college
    Style/Culture: The Great Depression
    Type/Theme: Surviving hard times
    Style/Culture: Dropping North from North Manchester
    Style/Culture: North Manchester, a town in northern Indiana
    Style/Culture: Knowledge of Manchester College
    Style/Personalore: Mom's degree from Manchester
    Style/Culture: Student lore

TC-3: . . . Mary Lyons and I roomed together.
    With the completion of the sentence, one aspect of the "Manchester

experience" comes into focus—the time-honored practice of rooming together in college dormitories. As we shall see shortly, part of the thematic emphasis of the story depends upon a deviation from this normal rooming situation. However, at this point, the listener is free to envision the typical dormitory setting and, more important, the special roommate relationship that is part of the "Manchester Experience" for both my mother and me. One might pursue the more universal track of psychological and sociological implications with which researchers have surrounded the tradition of rooming together, but my own response to this feature of life at Manchester is much more specific and is tied to the nature of the college itself. Manchester is sponsored by the Church of the Brethren, a conservative Protestant denomination. Until quite recently, the school was very restrictive in regard to student (and faculty) behavior. Smoking and drinking were not allowed, and it was not until 1965 that dancing was allowed on campus. Interaction between the sexes was usually supervised whenever possible. Especially when my mother was there, the greater part of every twenty-four hours was spent interacting with roommates or other dorm friends. The women at Oakwood Hall ate together family-style and were subject to the demands of a curfew and a weekend check list. Dorm life generally does bring with it this phenomenon of "much time together"; this alone is not enough to account for the special quality of roommate relationships so often visible at Manchester. Rather, much of it stems from the Brethren background of the college and the majority of its students. The Church of the Brethren, like many other Protestant denominations with historical ties to the Old Order Brethren, Mennonite, and Amish (Anabaptist) traditions, has encouraged an attitude of simplicity and unpretentiousness among its members. Girls, in particular, are expected to be modest and "innocent." Innocent, in this case, involves much more than simply being a virgin. Rather, Brethren girls are expected to enjoy, even prefer, the company of other girls. "Sisterhood" extends into adolescence and continues as the primary source of fellowship even after a woman is married. Very likely this is a result of the strictly observed separation of the sexes so obvious in earlier traditions of all Brethren cleavages (though it may well simply reflect America's greater tolerance for overt female friendships).[2] Though within the Brethren tradition men and women no longer sit on separate sides of the church and family eating patterns no longer demand that men and boys be served apart, still a basic notion remains that traditions of brotherhood and sisterhood dominate in an individual's experience of fellowship. A young woman is first of all a woman—not a sexual object, but a "sister" among sisters. And though it grows out of the general tradition of male dominance, the identification as sister is a positive one.

At Manchester, then, this proclivity toward extending sisterhood beyond adolescence is encouraged by the typical dormitory situation and the number of students with similar Church of the Brethren backgrounds. Growing out of this sense of sisterhood is a phenomenon that A. R. Radcliffe-Brown calls the "symmetrical joking relationship" (1965:90–91). In my mother's case, this joking relationship is easily seen in the affectionate teasing among friends and roommates. For example, she often tells the story of a typical dormitory prank involving her roommate and some friends. In a recorded version, she introduces the story with a succinct statement of the sisterhood phenomenon at Manchester: "It was my first year at Manchester, and we had a gang of girls." In the "Canary" story, Mary Lyons is understood to be a part of that sisterly tradition at Manchester. It is why she and Mom "got the giggles, of course" when the mosquitoes kept them awake all night. (See version #3 in the Appendix.)

Mary Lyons herself is treated referentially in the story. Mom knows that I know Mary Lyons. For several years she taught elementary school in Allen County; she lives in Andrews, a small community just six miles west of Huntington. Mary and Mom often see each other in town or at retired-teachers' meetings.

Analytical codes (Segment TC-3):
   Style/Culture: College rooming practices
   Style/Personalore: Roommate relationships
         at Manchester College
   Type/Theme: Roommate relationships
   Style/Culture: Traditions of the Brethren
   Style/Culture: Brethren sisterhood
   Style/Personalore: Mary Lyons

TC-4:   And we would live a whole week on about three dollars and some-
         thing worth of groceries between us. And we would live—or we slept
         in one house, and then we'd arranged with a lady a couple of houses
         down to cook on a little old beaten-up oil stove in her basement. And
         we would have—we'd buy a quart of milk for about a dime, and we'd
         buy a box of cereal, and we could get four bananas for a dime, and that
         did us for two breakfasts on just a little. And we could buy a pound
         of hamburger for twenty-five cents, or no, a pound of hamburger for
         ten cents, three pounds for a quarter. And we would—out of a pound
         of hamburger—we'd make our lunch and our supper. And her mother
         would give us leaf lettuce out of her garden and green onions out of

her garden. And she'd pick raspberries along her fencerow and bring
'em to us. Sometimes we'd have a peach or two—and I don't know
what else. We hardly ever had anything else to eat that whole summer.

This lengthy segment constitutes what Labov and Waletzky call the
orientation section typical in true stories (1967:32). The gist of this segment
is repeated in version #2 but is missing from version #3. Actually, the relevant
theme of enduring hard times is sounded in the conversation that precedes
version #3. Since version #3 was recorded only a week after version #2, there
was little need to elaborate on this thematic feature (at least for my benefit).
Mom merely says, before version #3: "I don't know how I'd a gotten along,
though, that summer if it hadn't been for Mary Lyons and her mother." In
version #1, however, the effectiveness of cumulative descriptive detail is played
to the hilt. Here is an example of narrative technique much more common in
written stories than oral (though the false starts and repetition—e.g., "out of
her garden"—definitely point to orality). The weight of the segment comes
with the consistent use of the modal auxiliary *would*. Indeed, the description of
the daily routine and menu oppresses and trivializes the audience's view until
they too long for some event, some relief from the monotony. This seems to be
the only structural strategy at work in this part of the story.

The major thrust of this segment is thematic and rhetorical. It is the discourse
itself that demands a plethora of descriptive detail building to a thematic
summation: "We hardly ever had anything else to eat that whole summer."
However, the particulars of this description represent for the most part cultural
details reminiscent of the era of the Great Depression. Food prices were low,
but money was scarce. It strikes me as impressive that Mom remembers these
details of food selection and pricing so many years afterwards. Whether or
not the items and prices are really accurate (and I have no reason to believe
they are not), they are rhetorically convincing and effective. Furthermore,
their numeration suggests how very attentive Mom must have been to the
management of living expenses. She says she kept a record of accounts with
all the food purchases itemized.

Home gardens were necessary to supplement the monotonous daily fare.
However, people were generous whenever they could be, making special
arrangements for people in need (the cook stove in the basement) or giving
them food out of their gardens (Mary's mother). The lack of variety was as
typical of the times as was the scarcity of money for food—as Mom says in
version #2: "We didn't *have* peanut butter." She adds in version #2: "I think
that's when I got real sick of corn flakes." Hearing the story now, the audience
senses the amazing absence of fast-food chains or restaurants of any kind.

Whatever Mom and Mary ate, they prepared themselves on their cook stove, and they bought perishables on a day-to-day basis rather than stocking them in a freezer or refrigerator. The only meals "out" (or prepared by someone else) were enjoyed when Mary went home to Andrews or when Mom was invited to dinner at the Dolby family farm in Huntington County. She and Dad were dating off and on that summer.

This also represents a counterpoint to or deviation from the typical college dormitory situation. Mary is a typical roommate, but they do not have a typical rooming arrangement. Perhaps this disclosure early in the story foreshadows some upcoming event that also in some way represents a deviation from the norm. In fact, at this point, the discourse presents us with an enigma: Does the strange housekeeping arrangement in any way determine the plot of the story? As we shall see, it does not. Instead, it is an early step in the development of a humorous motif and part of a developing symbol.

Analytical codes (Segment TC-4):
>   **Type/Theme: Surviving hard times**
>   **Discourse/Rhetoric: Descriptive detail**
>   **Discourse/Rhetoric: Subjunctive mood, Customary action**
>   **Type/Structure: Initial situation (Monotony to relieve)**
>   **Style/Culture: Life during the Great Depression**
>   **Discourse/Rhetoric: Detail as evidence of truthfulness**
>   **Type/Theme: Lack of variety**
>   **Style/Personalore: Mom or Mary's visits home or to the farm**
>   **Discourse/Rhetoric: Foreshadowing**

TC-5:   That was the same summer that on the Fourth of July I was wearing a wool skirt and a pink satin blouse because that was about the only clothes I had.

With this segment of the story, my participation as listener becomes more intense. By the end of the sentence, I notice that the theme of making it through a hard summer is sounded again. And I can easily pick up on some cultural references. The Fourth of July, for example. is mentioned *not* for the sake of accurate dating, or even for the sake of its symbolic overtones (celebration, winning, prosperity, etc.), though these are certainly present. Rather, the date is used here as it is traditionally used in American folklore and popular culture—to suggest midsummer. Unlike European tradition with its midsummer's eve on St. John's Day or the vernal equinox, American tradition expects corn to be "knee high by the Fourth of July," and children who sing of elephants jumping fences expect them not to come down "till the Fourth of July."[3] For most Americans, the hot and lazy days of summer begin with the Fourth of July; it is a time to wear the skimpiest or coolest clothing current taste and mores allow. The pink satin blouse is barely acceptable, but the wool skirt is definitely too hot for summer, especially if it is being worn on a day-to-day basis. The frequency with which the skirt is worn can be inferred to some extent from the generally referential use of "Fourth of July" along with the implied imperfect tense. In other words, we can assume that she means "*by the fourth of July I was still wearing a wool skirt.*" In version #3, Mom says, "I bet we had three dresses between us maybe," so the wool skirt and pink blouse really were "about the only clothes" she had. She describes the skirt in version #3: "This *wool* skirt with about five different colors of braid around the bottom of it—a really pretty skirt, but for July it was kinda hot!" Later Mom told me that the background color of the skirt was gray.

Here there is certainly a "lack to be liquidated" (see Dundes 1963; 1964a: 61–64). The storyteller needs some new clothing, something to break the monotony of the same tired outfit and something more suitable given the warm weather. Using the two stylistic reference points—the hot season and the winter clothes—the discourse presents a dilemma and demands a solution, or at least keys the listener's interest toward a solution. And the larger strategy of the type asserts itself as the plot poses its essential conflict, what Labov and Waletzky call the "complicating action" (1967:32–33). More accurately, as in some of Propp's Russian tales, the conflict is one not of action but of situation (1928 [1968]:35–36). Structurally, the conflict reverts to a functional potentiality that serves as a step in the procedure necessary to "relieve the monotony," the initial situational function. That is, "Wool skirt to replace" becomes the first function of the structure. It is important—though not yet apparent—that the structuring of the story is aimed at the *thematic* effort to relieve monotony rather than the specific desire to find clothing suitable for the hot weather. As we shall see, two otherwise unrelated events are structurally tied to the general procedure of that initial situational function though they have nothing to do with replacing the wool skirt.

Analytical codes (Segment TC-5):
    Type/Theme: Surviving hard times
    Style/Culture: July 4th as midsummer
    Style/Culture: Fabrics suitable for summer clothes
    Discourse/Rhetoric: Dilemma
    Type/Plot: Complicating action

Type/Structure: First function of procedure
(Wool skirt to replace)

TC-6:   And my dad had sent me a five-dollar bill in his letter.

Structurally, this segment answers the question of procedure in the previous segment with a thematic potentiality from another person's point of view. That is, the function "Wool skirt to replace" is met by or equated to the function "Help to give" from the point of view of "the helper," her father. The two functions would be equivalent:

Wool skirt to replace	vs. *Help to give (father)*
Procedure	vs. *Procedure of helping*
Wool skirt replaced	vs. *Help given*

Her father's procedure for helping is giving her money, in this case, five dollars. As an element of plot, this action is a first step in the resolution. Altogether, we have here a dominance of strategies of the type; this segment of the story is essential to the core that makes this story identifiable as an autonomous entity.

In addition to these structural strategies, there is in this segment a hint of the continuing theme of surviving hard times. As we shall see, in 1938 five dollars bought considerably more than it does now. And, of course, we must assume that it was then all the harder for Mom's father to spare the extra five dollars from his own household expenses. A very important stylistic strategy is at work in this short segment as well, one that is far less obvious than these dominant strategies of type. Mom's father (my grandfather) was often "guilty" of slipping his daughters or granddaughters money "on the sly." In fact, in both versions #2 and #3, Mom comments directly on his secrecy about the money: "And of course I wasn't to *tell* anybody that I had gotten it." Specifically, the "anybody" who was not to find out was Grandpa's wife, Mom's stepmother, Ruby.

Mom's own mother had died in 1927, a year after Mom's sister Luella (Susie) was born. Mom was sixteen when her mother died. In 1929, Grandpa (Charles William DeVault) married Ruby Chambers Emrick, a widow with a ten-year-old son named Chuck. Ruby was used to scrimping through the hard times; in short, she was penurious to a fault and seemed especially so when the times no longer demanded merciless economic watchdogging (at least such was my mother's opinion). Grandpa, on the other hand, delighted in slipping little gifts of money to his daughter, just as a surprise now and then—as a sign of his independence, perhaps as a sign of his southern upbringing with its emphasis on a gentleman's right to spoil the ladies in his patriarchal purview, but most certainly as a sign of his affection. This little custom continued to be a favorite indulgence of Grandpa's even after Ruby died (then the gifts were given to his granddaughters rather than his daughters). And the same secrecy prevailed even though his third wife was herself generous and appreciative of such signs of affection. Grandpa's secret gifts were given and received as intimate gestures, little love notes from a warm-hearted father and grandfather. He secretly slipped me a five-dollar bill just before I was married. I wish I had never spent it. He died the next spring.

Analytical codes (Segment TC-6):
> **Type/Structure: First function of action (vs. Help to give)**
> **Type/Structure: Procedure of first function (Money to give)**
> **Type/Plot: Procedure of resolution**
> **Type/Theme: Surviving hard times**
> **Style/Personalore: Grandpa's gifts of money**
> **Type/Theme: The stepmother motif in folklore**

TC-7:   And so I hurried downtown and—what's the name of that store over there at Manchester now?—advertises so much—German name?—Oppenheim's.

The rhetorical technique apparent in this segment is similar to that characteristic of the oral legend. Details are presented hesitantly; the audience is invited to supply information. In version #2, recorded a year later, Mom again appears to have temporarily forgotten the name of the department store in Manchester. In that version I respond with the name Oppenheim's; my participation along with her open request for that participation subtly disarms me, obliges me to accept her story as completely accurate. Furthermore, the direct request for this information underscores her own awareness of the stylistic device she has been employing throughout the narrative. That is, perhaps as a kind of metastylistics, she focuses on the very device of personal allusion in the styling of her story. She recognizes and seems, at this point, to delight in the intimacy that allows us to thus draw upon a common well of knowledge and experience. Again, in this segment anyway, I am the primary audience. The message is fuller for me than it is for Bobbie, who at this point can participate only as a witness to the dialogue (actual or implied).

The two hints or clues Mom gives—"German name," "advertises so much"—are presented as though she were simply ruminating aloud, trying to remember. In fact, she has momentarily forgotten, but the hints are voiced for rhetorical effect, though in this case she is using the hints herself as well as giving them to her listeners. Through dint of such memory-jolting, she remembers the name she has heard so often in advertisements on Huntington's radio station, the name of the long-established department store with the German name—Oppenheim's. Both of these hints, by the way, extend the stylistic allusion out from the realm of the personal—"that store"—to the realm of a larger cultural network involving the local radio broadcasting area and the general knowledge of German-sounding names.

Oppenheim's does advertise quite regularly in the local area, and of the major businesses in Manchester, Oppenheim's is one of the most strikingly "German-sounding" names. The store itself is an independently owned establishment that has carried a respectable line of men's, women's, and children's clothing for many years. Somehow they have managed to compete successfully with the discount chains. Their reputation is such that people travel from neighboring counties to shop at Oppenheim's, even with the lure of the large shopping malls of Fort Wayne only a half hour away. Mom's allusion to "that store" in her narrative builds upon this continuing popularity of the store rather than its more locally restricted reputation of forty years earlier.

Analytical codes (Segment TC-7):
   Discourse/Rhetoric: Request for audience response
   Style/Personalore: Oppenheim's
   Style/Culture: German names

TC-8:   Well, they were having a sale, and in the window was a *bright-yellow dress* for three dollars or two-ninety-nine or something like that. So I went in and bought it. Boy, was it yellow! And then I had two dollars left, so I bought a pair of shoes.

It is imperative for this segment of the story that the listener conscientiously, energetically enter into the performance; otherwise the point of the story is lost, or perhaps only obliquely voiced later by the teller. John A. Robinson (1981), writing on the genre personal narrative, puzzled over precisely this phenomenon of listener participation in reviewing another of my mother's stories published earlier in a journal article (Stahl 1977b). Robinson appraised the performance accurately, but he seems to have been dissatisfied with stories of this sort: "In this case the narrator disregarded both of the constraints implied by Labov and Waletzky: not only is the point not explicit, but the responsibility for making the point has been delegated to the listeners" (Robinson 1981:68). Similarly, in the "Yellow Dress" story, the responsibility for realizing the point is handed to the listener, especially in this version of the story. In versions #2 and #3 the listener is given some help in correctly assessing *before* the punchline Mom's own attitude toward the yellow dress. In version #2 she says: "Anyhow, I had about two-ninety-eight—. They had a yellow dress; oh, it was as yellow as a dandelion. Real yellow, but it *wasn't wool*, so I bought it." And in version #3 she says: "In the window was this dress for two-ninety-eight or something like that—and *yellow*—as a pumpkin or canary or something. Boy, it was—it was *nothing* but yellow, didn't have a white collar on it or anything, just yellow! But I bought it, and they had a pair of sandal shoes for a dollar-ninety-eight, so I bought those, and there went my five dollars."

In both of these later versions—but especially in version #3—it is clear that the yellowness is objectionable, that Mom is buying the dress only because it is not wool and *is* inexpensive. In both cases, the use of the conjunctions *but* and *so* suggests a concession has been made; she implies that she bought the dress even though it was bright yellow, despite the fact that it was yellow. In version #1, however, this objection to the yellowness of the dress is underplayed, or rather the listener is forced to rely upon more subtle clues and is expected to participate by actively inserting elements of personalore into the story *as it is heard*. Strategies of discourse and strategies of style are employed here very skillfully and effectively—though the teller risks losing the point if the audience does not participate. The simple strategies of emphasis ("*bright-yellow*") and mild expletive ("Boy, was it yellow!") might easily be missed by themselves. However, as listener, I am thus alerted to a fact I already know about the teller: that she would not normally wear a bright-yellow dress.

The "jazz age" had ushered in a new and varied set of women's fashions. By the 1930s, Mom's wardrobe was no longer dominated by the shapeless middy blouses and cotton print dresses she wore as a teenager in Michigan. Instead, she was wearing fashionable knits and blouses and dresses made of silk or new synthetic weaves. Even lounging pajamas were permissible at informal gatherings. Nonetheless, even as fashion allowed brighter colors and richer fabrics, a conservative Brethren background encouraged moderation—feminine pastels, standard gray and navy, occasionally colorful prints, but never bold, bright, brassy solids in the more intense shades of red, green, orange, or yellow. Such colors even now are considered flattering only on someone with a dark complexion. Not only does a pale-skinned person look "washed out" in such colors, but dominant American convention surrounds such bright colors—especially red, but also any "gawdy" clothing—with connotations of passion, emotional fire, exhibitionism, or adultery. Yellow itself has any number of traditional meanings. The Thompson index lists a motif of color symbolism that identifies yellow as a lucky color. But, in Mom's story the specific color of the dress is structurally less important than the overwhelming intensity and starkness of the color—as Mom says, "it was *nothing* but yellow!"

Ishmael was appalled by the whiteness of the whale, and Melville expounded the terror of that whiteness through many pages. Perhaps there is some similar deep symbolism in the yellowness of the yellow dress, but for Mom the dress seems not so much an anathema as an embarrassment. In fact, I would argue that herein lies the basic traditional motif that ties this particular story—and by extension, its genre—to the great store of American humor. Easily, the string of circumstances that makes necessary the purchase and wearing of the yellow dress is seen as typical of situations antecedent to any motif of discomfiture. Unlike Hester Prynne's scarlet letter, Mom's yellow dress is worn through her own choice, and unlike the scarlet *A*, the dress is perceived as a reflection of the wearer's taste, not as a sign of her sin. Precisely this is the source of discomfiture for the wearer: people seeing her in the yellow dress will assume that it accurately reflects her taste, and perhaps her character as well. Or she may worry that people will figure out the truth: that the obviously inexpensive yellow dress is the only one she could afford. In either case, she stands to be embarrassed, though perhaps more thoroughly by the former assumption than the latter.

The *Motif-Index of Folk-Literature* (vol. 5) lists a general category for the humor of discomfiture. Perhaps following the motif identifying embarrassing nakedness (X52, Ridiculous nakedness or exposure), one could suggest a similar motif identifying embarrassing clothing, such as X62*, Ridiculous clothing, or a subcategory such as X62.1*, Woman embarrassed by necessity of wearing bright-yellow dress. Whether there is any point in compounding such motifs for nontraditional personal narratives is perhaps a question only Stith Thompson could have answered. For our purposes, it is enough to note that the perception that sees humor in the experience of buying and wearing the yellow dress and infuses that sense of a humorous motif into the telling of the story is the same perception that has always worked to give us our stock of traditional tales and anecdotes. A motif is perceived and used by the teller whether our indexes recognize it or not.

Still, it is the purpose of the index to catalogue such motifs, and only to catalogue them. A motif is not a generative unit; it is a descriptive tag, an analytic construct. The ongoing plot, however, is built upon a compelling structure, a procedural braid emanating from that initial structural situation represented by the infinitive phrase "Monotony to relieve." Two actions represent potentialities in the narrative structure at this point: buying a dress and buying a pair of shoes at the combined cost of five dollars. With the realization of those two potential actions, the plot continues as a somewhat unsatisfactory resolution.

The discourse provides rhetorical signposts that lead the listener gloomily toward the inevitability of the purchase. Nowhere does the discourse allow the intrusion of other possibilities: "They were having a sale," and "in the window" was the yellow dress; the dress cost "three dollars or two-ninety-nine or something like that"; those are the only facts. The discourse assumes a causal relationship and snares the listener with the favored *ergo* of every American child—*so*. She says, "So I went in and bought it." Why? Because it was on sale, and in the window and cost only two-ninety-nine. Were there other, more acceptable dresses in the window, or dresses not on sale but under five dollars, or some on sale but not in the window? Did she need to buy the shoes, or were they simply an afterthought? The discourse is ambiguous, and this very ambiguity is skillfully mustered through the common implication that one thing is a consequence of another if the two are joined by that bane of composition teachers—*so*. Once caught, the listener readily accepts the sequence that follows: "And then I had two dollars left, so I bought a pair of shoes."

Analytical codes (Segment TC-8):
> **Discourse/Rhetoric: Use of conjunctions to indicate concessions**
> **Discourse/Rhetoric: Emphasis; expletives**
> **Style/Personalore: Mom's taste in clothes**
> **Type/Symbol: Bright colors and emotion**
> **Type/Motif: Z148, Yellow as a lucky color**
> **Type/Motif: Unindexed**
> **Type/Structure: Second function**
> > **(Dress to buy and Shoes to buy)**
> **Type/Plot: Resolution**
> **Discourse/Rhetoric: Ambiguity of *so* in English**

TC-9:   And so I went home, back to the room. . . .

If this were a fairy tale, this segment would represent the important function Propp identifies as "the hero returns," designated by a downward arrow [↓]. In the more generally applicable structural model I have been using, this segment is something of an anomaly since it seems to represent neither a procedure for buying the dress nor a result of buying the dress. "Returning" itself is not a requirement of the genre in this case, or even of the specific plot. Rather, the structural strategy at work thus far would demand some thematically relevant result from the purchase of the yellow dress.

In this version of the story, this next structural step seems to be hidden or implied. However, in both version #2 and version #3, the necessary sequential step is stated directly: "So I came home and put on my yellow dress." It is important for the structure of the story and for the resultant humor that the teller actually wear the yellow dress. In version #1 we must simply assume that Mom does put on the dress, and perhaps, judging from the later versions, we might guess that she would not typically leave this important structural step to be filled in by the listeners.

Analytical codes (Segment TC-9):
   Type/Structure: The hero returns (Propp)
   Type/Structure: Internal function (Yellow dress to wear)

TC-10:   . . . and Mary said, "Oh, where did you get such a pretty yellow dress?!"

At long last some dialogue breaks up the long epic narration. Mom's stories tend to be told almost entirely in epic prose. Small segments of dialogue are thus foregrounded both in relation to the story in which they are embedded and in relation to the listener's general sense of the teller's personal style. This segment and the one that follows represent "essential idiosyncratic formulas" of the story.[4] In other words, the formulaic exchange is found in all three versions and would, we assume, be found in any version of the story. However, the fact that the exchange is presented as dialogue rather than as indirect quotation reflects a time-honored rhetorical strategy. Tales, ballads, toasts, hero tales, epics, legends, modern novels and short stories, biographies—all forms of narrative depend upon the immediacy of dialogue to enliven lengthy descriptions or epic segments that have retarded themselves to a standstill. The brief switch to dialogue serves this superficial function, then, and as we shall see allows a more subtle manipulation of the listener's response through the discourse as well.

Before looking further into this rhetorical strategy, I should admit—with due apologies to my informants—that in my own thinking I treat reported dialogues as though they were fictions. To be sure, as listener I regard the stories—the personal narratives—as true. But our literary and dramatic traditions have taught us to expect the subtle editing of dialogue for rhetorical effect. Someone telling a personal narrative must select segments of dialogue, modify them slightly as rhetorical sensitivity dictates, and present them in the context of an as yet unfinished story. Such modifications are slight; otherwise, the dialogue would not have been perceived by the teller as an integral part of the story. But the modifications are allowed and perhaps unconsciously recognized by the listener, for dialogue—much more than epic prose—is the means by which the teller gives an independent existence to the characters in the story.

Like Pirandello's *Six Characters in Search of an Author*, Mom's "Mary" is now suddenly a separate entity, a "character"—not simply Mom's roommate of the epic sections, not Mary Lyons who now lives in Andrews, but "Mary," a complicating new element in the discourse. The teller must present her conversation realistically, yet the teller's interpretation and use of the character's words must dominate. Thus Mary asks, "Where did you get such a pretty yellow dress?!" The question jolts the listener. What does she mean? Surely, Mary does not want to know if Mom bought the dress at Oppenheim's. No, the listener knows immediately that the question must be translated.

Perhaps Mary (like the listener) is drawing upon her personal information about the teller and is actually asking, "How can you afford a new dress? Where did you get the money for a new dress?" She may even be a bit hurt that she did not know about the money, that she did not get to share the fun of spending it. Or perhaps instead she is simply using a fairly common linguistic switch, masking a direct comment as a question. She would have no real need to do this if her comment were simply a positive reflection; she would say, "Oh, I like your new dress," and have done with it. But the discourse demands a different kind of comment from Mary: she must in some way comment on the objectionable yellowness of the dress while keeping in character as friend and roommate. The question, "Where did you get such a pretty yellow dress?" conveys the implied comment so necessary to the ongoing discourse—"I notice you are wearing a new and very yellow dress." As we shall see, this implied statement rather than the superficial question is the message to which Mom responds in the second part of the dialogue.

Analytical codes (Segment TC-10):
  Discourse/Rhetoric: Epic prose in narrative
  Style/Personalore: Dialogue foregrounded in personal style
  Discourse/Rhetoric: Dialogue
  Discourse/Rhetoric: Reported dialogue as fiction
  Discourse/Rhetoric: Narrative characters
  Discourse/Rhetoric: Implied statement

TC-11:   And I said, "Yes, I look like a damn canary!"

The brief interlude of dialogue continues. As suggested above, the speakers of dialogue gain a new dimension for the characters they represent. As suggested in Chapter 2, there are three important dimensions that present themselves simultaneously when the characters—especially the character called "I"—speak. There is, of course, the teller herself, my mother. I have a current sense of her personality developed through a long and intimate association. It is belief that makes my sense of her personality a real configuration for me. For our purposes, I would consider my current sense of my mother's character as an element of personalore, a typically nonverbalized cluster of information and feelings I bring to the story. Furthermore, in this case, I also have a current sense of who Mary Lyons is, though obviously my sense of her character is not founded on so intimate a relationship as is my sense of my mother's character. Again, part of my response to the characters in the story involves my current sense of their personalities as my contemporaries. I should also mention at this point that the use of "I" in the dialogue has yet another dimension for the teller herself. As listener I cannot readily appreciate this function of the word *I* except as it is reflected in the discourse as a "shifter," or a reminder that in the context of the storytelling the speaker must have some means of self-reference.

A second aspect of the characters in the story relates, as did the first, to their personalities, but in this case, the personality and other personal characteristics are ones I as listener would associate with the characters at the time of the incident related in the story. These characters are most like the ones usually found in written literature, especially short stories. They are what literary critics would call "static characters"; they do not change over the course of the story. Rather, the story serves to reveal something about them, something assumed to be a stable part of their personalities. As listener, I must accept the "I" in the dialogue as someone who is both the same person I see before me and also that person she was some forty years ago, a person I know only through photographs and verbal reminiscences such as this one.

I can, perhaps, bring the two aspects together through the creation of a composite, or more accurately cumulative, image of the personality represented by "I" in all the stories my mother tells. This "dynamic" character becomes visible only because I have heard many segments of my mother's repertoire. Thus over a stretch of time, I do hear a "saga," as Richard Dorson (1952:249–72) suggests in his comments on Michigan "sagamen." I create for myself as listener the notion of a stable character who remains identifiable yet changes and grows. But if there is to be a *Bildungsroman* or saga that I am to perceive, then it is I as listener who must create it and give its character a stage on which to perform—like Pirandello's characters—in my mind.

On a simple, narrative level, the "I" of the story is the main character or, structurally in Propp's terms, the "hero" of the story. That is, the characters—both Mom and Mary Lyons and, though absent, Mom's father and stepmother—are the *dramatis personae* of this rather brief plot. The story is not a fairy tale, so the characters do not represent Propp's character prototypes exactly, though they do share some of the "spheres of action" Propp identifies. Propp argues that the actions of all *dramatis personae* are to be defined and evaluated "from the viewpoint of their meaning for the hero and for the course of the action" (Propp 1928:81). Thus, the "course of the action" demands that Mary be a foil for the hero. Similar to the role of the "straight man" in comedy routines, Mary's "sphere of action" is that of helper (again, using Propp's term). The "task" she helps the hero accomplish is, however, related not to the plot of the story but rather to the development of a direct thematic statement. Her initiation of the dialogue invites the articulation of the story's primary motif—discomfiture—in the form of a verbal, almost jokelike simile. The "I" of the brief dialogue is the plot's main character, and she is the "hero" who with Mary's help creates the verbal climax of the story.

As suggested earlier, the emphatic "Yes!" in response to Mary's question is in fact what Mary Louise Pratt (following Grice) would call an example of implicature through flouting of the literary cooperation principle (Pratt 1977:158–59). That is, Mom responds not to Mary's actual question but rather to her own overwhelming sense of how she must look in the yellow dress. In effect, she agrees with a statement she thus attributes to Mary—i.e., that she looks like a "damn canary." As a strategy of rhetoric, the "Yes!" answer violates a maxim of relation; it does not represent a proper response to the words preceding it. However, it does imply successfully that Mary *knows* and probably agrees that the real issue is not whence the dress came but rather how Mom feels she looks in the bright-yellow dress.

The next obvious rhetorical strategy is the invocation of a standard poetic device—the simile. Proverbial comparisons—"like a drowned rat," "like a chicken with its head cut off," etc.—are fairly common in ordinary speech. And the creation of new, context-specific similes modeled on these traditional examples is not unheard of by any means, though when generated spontaneously in oral speech, they are appreciated as "poetic gems" all the more because of their seeming flash of inspiration. Mom's simile does have this insightful appropriateness as an attribute, and of more significance to me, it suggests the storyteller's own image of herself as someone who enjoys and creates poetry. In this sense, the choice to cast the comment in the form of a simile represents a strategy of style that draws upon both the cultural tradition of poetic devices and the self-image of the storyteller (at least as I recognize that image).

Mom grew up writing poetry—as we all write poetry—as an assignment at school, as exercises in English classrooms, perhaps a few as sincere expressions of adolescent doubts and longings. But she continued on occasion to write poems as an adult. Always her poems are conventional in rhyme and scansion, and this, Roger Renwick (1980:158) suggests, is typical of modern "domestic" or "occasional" verse. She seems to enjoy the challenge of a regular meter and rhyme scheme. In 1959, one of her poems, "Castles in Spain," was published in the *National Poetry Anthology*.[5] She keeps the one-volume anthology on a shelf upstairs. In it are countless slips of lined composition paper with more poems—some of them Mom's, some of them grade-school productions by my brothers or me, a few we wrote later in high school or college. Her own poems, like her stories, tend to be short and build to a concluding twist or punchline. I can remember hearing "Castles in Spain" as a child, and to this day I must remind myself, when I hear people talk of building "castles in Spain," that it was my mother who borrowed from tradition and not the other way around. Here is her poem:

> Castles in Spain
> Airy and fleet are my castles in Spain,
> Framed in a circle of rolling mist,
> Spangled with diamonds and studded with stars,
> Often blooming with hundreds of flowers
> Where my winged thoughts keep their tryst.
>
> Bird notes from fairyland float through the trees;
> Hornpipes from elfland call down the hollow;
> A ripple, a splash, from its broad shining bay,
> A wave from the deep washed my castle away—
> I'll build me another—tomorrow!

Literary critics often proclaim that similes are a poor man's metaphor, that "real" poets throw themselves directly into their imagery ("I should have been a pair of ragged claws/Scuttling across the floors of silent seas"), while lesser poets resort to the prepositions and conjunctions that spell out the comparisons at the base of their poetry. And, while it is true that the use of *like* or *as* or *than* is a hallmark of popular or folk poetry, still this in itself does not imply that this poetic device is necessarily inferior to the metaphor with its directness and complexity. In Mom's answer to Mary, she does not at all want to equate herself and a "damn canary." She does not want to get inside the image of a canary and draw lines of relationship between some charged symbolic configuration and her own self-image. Rather, she wants to say that *in regard to the yellowness of her dress* she looks *like* a canary; that is, like a canary, she is completely covered with yellow and nothing but yellow.

I am not suggesting that there is no significance (beyond the yellowness) in the choice of a canary as the object in the simile. It is significant that Mom chose "canary" rather than, say, a banana, a lemon, a pumpkin (which she does mention in version #2), a dandelion (which she mentions in version #3), or a daffodil. These other candidates for "yellow object" are all passive fruits or flowers—with symbolic characteristics of their own, of course, but without the animal liveliness and fablelike symbolism of the canary. There is no denying that the canary in Mom's simile invokes its own store of traditional symbolism. However, I would stress again that Mom does not grasp *all* of the characteristics of the canary as her *intended* comparison. As listener, I may bring many cultural or personal associations to my understanding of her simile, but I recognize that her primary literary intent is to make the comparison of yellowness through a simile that is new but aesthetically acceptable and effective. On the other hand, it is the fuller symbolism of the canary that makes the simile more effective— for me—than would a "yellow" simile with any other object.

Canary is a stylistic and essential choice, then, and one Mom made forty years ago when the dialogue really took place. Though perhaps not intended, the symbolism of the canary has been recognized and appreciated not only by myself as listener but also by Mary Lyons as the original audience for the simile. This recognition—or perhaps expansion—of the original simile into a metaphor or transformation came home clearly to me at my parents' fortieth wedding anniversary celebration (they were married May 19, 1940). An open house was held to celebrate their anniversary on May 20, 1980, at the Evangelical United Methodist Church in Huntington, and Mary Lyons came bringing a gift reminiscent of that period forty years before—a ceramic canary.

Certainly, for Mary, the canary *had* become a symbol. And while a symbol has many simultaneous meanings, usually the varied meanings are assumed to arise from shared tradition—culture—rather than from personal associations. That is, if the canary is to be viewed as a symbol, I should outline a vast compendium of collectively held beliefs, customs, traditional stories, proverbs, or artifacts that embody that symbol and impinge upon the meaning Mary or I or anyone else attaches to this specific manifestation of the canary. And if I were confined to the ceramic bird and its abstract referent in the plot of the story, then indeed I would be bound to "the strategy of the type," to a general survey of the symbol in folklore and culture. I could start with the wide-ranging symbolism of birds in general—as Cirlot (1962:25) says, "every winged being is symbolic of spiritualization." I could ponder—as have generations—why the typically caged canary-bird yet sings. I could review the conflicting beliefs and customs surrounding canaries: they bring good luck; they bring bad luck; dead, they portend human bloodshed; singing, they promise a long and healthy life.

I shall not deny a rightful place to the collective level of the symbol represented by these characteristic interpretations; not surprisingly, as Umberto Eco (1976:62) suggests, the content of such a symbol is typically defined as a "cluster or system of interconnected *cultural* units" (my emphasis). Even so, I do feel that the same definition might function within a much more restricted system of intimacy. In other words, "canary" may function as a symbol both at the level of universal or cultural units and at the level of units of personalore. Unlike the amorphous attachment of associations that surround each segment of the storytelling, this more pronounced and often conscious clustering of personal, intimate, cultural, and universal associations around the image "canary" follows the procedure of symbolizing more commonly recognized by literary critics, sociolinguists, or cultural anthropologists (with the exception that both intimate and personal symbolization are often neglected or even rejected or denied). Formally, these personal associations (with the object "canary") represent aspects of style, but functionally they represent the larger strategy of the type, the "multivalency of meanings" commonly ascribed to the symbol.

I can most easily demonstrate the intimate symbolism of the canary and its yellow color by turning again to the storytelling situation. Bobbie, you will remember, is listening to the story as I am. Because she knows Mom and knows me, she will share some of the meanings I attach to the canary. She will also have her own personal associations as well as the backdrop of universal or culturally determined symbolism. But she will not share those associations tied to my personal life history that come to the fore in my interpretation of the significance of the canary. However, Mom and I will in fact share a number of these associations, as well as some spawned by her life history (at least as I know it). These mutual associations (personalore) represent in this case a kind of intimate symbolism; the associations that are strictly individual revert to the level of style, unless, of course, they independently represent a level of personal symbolism that has evolved over time.

Appreciation of a symbol is covert; by definition a symbol must be unfathomable. Unlike the strands of meaning that attach to the story by association (the kinds I have outlined thus far), a symbol lives and does itself attract strands of meaning. The symbol is not embedded in the text, nor is the text simply a covering for the symbol. The symbol is not "the meaning" of the text, and the text is not simply a manifestation of the symbol. Both the text and the symbol are real entities I hold in my mind. Both are amorphous but may be represented (respectively) by the words of the text printed above or by the image of a canary. Mary Lyons's ceramic canary is a sign, a direct and efficient reference to the story. But it is also a symbol, and one that I cannot assume is immediately lucid. Even if I were to exhaust all of the archetypal, psychological, or cultural references that might exhume the symbol from its unconscious or cultural depths (and I certainly will not be able to do this), I would not yet have laid bare the meaning of the symbol. Much of the meaning of any symbol is bound up in subjective and intimate procedures of symbolization. My subjective interpretation of the symbol (canary) necessarily draws upon these additional explanations in "private" symbolization as well as those "public" explanations that reflect collective (universal or cultural) knowledge. To reinterpret Raymond Firth (1973) but slightly, both intimate and subjective symbolization are private dimensions of the symbol, and these dimensions are as true to the meaning of the symbol as are the public dimensions recognized in native or scholarly analysis. My subjective interpretation of the symbol "canary" is something I would normally not articulate; rather, I would grasp it as a gestalt.

At least three levels of identification function in my recognition of the symbol. At the first level, the canary—like any bird—symbolizes the soul (or in Freud's scheme, the superego). The canary is capable of flight; like the human imagination it rises above the mundane, it transcends; it leaves the brown earth and approaches the yellow sun and brings that yellow brightness back to cheer those earth-bound creatures it left behind. At the archetypal level, identification with the canary captures only these positive universal images of free flight, assent, brightness, and compassion. It is at the second level—cultural symbolization—that the negative images emerge to coexist with the positive. I have already mentioned that the color yellow can be seen as both good and bad, lucky or unlucky. And there are both positive and negative beliefs in tradition surrounding birds in general and canaries in particular. However, "civilized" culture has produced a particularly evocative image through its practice of selectively breeding canaries and selling them as caged pets. Because of this practice, our image of the canary includes this notion of the caged, restricted spirit. But unlike the caged lion, the canary still sings. In fact, the beauty of the canary's song and plumage is the reason for its capture and display. An American proverb asserts, "It is the beautiful bird which gets caged" (see Barbour 1965:16).

There is an indictment in the image. We exaggerate the canary's superficial characteristics to an unnatural state—the Harz Mountain songster, the Manchester show bird—and we deny it the natural grace of a free spirit. We make it an object of display and an item of commerce; we laugh at its frantic efforts when it sees how unbalanced are the odds when "Puddy-Tat" tries to raid the cage. We are the gods who have damned the canary, ignored its natural symbolism as a spirit that flies, made it a slave and denied its soul. But the canary sings despite its cage. Like Prometheus or Sisyphus, the canary is an existential symbol. It asserts its spirit in the face of the absurd and unfair condition of its existence. This, I think, is the source of Mom's ambiguous identity with the canary. Or, at least it is the cultural imagery most prominent in my interpretation of the symbol.

There is an interesting story collected by Linda Dégh from a Transylvanian herdsman. It tells of a hunter who pursued a yellow bird for seven years, trying to shoot it down. Finally the man died, but there was no one to bury him. Some time later his skull split in two, and the rains filled it with water. The yellow bird he had pursued for so long came to drink, and as the bird alighted on the skull, the parts snapped together, trapping the bird inside (1965a:199–200). This is a strange reversal of the typically ironic plot in the Old World narrative of Oleg's Death. As Max Lüthi (1967) demonstrates, in that narrative tradition, the motif "Death by one's own horse" suggests a theme of hubris—man through his pride is the greatest danger to himself. In the Hungarian story of the hunter and the yellow bird, it is the man who is able to harm the bird, even after his death, and again because the bird chooses to flaunt his triumph by drinking from the skull (it is clear that he knows it is the hunter's skull). In life, the hunter was obsessed with pursuing the bird; like Ahab, he seemed to both hate and identify with his quarry. In death, the hunter captures the yellow bird; but, as the bird asks, "Of what use is that to you?" Obviously, the bird is of no use, except as a symbol. As long as the bird was free, the man was free. But the man wanted the bird brought down; he envied its flight. In the end the hunter captured the bird, but his prize was doomed—like the man himself—to a dreary, unsung death, since no one was there to nurture the bird in its ghastly cage.

It is common in cultural symbolism to thus identify with birds and with the treatment we often inflict upon birds. As the Psalmist says, "Our soul is escaped as a bird out of the snare of the fowlers: the snare is broken, and we are escaped" (Psalms 124:7). The once-snared bird that knows the joy of escape is the psalmist singing (cf. Motif B375.3, Bird released: grateful). The caged bird knows that it can fly. Its flight—when caged—is all potential, is idea, is an untangible reality that is not physically actualized but yet has its effect in mundane reality—the caged bird sings. The canary on display in its cage signals man's preoccupation with his own soul. We see our own great potential; our souls would fly were they not fettered by our three-dimensional world. We cage the canary as a symbol—a bit of yellow that would fly to the sun.

Both the song and flight of the canary are images Mom readily draws from the stock of cultural symbolism and assimilates into that more intimate symbolism she and I share. You may recall, in her poem "Castles in Spain" she gave an obviously birdlike animation to the traditional image of "winged thoughts," and she filled the air around her imaginary castle with "bird notes from fairyland." These clues simply reinforce for those who know my mother the positive symbolism they would attach to her creation of the canary simile. For example, most people who visit my parents' home do notice the yellow lovebirds in the kitchen. The yellow lovebirds are neither expensive nor unique; they are not regarded as a special memento to the fourth-grader who gave them to Mom twenty years ago. Rather, they remain because Mom wants them there. She is quick to squelch any roughhousing in the vicinity of her birds. Some years ago, the birds and their swing did fall; one bird's tail was broken. Most mass-produced decorative pieces are basically "throw-away art," something to be tossed out when broken or to be sold bargain-rate at a white elephant sale when no longer interesting or appropriate. But Mom was not about to throw away her canaries—then or now. Instead, she asked Dad to glue the tail back on and attach a new (and *stronger*) chain to the swing. Obviously, the yellow lovebirds are a precious item, something of significance to Mom and consequently to her family. She has invested some of herself in the display and maintenance of these symbolic figures, and the family recognizes this investment and identification as clearly as it recognizes the association between Mom and her place at the kitchen table, her living-room chair, her golden chalice saved from the dinner set used on the farm in Michigan, her 1938 Macmillan dictionary given to her by Dean Davenport, her story of the yellow dress.

An almost superstitious aura surrounds the birds, as though they were some sort of subconsciously recognized totem or life-token. At a cultural level of symbolism, the birds may well represent the general motif E732, Soul in the form of a bird, but at the intimate level of symbolism, they represent Mom's identification with and affection for birds and her obvious appreciation for their close relationship with humans generally and herself in particular. It is significant, I suppose, that Mom has never kept a live canary as a pet. We did once have a green parakeet named Pete. He had been given to my brother Dick as a "gift" from someone on his paper route. Actually, the poor little bird was sick (literally lousy) and permanently lamed in one wing. But, rather than let the bird die—which I am sure the "benefactor" fully expected—Mom gently bathed the scrawny little fellow in Lysol every day until he was cured. Pete never could fly, but he learned to talk early and long. He died in 1963 after a long and noisy life and was buried out back by the pear tree. Mom prefers to see birds in the wild. In fact, this, I think, is part of her fascination with birds: they are so willing to openly share the immediate environment—even in town—with humans, and yet they are not domesticated but free.

I can remember that Mom was intrigued by my Great-Uncle Fred's beautiful white pigeons that nested in the dovecote above his small barn. Uncle Fred lived just across the street in Huntington. The barn and dovecote (and "cow pasture" with no cows) attest to the fact that Vine Street had once been beyond the outskirts of town. Uncle Fred fed his pigeons well; they fattened and multiplied—and stayed. Aunt Opal finally protested that there were just too many birds. He couldn't stop feeding them; that would be cruel. He couldn't eat them; they were his pets. Finally, with a sad heart, he sold them and boarded up the cote. As much as she enjoys birds, Mom has never done what I am sure she would consider a disservice to the birds by making them dependent upon her. To be sure, she worries over the birds that come to the bird feeder during the winter, knowing that the food she and Dad give them may well be sorely needed. And she is saddened by the sight of frozen birds that could not survive the long subzero nights. But the birds are free, free to come to the bird feeder and in exchange bring some pleasure to the watchers inside the house. Mom faithfully keeps a record of the birds that visit the bird feeder, identifying them by species, noting when there are pairs, and counting their number. On sight, she can name most of the birds that winter in northern Indiana as well as those that migrate through the area in the fall and spring.

Uncommon visitors are a welcome challenge. She keeps two bird books handy on her utility table: a facsimile edition of John James Audubon's *Birds of America* and a more recent publication of the National Geographic Society titled *Song and Garden Birds of North America*.

Mom's birdwatching, her anecdotal reaction to Uncle Fred's pigeons (Mom often tells people about Uncle Fred and his pigeons, though both Fred and Opal died years ago), her attachment to the yellow lovebirds—these "characteristics" are some of the ones I experience as creating an allusive field in the intimate level of symbolization in my image of the canary. The universal, cultural, and intimate levels of identification in the symbol of the canary combine with the personal and cultural associations with the color yellow to create a positive imagery in the canary simile. Overall, as a symbol, the canary is an attractant, something with positive emotional, aesthetic, even spiritual attributes despite its philosophical image as a restricted spirit.

There is a problem, however, in this image of the canary as an attractant. A Brethren background and feminine modesty are hard-pressed to accept either the yellow dress *or* the metaphor of the canary precisely because they seem designed to attract attention, perhaps even sexual attention. Some years ago, Richard Dorson collected a recipe for a love potion from a Potawatomi Indian living in Michigan's Upper Peninsula. The potion was to be made of powdered canary root. The root was also useful in hunting and fishing, as his informant, Alec Philemon, said: "If you rub that root on your hook you can make fish and animals come to you. You know a canary is a nice bird, sings pretty. If you see a canary you'll want to go up and look at it. Well, it's the same way with the deer and the bear, when you use the root. They'll come up to look at you, you aim your gun, down they go. It's like you were a big canary. I looked all over for that root, never could find it" (Dorson 1952:36–37). The canary, like the canary root, attracts attention, positive attention, perhaps even that of a lover. Mom may have been reluctant to wear the yellow dress because it made her more attractive, blatantly so. Though there certainly is nothing scandalous or particularly sexy about yellow clothing in general, by invoking the symbolism of the canary, Mom seems to suggest that wearing the yellow dress is an open admission that she hopes to attract someone. Indirectly, donning the yellow dress represents a youthful, enthusiastic willingness to be beautiful, exciting, daring, wonderful—all the things a lover should be.

At this point in the story, meaning is generated (in my perception) through a tension between two levels of strategy of the type—the level of symbol and the level of structure. Or more specifically, there is tension between the superficial structure of the narrative and the psychological implications of the symbol. The canary, as symbol, is an attractant; it represents a blatant, exuberant statement of willingness to attract someone, to engage in life and love. From most perspectives, the symbol is positive; the willingness it represents is not a crude, jaundiced "offer" but rather a joyful, sunny rush of feeling, the canary's ecstasy of song and flight. In contrast to the symbol, the structure of the narrative paints a rather dour picture. The key word that sets up the tension between structure and symbol is the word *damn* in Mom's reply to Mary. Mom says, "Yes, I look like a damn canary," not simply a canary.

The tone of mock disgust is a secondary clue that Mom intends *canary* to be interpreted in a negative light. Had she said something like, "Yes, don't I just look like a canary!"—even if spoken in a half-mocking tone, the listener would jump immediately to a positive semantic, and the motif of discomfiture would never have developed.

The word *damn*, then, is a highly charged word modifying the already ambiguous word *canary* and almost single-handedly deflecting the superficial structure into a negative direction. *Damn* reinforces the ambiguity of the symbol, bringing to the fore again the notion that the canary—bred and caged as it is—is "unnatural" either because we have "damned" it (enslaved it) or because it is "damnable" (certainly a projection in which we blame the victim for tolerating its enslavement). And yet the canary is a positive symbol. The temptation is strong to hear only a positive tone in the word *damn*. And this is possible in American folk tradition since *damn* enjoys a most ambiguous usage itself. *Damn* is a curse word with a variety of inhibitions and inducements attached to its use, and these of course affect its meaning in specific contexts and in the speech of specific individuals.[6]

In Mom's case there are several strong inhibitions against its use and, I would guess, at least as many inducements toward its use *aside from the simple demand of the discourse* that she somehow express her dislike for the yellow dress. One inhibition is Mom's religious background: cursing is blasphemous; a good Brethren does not curse. Another inhibition is Mom's sex: ladies do not curse or use foul language. And I think we could say that Mom has a personal (family-based) inhibition against using the word *damn*. Her vocabulary is instead replete with traditional euphemisms; this story is one of the few times I have ever heard her use the word *damn*. Never have I heard her utter *damn* or any other potentially blasphemous word in a context (of despair or anger) that would actually constitute blasphemy. Even simple profanity as in the story is rarely a part of Mom's speech.

The inducements to use the word *damn* obviously won over the inhibitions both at the time of the experience and with the initial telling and many retellings of the story. I can imagine that there might be some storytelling contexts in which Mom would substitute a word such as *darn* or maybe *dumb* for the word *damn* in her reply. It is, after all, the only potentially offensive word in the story. Obviously she does not feel a need to alter the sentence in my presence (or Bobbie's), though I suspect that this is because I am now an adult; both Mom and Dad have always been very conscientious in their avoidance of profanity or "improper" language or stories in front of children.

In looking at the original sentence in its initial context, we can see other inducements to use *damn* and ignore the inhibitions (or rather play on the tension between the two). For a college senior (as Mom was in the story), there is a certain peer pressure to appear worldly and uninhibited, to rebel against family inhibitions and exhibit new signs of strong self-identity (or more accurately, a new group identity). Many a "good" girl learns to swear (and smoke, drink, etc.) in college because of peer pressure. Besides, women had "come a long way" since the passage of the Nineteenth Amendment, and the age of the flapper ushered in new values and standards of behavior.

Folklore of the time had already picked up on the more acceptable use of *damn* and other profanities in popular expression and everyday speech.[7] Another short anecdote Mom often relates centers around a candy bar she and her friends created and marketed under the name "Dam-fine-O." The name (aurally) can be interpreted as either "Damned if I know" in response to a question about the name of the candy, or simply "Damned fine-o" as a testimonial to the quality of the candy. In either case, they felt free to use the erstwhile taboo word *damn* in a humorous and public context. And finally, I might add that integrity and aesthetic sense seem to converge and compel her to tell the story (and recreate the dialogue) as it happened. She said *damn* then and sees no reason to lie about it now. (Besides, Mary Lyons corroborates her story and dialogue.) By now, "damn canary" simply sounds right. Anything else would be a self-imposed bowdlerization.

I would like to go back now to my earlier assertion that the conflict between structure and symbol is an important element in my sense of meaning in the story. The structure can be abstracted at various levels (as I shall demonstrate shortly), but none of these structural schemes alone conveys the psychological meaning of the story. To a great extent, the psychological meaning of the story grows out of the apparent failure of the structure to accommodate the positive aspects of the symbol (the canary as attractant). This failure coupled with the charged modifier *damn* is a clue that the "psychological structure" is not derived from the plot as *presented* but rather represents a special kind of nonverbalized folklore, what we might call an "inverse narrational value endorsement."

Narratives support or endorse certain values through their repetition; personal narratives often serve to articulate or represent values that in fact become values only through the effect of literary foregrounding when the story is first told and then repeated as part of the teller's repertoire. Narrational value endorsement is simply a recognition of this effect; it constitutes an abstract category into which various specific values might be slotted and thus endorsed by the storyteller. When this effect is inverted, the result is a *seeming* ambiguity in regard to the value involved. In fact, however, the listener's response to such an inversion is very likely an acceptance of the underlying endorsement. In other words, as listener, I am convinced of the teller's allegiance to the positive value of the canary symbol despite her presentation of a plot structure that would seem to support the opposite value of inhibition. In effect, by allowing the canary symbolism to win over the motif of discomfiture inherent in the plot, the teller endorses the value of assertion and attraction implicit in the symbol. At the same time, however, she projects responsibility for this new value onto her father, her roommate, even the clothing store—anyone but herself.

This particular narrative value endorsement involves in part what Alan Dundes (1980a:51) describes as a narrative "projection inversion." That is, the teller hopes to establish other characters in the story as the perpetrators of the positive valuation of the yellow dress and its symbolic overtones. However, it is ultimately the teller herself who chose to endorse the value of attractiveness, though she presents herself in the plot as the antagonist opposing this value. Before looking further to the psychological structure, let me briefly present an analysis of the plot structure in the "Yellow Dress" segment that allows this psychological structure to develop.

I see three general levels of plot structure. Each level is identifiable by the size of the abstracted unit involved—large, medium, or small. Various schemes may be slotted into these three levels. For instance, at the level of the large structural units, we have a "problem/solution" structure something like Alan Dundes's (1963) "lack/lack liquidated" sequence with, in this case, a lack represented by the "lack" of appropriate clothing and the "liquidation" of the lack manifested in the purchase of an appropriate summer-weight dress and shoes.

We might instead follow the cyclical (large-level) scheme of Claude Brémond and view the structure as the development of action from a "state of deficiency" through a "procedure of improvement" to an "improved state" (Brémond 1970:251). Or again, as my adaptation of Brémond suggests, we might specify the overall thematic goal in structural terms as a procedure that relieves the initial monotony of the long summer.

> *Monotony*
> *Procedure for relieving monotony* —[Plot]
> *Monotony relieved*

All three of these large-unit schemes view the action of the story as the means by which a negative state is neutralized. The structure in these terms is too abstract to create a sense of tension between itself and the primary symbol in the story. Though they do not point to a negative resolution, neither do they parallel the positive lines of the symbol. They simply represent the narrative tendency toward equilibrium.

The medium-level schemes for structural analysis contrast very sharply with the positive ambience of the symbol. Whether one looks to Propp or Dundes or Lévi-Strauss for a model to adapt for structural study at this level, the analytic schemes at this level point to a negative closing or failure in the plot of the Yellow Dress segment.[8] If the plot is treated through its chronological progression, it generally represents a cycle from a state of dissatisfaction through an action and a return to dissatisfaction:

> Discontent (dissatisfaction with clothing)
> Receipt of gift (money from her father)
> Misuse of gift (money spent on inappropriate clothing)
> Discomfiture (embarrassment at wearing dress)

If, on the other hand, the story is treated with greater attention to paradigms of cultural meaning (adapting Lévi-Strauss 1958), then the negative structure is represented by the failure of the plot to mediate significant opposites:

> NATURE Situation: inappropriate clothing
> (Undervaluing of the environment)
> CULTURE Action: purchase of the dress
> (Undervaluing of taste)
> FAILURE TO MEDIATE NATURE
> AND CULTURE Consequence: discomfiture
> (Failure to mediate between the environment
> and taste)

Even at the level of small units of structure (i.e., greater detail in the abstraction of functions), discomfiture is the primary result of the purchase of the dress. (I shall summarize this third level of structure separately in the review at the end of the instructional text.) Consistently, the message of the plot structure seems to be a negative one, a contention that the storyteller really should not have bought the yellow dress because she does not like it and feels uncomfortable wearing it. It is important for our perception of "projective inversion" in the story that we recognize this negative structure in the plot. In psychological terms, we must be able to see how the story *as told* allows Mom to project blame for her discomfiture onto the dress itself and (indirectly) onto her father for giving her the money to buy the dress and onto Mary for liking it.

In the discussion of the canary as symbol, I concluded that the dress symbolically represents the willingness of the heroine (Mom in 1938) to attract attention to herself. If the plot structure were not negative, Mom would, in effect, have been saying (1) I bought this dress because I want to be attractive (like a canary), (2) my father has given me the means to attract a suitor, and (3) I am ready to cast off my daughterly inhibitions, attract a suitor, and marry. However, the structure of the plot denies these statements. Therefore, to see the psychological structure, we must hear first the projection: women who wear bright-yellow dresses are like canaries; they enthusiastically solicit the attention of men. It is easy to see how the dress and her father (who gave her the money) are made responsible for her "taboo" behavior. If her father, of all people, *encourages* her to make herself attractive to other men, what choice does she have but to deny her value of inhibition and symbolically leave the nest and engage in life and love in the big world "out there"?

By professing discomfiture in the plot of the story, she is able to deny (to herself) her own *interest* in attracting the attention of a lover while at the same time reaping the benefits of her purchase. In fact, over the course of that summer she was dating three young men (including my father, whom she married two years later). In version #2, you might notice a joking exchange between Mom and Dad on the subject of these other two suitors—Glenn Beery and "Puffy" Plasterer. By insisting that she is embarrassed by the message the yellow dress conveys, Mom is able to project her own desire to be attractive onto her father. *He* is the one who has encouraged her to attract a lover; she obediently follows his suggestion, but he is responsible for the change. Superficially at least, she remains a modest, self-effacing young Brethren woman who condemns new bright-colored clothing as ostentatious. But her father's gift has forced her to actively seek to be attractive.

Through this "projective inversion," she is able to maintain the illusion that the yellow dress is a source of personal discomfiture and to decry any interest in attracting suitors. Much in the story could be analyzed as a fairy tale with all the psychoanalytic apparatus often used in such studies. (There are, conveniently, a father, stepmother, heroine, helper, and three suitors.) My tendency in this instance, however, is to hear what is most meaningful to me. I think Mom found a complex and clever way to use "projection inversion" (not that she would use that term or necessarily recognize the concept) to endorse those symbols and behaviors that celebrate life, and especially a natural delight in physical attraction.

Analytical codes (Segment TC-11):
 Discourse/Rhetoric: Dialogue
 Style/Personalore: Personalities of acquaintances who are
   characters in the story
 Discourse/Situation: Self-reference by the speaker
 Discourse/Rhetoric: "Static characters"
 Discourse/Rhetoric: "Dynamic characters"
 Discourse/Rhetoric: Characters as *dramatis personae*
 Discourse/Rhetoric: Flouting the cooperation principle
 Discourse/Rhetoric: Use of simile
 Style/Culture: Poetic devices
 Style/Personalore: Mom's poetry writing
 Type/Symbol: Canary
 Style/Personalore: The significance of the canary to Mom and
  Mary Lyons
 Type/Symbol: "Intimate" symbolism of the canary
 Type/Symbol: Universal (bird, flight, yellow)
 Type/Symbol: Culture (Caged bird, human envy of the bird's
  flight)
 Type/Symbol: Culture (Song as witness to the potential for
  flight)
 Type/Symbol: Intimate (Ceramic yellow lovebirds)
 Type/Motif: E732, Soul in form of a bird
 Type/Symbol: Intimate (Birds in close relationship to humans)
 Style/Personalore: Pete the parakeet
 Style/Personalore: Uncle Fred and his pigeons
 Style/Personalore: Mom's birdwatching
 Type/Symbol: Cultural and Intimate (Canary as attractant)
 Style/Culture: *Damn* used to express negative tone
 Style/Culture: Ambiguous meaning of *damn*
 Discourse/Rhetoric: Expressing a negative
 Style/Culture: Religious prohibition against swearing
 Style/Culture: Bias against women swearing
 Style/Personalore: Mom's use of euphemisms
 Discourse/Situation: Adult audience
 Style/Culture: Peer pressure in the 1930s
 Style/Culture: Folkloric use of *damn*

Style/Personalore: "Dam-fine-O" candy bar
Type/Structure: Psychological structure (narrative
         value endorsement)

TC-12:   I hated the thing, but it's the only one I could get for that price, so that's
          what I got.

In this comment that closes the "Yellow Dress" segment, Mom lets rhetoric
pay the piper. She *says*, "I hated the thing," but in fact she reaped the rewards
of wearing a new and attractive dress. By claiming to dislike the dress and to
resent having to wear it, she denies her own interest in being "like a canary"
and indirectly faults her father for making it necessary that she thus proclaim
an interest in being the object of love and attention from young men outside
of her family.

Other cultural elements would include such things as the fear of
assertiveness common among many women. Not only do many women fear or
avoid assertiveness, but often their speech reflects this fear through appeals to
others for authority when an assertion is tentatively made or through obvious
awkwardness in accepting a compliment (Kramer 1974; Lakoff 1975). Mom
was pleased that Mary thought the dress pretty, but her reply was the near-
proverbial "This old thing!?" so often comically represented as the stereotypical
response of a woman when complimented on her dress. Mom is not at all
confident that she does look pretty in the yellow dress. Her transferral of the
final authority to Mary (or others generally) would be judged typical behavior
for a young woman. She still needs some reinforcement of her decision to try
something new. She asks for this reinforcement by challenging Mary with a
negative statement. She carries the challenge on to the listener by reiterating
her dislike for the dress: "I hated the thing"—and by reiterating her practical
rationale for buying it: "It's the only one I could get for that price." Like Mary,
the audience must lend authority to the decision she has made.

Finally, I would return to the symbolism of the canary in a more superficial
sense and view Mom's closing words in the "Yellow Dress" segment as a clear
statement of her reluctance to "leave the nest." She knows the time has come to
cast off the camouflaging feathers of childhood and take on the brighter colors
of the adult, to leave the nest and her parents (real or substitute—Manchester
was certainly *in loco parentis*) and fly out into the world where a mate and
her own future family await. (Mom was in her middle twenties in 1938.) It is
the disquieting thought of leaving the known and reaching for the unknown
that bothers her. She "hates" to leave the known—her conservative Brethren
tradition, her family, her dormmates, even her personal habits and tastes (the

wool skirt and satin blouse). She "hates" the yellow dress as a subjective symbol of that leave-taking. It is a tribute to the comfort the nest has provided that she so hates to leave it. Yet, as in the fairy tales, the child must "go out into the world," mature, and marry. I find it significant, personally moving, and instructive (certainly, a visible function of the storytelling) that Mom was so very sensitive to the drawing power of her primary family, the family of her birth (cf. Goode 1964). And it reminds me as listener that I went through much the same sequence of feelings when I earned my college degree, later married, and later still started my own family. To me, it is as though she felt that great sweep back in time and forward to the future where children must always leave what they love and themselves produce a world their children will be just as reluctant to leave. James Agee said it, too: "Just one way, you do get back home. You have a boy or a girl of your own and now and then you remember, and you know how they feel, and it's almost the same as if you were your own self again as young as you could remember" (from *A Death in the Family*).

Analytical codes (Segment TC-12):
 Style/Culture: Women's avoidance of assertiveness
 Type/Theme: Reluctance to leave the nest

TC-l3: That was the same summer—that was the broke summer—but anyway, Mary and I were getting awfully bored and we wanted to go to the show. But between us we had a quarter, and neither one of us wanted to go by herself, so we stayed home. And that night my name had been drawn for a hundred dollars—Bank Night. And I wasn't there to claim it, so I didn't get it. —Sad!

Here Mom brings us back to the theme of surviving hard times and the initial structural abstraction revolving around the monotony of "the broke summer." Though it cost only a quarter to get into the movie theater, money was scarce enough that even a quarter was hard to find, especially for inessentials like entertainment. In contrast, food prices were even lower (remember the three pounds of hamburger for a quarter), while luxury items were completely beyond the budgets of most Americans living through the Great Depression.

The irony of the little sketch is that had Mom gone to the show (without Mary, of course), she would have won one hundred dollars, a most significant sum given the hard times. As is typical of such "misfortune stories" (cf. Brandes 1975), a direct causal line can be drawn from the misfortune back to an earlier decision, in this case Mom and Mary's joint decision that since they did not have enough money for them both to go, then neither of them would go. Hindsight of course urges that Mom should have shown some initiative: You cannot win at Bank Night (or life) unless you leave home and go to the show (go out into the world).

As she explains in version #2, she was not aware that her name was in the hopper. Significantly, it was one of her dates (Glenn Beery) who had entered her name earlier in the summer. (Perhaps if he had seen her in her new yellow dress, he would have asked her out that night.) As it was, in true fairy tale fashion, she passed "the test" with an absence of greed and an appropriate display of compassion and loyalty (by not going without Mary). But in contrast to the typical fairy tale hero, she was not rewarded with riches for demonstrating her good character.

Analytical codes (Segment TC-13):
    Type/Theme: Surviving hard times
    Type/Structure: Initial situation (Monotony to relieve)
    Style/Culture: Twenty-five-cent movie admission (1930s)
    Type/Genre: "Misfortune story"

TC-14:   That was the same summer we stayed up all night swatting mosquitoes because our screen had holes in it—let the mosquitoes in. We couldn't go to sleep.

One might be tempted to hear this final segment of the story as an afterthought; it hardly seems significant in any way, except maybe as a sign that they were too poor to patch the screens. Nevertheless, there is a clue in the overall rhetoric of the story that suggests that the closing segment is significant and is in fact a part of the structural unity of the story. If you look at an unsegmented presentation of the text (see the Appendix), you can more easily see the repetitious phrase that indicates the start of each new segment of the story. The story begins, "When I was at Manchester *that last summer* . . ." (my emphasis). The next "paragraph" begins, "That was the same summer . . ."; the third segment begins, "That was the same summer—that was the broke summer . . ."; and this last segment as well begins, "That was the same summer . . ." If nothing else, the repeated phrase is a rhetorical device that ties the four segments together temporally.

Thematically, the four segments all point to problems of living through the years of the Depression, especially "the broke summer" (though the theme is sounded only minimally in this last segment). In fact, because of the linear development of the story, reference to "the broke summer" becomes (by the third segment) an element of personalore growing out of the story itself.

However, the structure of the story is the analytic aspect most clearly affected by the "connections" implied by the rhetoric. Much earlier in the instructional text I suggested that "Monotony to relieve" was the primary structural impetus in the story. With that in mind, we can look to each of the four segments of the story as a new and specific illustration of how monotony was relieved that summer. The most important segment—important in terms of the greater meaning of the story—is the second, the "Yellow Dress" segment. Here change is brought about through intentional action by the story's main character. The purchase and wearing of the yellow dress represents a spontaneity, a willingness to change her self-image and break away from her own monotonous attire and grooming habits.

Nevertheless, if we survey the Simplified Structural Chart (see figure 5.1), we can easily see that all four segments are representational movements from a state of boredom to one of excitement, improvement, or action. Segment one is situational; however, the "situation" extends beyond the time of the story action and into the time of the storytelling. The improvement can be perceived only from the listener's point of view (personalore and cultural cues) since the storyteller herself does not directly mention anything about her own current economic situation.

In this simple structural scheme, the second segment seems no more prominent than the other three segments; it too involves a clear movement from monotony to change. The third segment actually seems more complicated structurally. Here the consequence (C) is not a goal but a result; Mom did not even know that her inaction (not going to the show) resulted in the loss of a potential one hundred dollars until the fact was conveyed through the attention and interaction of her friends who did go to the movie. In a traditional plot (a *Märchen* or romance), segment three would have been reversed (to a positive monetary outcome), and segments one and three together would have been the essential plot pair (lack/lack liquidated in Dundes's scheme; a/K in Propp's); the heroine would have won the reward and married the prince.

But in this realistic (nonfictional) plot, the attention and interaction with friends must be accepted instead as a positive consequence; the event "makes a good story" and stirs the admiration of her friends. She is consoled by her recognition as one of the souls fate has singled out to treat with such irony. The fourth segment would hardly qualify as an incident at all *outside of the context of the overall plot.* In Labov and Waletzky's terms the segment represents only a "complication"; theoretically (but not in the real world, I am sure) the mosquito-swatting segment represents what Labov and Waletzky (1967:41) call "the simplest possible narrative," a complication without a clear resolution.

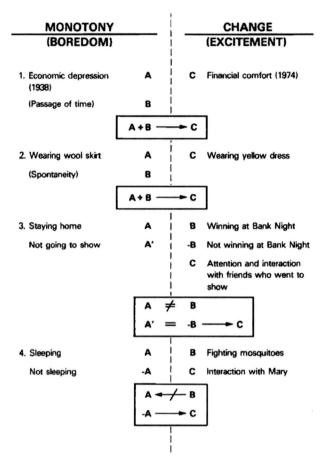

Figure 5.1

But because the incident is a segment of the larger plot, the listener is able to (in fact, must) provide the necessary consequence (interaction instead of sleeping) and positive evaluation (the perception of movement from potential inaction or monotony [sleeping] to action).

Alone, segment four would be negative, a complaint. What good could come from losing sleep and fighting off mosquitoes? Only in the context of the whole plot structure does the "good humor" of the last segment come through. Mom and Mary "got the giggles, of course" (see version #3 of "The Yellow Dress", in the Appendix) as a response to the absurdity of their situation—two grown women kept awake by a tiny mosquito. The listener appreciates the segment as one last illustration of how the monotony of that long "broke" summer was relieved.

Analytical codes (Segment TC-14):
  Discourse/Rhetoric: Repeated phrase ("That was the same summer")
  Type/Theme: Surviving hard times
  Style/Personalore: The broke summer of 1938
  Style/Personalore: Mom's current economic situation
  Type/Structure: Four-part structure (simplified)

"The Yellow Dress" in Review

The prominent theme of the story is economic survival. The 1930s were hard years in the United States. Probably Grandpa DeVault was able to survive the worst years because he was a farmer and a landowner. Even so, sending a daughter to college was a luxury he could not afford. By starting college later, by working part-time jobs during school and summer jobs in between, by borrowing money, even by teaching a class, Mom was able to pay her own undergraduate tuition and most of her living expenses. The five dollars her father sent was a welcome gift. But for me (and Bobbie) as audience to the storytelling, the five-dollar gift is a subtle clue that *most* of Mom's college expenses were met through her own efforts. Mom would never come right out and say (to me, for example), "Just look at what I endured to be able to complete my college education. I couldn't depend on my parents for money to go to school, but I wanted to go badly enough to suffer even that miserable 'broke' summer. I can laugh at it now, but at the time it was a pretty trying situation. I wouldn't wish such a time on you, but I hope that by hearing my story you appreciate even more the money we have spent to help you through school and the comparative 'good times' we enjoy now in America."

She does not resort to such obvious preaching; the story does it much more graciously. I am more inclined to accept the lesson in its narrative guise. In 1972, when version #1 was recorded, I was still in graduate school, and though the times were not so bad generally, my own economic situation was the typical substandard one of most graduate students. Most of my parents' financial support had come during my undergraduate years; graduate school would not have been a possibility without that earlier help from them. Mom's story is not a game in one-upmanship. Rather, she likely feels I can appreciate this latent message of her story all the more, now that I am experiencing something analogous to her "broke summer." She offers clear evidence that she can sincerely empathize with me as I endure a period of economic hard times for the sake of furthering my education.

The story functions as an exemplum or parable, then, as, for example, do the "yarns" based on personal experience told by the La Have Island fishermen in Richard Bauman's (1972b) study. There are a number of other less prominent functions of the story and storytelling. Sociability is certainly part of the *raison d'être* of the genre generally and this storytelling in particular: the men are out working in the garage, the children are playing, and the women are talking in the kitchen. "Talking" often involves the exchange of personal narratives as a way of reinforcing the intimacy of the particular social relationship. When grown children (or in-laws) do not live in the parents' home or see them on a day-to-day basis, the exchange of such stories is a particularly effective way of reestablishing the sense of intimacy that otherwise fades without daily interaction and local interests in common.

The structure of the story reflects the dominant theme of surviving hard times, and it is this theme and structure that enable the story to serve so well its primary didactic function. The message (usually) to the audience of the story is that an economically difficult period can be endured with good humor if one learns to appreciate those precious intrusions into the monotony that is so often a stifling companion to hard times. (Many social theorists blame simple boredom for the rioting during the "long, hot summers" when a high number of youth are unemployed, bored with their inactivity, and unable to afford the kind of entertainment that would distract them from the monotony of their lives.)

The structure of Mom's story is a sequence of actions that in some way relieve the monotony of "the broke summer." Using my adaptation of Brémond's model, I would represent the full narrative structure (small units) of Mom's story as indicated in the chart in figure 5.2. The functions immediately within the largest level of structure (Monotony to relieve) are the three primary actions of the plot—(1) replacing the wool skirt with the yellow dress, (2) interacting with college friends (after losing out at Bank Night), and (3) interacting with Mary (swatting mosquitoes). The three functions in the story are parallel rather than internally dependent. They are each a separate illustration of *a* procedure for relieving the monotony.

This view of the structure is from the perspective of the storyteller and her literary goals relative to the main character. Each of the three main segments of action (labeled [1], [2], and [3] on the chart) is independently a "sufficient" fulfillment of the largest triad (Monotony to relieve). Nevertheless, the effect of the three segments is cumulative—which only makes sense in light of the quantity of intrusions (in this case, three) necessary before a person feels monotony has in fact been relieved. The internal development of each segment—the *procedure* for replacing the wool skirt, the procedure for seeking interaction—reflects the intradependent sequence of literary goals that directs the presentation of the plot. Each new function cannot be completed (the third line of the triad) until all of the functions within its triad are also completed.

With the completion of the final triad in each segment, the links in the chain of previous literary goals reaching back to that initial triad are simultaneously fulfilled (if they had not been completed earlier). The structure can be analyzed, then, in terms that clearly point to the traditionality of that structure, especially in such standard functions as "Help to give" or "Test to pass." But the greater value of such a structural analysis is the frame it provides for abstracting less prominent themes and cultural values from the narrative.

The problematic economic situation in the 1930s is the most obvious

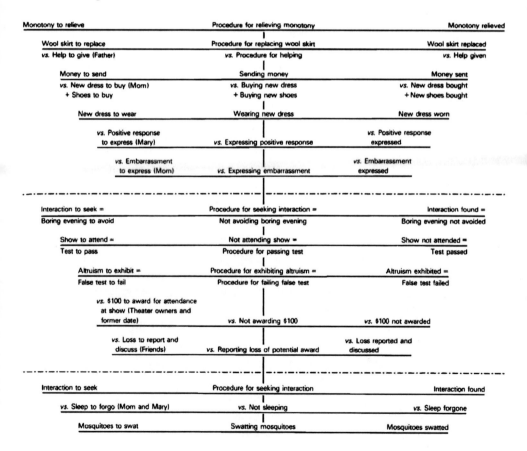

Figure 5.2

theme, and the closely associated theme of boredom is prominent to some extent as a consequence. Friendship is another theme; in all three action segments, friendship is emphasized either through some form of positive social interaction—Mary's compliment on Mom's dress in the first segment, the gamelike activity of swatting mosquitoes and the accompanying laughter in the last segment—or through some obvious symbolic action that recognizes and reinforces the friendship—Mom and Mary's mutual agreement that if they could not both afford to go to the show, then neither of them would go. A less obvious theme is the absence of men—not simply that they are not a part of the story; they *are* a part of the story, but primarily through their absence. The letter and five-dollar bill from Mom's father are the only obvious clue to this theme of absence. However, the absence of men is clearly a part of the story if we look to the roles men typically fill in the real-life situations around which the story revolves.

In regard to the first action segment, a man—the father—is usually expected to provide for his family, especially his daughter. In this case, the daughter has left the home and gone to college. The home and sustenance the father would provide for her cannot be portioned off and sent along with her; neither can the father himself. He sends a token, wishing of course that he could be of more help. The five dollars is a help, but it is also a reminder that the father is not there. In the second plot segment the absent man is any young man who would fill the role of date. As I mentioned earlier, version #2 of the story suggests three potential candidates for this absent date: Dad, Glenn Beery (the young man who enrolled Mom in the drawing), and Puffy Plasterer (the one Dad guessed had put Mom's name in the drawing). Of the three likely suitors, not one is available to take Mom (or Mary) to the show. And finally, in the last segment, we can infer the absence of men from the fact that the screen had holes in it. Typically, home repair jobs are handled by men—husbands, grown sons, or paid repairmen. Such conventional sex-role stereotyping allows us to assume that if there were a man around the house, the screens would have been fixed.

One other theme—and one that easily overlaps into the illustration of cultural values—is personal responsibility. The story involves no heavy responsibility or decision making; rather, the decisions that are made are simple everyday decisions—what purchase to make at the clothing store, whether or not to go to the show, perhaps even whether or not to leave the window open. Thematically, however, the decisions, minor as they are, require that Mom accept responsibility for the consequences of her decisions. *She* is the one who decides to wear the yellow dress, though it does not fit her previous self-image; she is the one who decides to stay home rather than go to the show. Fate does not cheat her or embarrass her; she makes the decisions herself and acts on them. Accepting responsibility for decisions is a sign of maturity and a positively valued characteristic in our culture.

Other values given some prominence in the story include the "prize" of a college education, a prize made increasingly valuable through the sacrifices made in its behalf and the personal investment of time and money. Money itself is valued positively in the story. Human avarice gives money its bad name; in this story, money is treated with respect for its power and scarcity and with great care in its apportionment. A related value is practicality; Mom cites this value as the primary influence on her decision to buy the yellow dress. She could buy the inexpensive dress *and a pair of shoes* for five dollars; buying a prettier, more expensive dress might be an appealing alternative, but it would not be as practical.

On the other hand, we can see that the story illustrates as well a concern with aesthetics. Mom is probably pleased that Mary finds the dress pretty, but she knows—from her own perspective anyway—that she has let practicality be the first priority. Her frustration with having had to make the decision in favor of practicality simply underscores the strength of her attachment to the positive values of beauty and good taste—which she feels have been somewhat compromised.

Altruism is a highly valued trait, one expected—nay, demanded—of mothers, nurses, perhaps women generally. As in Mom's story, altruism usually does not mix well with the egocentric (male-dominated) world of moneymaking. By including the second action segment in the story (by telling it at all), Mom asserts her own conviction that the altruistic stance she and Mary demonstrate in their refusal to abandon a roommate and enjoy the show alone is of greater value than any monetary reward.

In addition, all three action segments illustrate the premium placed on a "good sense of humor." The incidents in the story are not particularly funny; instead, at base, are rather sober accounts of how "a good sense of humor" is necessary if a monotonous, "broke" summer is to be tolerated. On the other hand, if the audience shares that value—appreciation for the ability to laugh at oneself, to see humor in situations that are not so much funny as ironic—then they will likely find the story amusing as well.

Finally, I think the story serves a metanarrational function; it explores the question of how to evaluate experience within the context of the experience story itself.[9] The canary, you will recall, is the primary symbol in the story; it represents Mom's willingness to attract to herself new experiences, a welcoming of new relationships. Some of the less prominent symbols and images work along with the primary symbol to reinforce this positive evaluation of "new experience." This other imagery in the story is less vague about just what kind of new experience is to be sought or at least welcomed. Certainly sexual experience is part of the new experience alluded to symbolically, but the more direct concern of the story is, again, the experience of leave-taking itself. The contemplation of any new experience involves both a projection into the future and a reassessment of the past. In the context of the story, the storyteller is again at that point of contemplation. Just why *would* anyone fly to experiences she knows not of? Or to reverse Hamlet's query, why would anyone choose to "leave" an experience that has been good? By telling the story of the yellow dress, Mom considers again the painful necessity of that decision.

The experience in this case involves the archetypal nurturing family, the safe and loving household where love is given rather than earned, where, as Frost says, "when you have to go there, they have to take you in." In the story the experience of home must be recognized as the symbol it is; if the canary is to fly, it is the home it flies away from. Symbolically, the story divides the home into its components and exposes these components as independent, as separate, though perceived normally as unified in the symbol. Once the components of home are exposed as separate people with independent lives, the child, like the novelist, can never go home again. The child teaches itself to be aware—to see the pattern of the symbol in the home, in the people it calls home, and then, courageously, to see the awful, unknown, and independent reality of the persons behind that pattern. The child must grow to its own independent personhood. It must perceive pattern in its experience and then look beyond the pattern to the wonderful uniqueness of each new experience.

Mom slowly carries out this painful task through her telling (and retelling) of the story. The clearest image of this "breakdown" of the home is in the long introductory section. The home in Manchester is literally divided—she and Mary sleep in one house and prepare their food in another. In version #2 Mom comments directly on the unusualness (and thus potential significance) of this sleeping-and-eating arrangement; she says, "And that was really kinda funny when you stop to think about it." The symbolism was grasped intuitively and returned as a puzzle for the listener. The food imagery of this first segment is associated with Mary's mother, who brings them lettuce, onions, and raspberries from her garden. The money—five dollars—of the second section is associated with Mom's father. The traditional image of the mutually supporting parents is broken up into the stereotypical roles—the nurturing mother and the financially supportive father. The symbolic parents are from two separate households;

they and their roles must be viewed apart.

The third segment of the story is a symbolic exposure of "the brother." Older brothers are notoriously ambivalent toward their social role relative to younger sisters. Typically, older brothers are a source of pride to younger siblings, especially sisters. Even among today's sophisticated children, sisters enjoy being escorted to social events by their brothers, especially if the brother is popular and good-looking. In Mom's story, the absent "date" is of course a potential mate or lover, but he is also by his absence a reminder of the brother who would otherwise serve as the platonic suitor-substitute, escorting his sister to the show—and perhaps teasing her by entering her name in the Bank Night drawing without telling her.

In the last segment, Mary represents "the sister." Like sisters, she and Mom competed for the attention of the brother in the segment before. Like sisters, they are happily playing together again in the last segment. But Mary is a playmate, and swatting mosquitoes is, after all, a childish game. The sister, the brother, the mother, the father, the home—all are images that Mom had assumed were really represented by her real experience of home. Now she sees that the experience of home itself is breaking down; she must leave the nest because it is no longer the nest she knew. The experience of home has passed already; she now has only to deny her loyalty to that lingering image.

Loyalty is what makes the leave-taking so painful. It is what makes any change, any new experience, painful. Here is the story's comment on its own genre. When an experience is evaluated positively, it will be repeated or maintained sometimes to the exclusion of new experiences. Mom wanted to wear the yellow dress, to welcome new experiences, but all of her own best feelings berated her for her disloyalty to her "old" self-image, her previous well-ordered store of experiences, her predictable taste. Indeed, she "hated" the yellow dress for what it represented: change—a specific new experience and the general notion of new experiences. Poets of every age hate change, or rather they celebrate our great loyalty to our personal past, our great attachment to all the things that have changed us into what we are now and our dread of all things that would bring us away from that self our past has made. Some changes truly are worthy of that dread—the death of a loved one, the loss of health and vitality, exile, imprisonment. But most of our dread is that we will somehow dishonor or betray our present experience and the investment of self it has demanded by replacing it with a new experience. The challenge is to feel loyalty, appreciate its powerful attraction, and then move on to new experiences. Mom is able to do this herself by wearing the yellow dress. She challenges her listeners to do the same through her telling of the story of the yellow dress.

And what about *this* listener? All of the preceding is my interpretation, my suggestion of the function her telling and my listening serve (and, as Elliott Oring [1976] argues, this commentary on function is still interpretation rather than explanation). I grasp the challenge she extends primarily because I hear the story as a cautionary tale; its function, for me, is attached not only to its thematic message (surviving hard times) but to its symbolic message as well. No platitude or fairy tale, no song or poem (not even her own) could move me to an acceptance of the symbolic message so easily yet firmly as does this story. For the story conveys an attitude—Mom's subtle suggestion of how to handle the very human desire to remain loyal to the past yet move on to new experiences.

Unlike the poets who break their hearts and ours with laments for the falling leaves and "Time Long Past," Mom cautions me to accept the truth that "nothing gold can stay" and move on to find more gold in each new experience. Frost and Shelley might wish to do the same through their poems; perhaps they succeed. Mom succeeds for me because the symbolism in her story is both universal and intimate. I know how difficult her leave-taking must have been; my own has been so smooth she may doubt whether I have given it much thought. In contrast, she lost her own mother when she was barely sixteen; her father and "home" became all the more precious and significant. Leaving something that valuable is hard, but once done, the leave-taking itself is a symbolic experience, valuable for the lesson it carries. The lesson it bears is an attitude, a chosen stance, a world view. It is the stuff of literature, the core of a personal narrative.

Epilogue
Hearing Tradition in the Personal Narrative

The personal narrative is an anomaly in the folk narrative taxonomy; its content is not easily classified as traditional. The notion of "tradition" implicit throughout this book would seem to be somewhere between what Dan Ben-Amos (1984) identifies as a concept of "tradition as canon" and one of "tradition as mass." However, it would be unfair to assume that a full-blown definition of tradition has been presupposed in discussing the personal narrative. Quite the contrary, because the focus has been upon oral literary texts only, the concept of "tradition" involved is roughly equivalent to the notion of "embedded folklore" long in use among folklore-and-literature scholars. The allowance for what constitutes folklore has been expanded, yet this expansion has occurred only within the confines of what might be construed as traditional or folkloric material embedded within an oral literary text.

From the perspective of literary folkloristics, as Richard M. Dorson suggests, the folklorist "must prove that the saying, tale, song, or custom inside the literary work possesses an independent traditional life" (1957 [1971]:197). Dorson demanded such "corroborative evidence" from critics presuming to interpret literary texts based on folklore materials. Alan Dundes (1965b) pushed the requirement one step further and called for the identification of "folklore in culture." What Dundes in fact presented by way of demonstration was a narrative text he collected from a Prairie Band Potawatomi in Lawrence, Kansas. He then discussed various details of the text as either borrowings from European culture or overlays from Potawatomi culture and pointed to the advantage an interpreter of the text has in knowing what elements of the story represent the storyteller's own cultural interpolations. In effect, Dundes has demonstrated that the folklorist's task is the same in studying either a literary or an oral literary text, and that task is, first, to identify the folklore embedded in the text.

Both Dorson and Dundes regarded the identification of embedded folklore as an objective, scholarly activity, something folklorists are especially well trained to do. The folklorist must be prepared to undertake, as Dorson suggests, a "tedious search through glossaries, indexes, field reports, town histories, and other available sources" in order to properly "corroborate" embedded folklore (189). From my own perspective, this identification of tradition is not nearly so empirical as practitioners have claimed, though certainly skill does come with practice. Instead, the recognition and identification of folklore, as well as the formulation of an interpretation, involve subjectivity in ways I have tried to demonstrate throughout this study—in the selection of focus, in the recognition of conceptual, nonverbalized folklore, in the identification of private folklore, in the contextualizing of the instructional text.

An individual listener/interpreter responds to a narrative performance from the perspective of personal reality, and that personal reality is grounded in a multifaceted social base, as Richard Bauman (1972a) has suggested with regard to folklore generally. Especially in the personal narrative, the embedded folklore is perceived by the listener as a thick web of shared traditions connecting the teller's personal reality and personal sense of history to those of the listener. Identifying these traditions is the listener's first step in responding to the narrative. Though the listener may be unaware of this process of identifying folklore, the listener may well *experience* a redundancy of meaning, a feeling that these same embedded items or processes have meant something personally before now.

In all communications some commonality of meaning is assumed. Julienne Ford (1975) identifies this common frame as a "social world": "A social world is a set of taken-for-granted-meanings" (171). Someone listening to a personal narrative projects this assumed meaning onto the storyteller and basks in the resultant sense of community, of *shared tradition*. As Roger Abrahams (1963:107) says: "When the experience can be shown to be extrapersonal, the narrative achieves psychological importance for the group as well as the individual. Thus we can relate the implicit values of the story to the lives of those in the group."

For the teller of personal narratives and the listener, tradition represents a leap of faith, a belief that personal reality has been shared. More often for the folklorist, tradition is, as Dan Ben-Amos (1972: 13) argues, an "analytical construct." It is a scholarly abstraction devised by the folklorist—usually for the purpose of demonstrating evolutionary theories.[1] The process of abstracting significant, redundant content from a narrative and identifying it as tradition is a basic, but subjective, skill essential to the discipline. All of the tools of folkloristics—the type and motif indexes, the ballad catalogues, the riddle and proverb dictionaries, the compendiums of folk belief, children's rhymes, dances, games, and customs, the taxonomies of house types, farming tools, quilt patterns, even the bibliographies, libraries, and archives—all serve this one basic objective, to aid in the identification of *tradition* in that whole range of artistic, social, communicative activities usually called folkloric.

Among the consequences of the rise of reception theory, deconstructionism, and performance theory is an uneasy ambiguity about the role tradition can play in the interpretation of texts.[2] As folklore-and-literature scholars have insisted repeatedly, the identification of folklore or tradition does not in itself constitute an exegesis. Furthermore, the subjective nature of criticism (see Bleich 1978) prohibits the easy assumption of collectivity with regard to the meaning of traditional content or pattern when it is identified. It has, however, been my contention throughout this study that tradition is significant in the individual's sense of personal reality. Tradition informs the interpretive context in which an individual listener hears potential texts, such as personal narratives. By identifying tradition in a given listener's interpretive context, the scholar creates an instructional text, which in turn allows the process of interpretation itself to be examined.

In my interpretations of "Koo-Nar, King of the Rats" and "The Canary, or The Yellow Dress," I devised instructional texts with the objective of disclosing the process of selection and response essential in any hearing of verbal performance. What was selected was a personally significant mass of traditions accepted as allusions within an aural text. Only then was I able to offer an interpretation or review based on the cumulative effect of having selected those allusions as meaningful. That elaborate interim step of identifying the traditions and analytical frames that guided my interpretation was an essential part of the literary folkloristic methodology I have invoked. It is this step which distinguishes this interpretive practice from an exegesis based on a conventional analytical scheme alone. To have argued only that Larry's story represents a self-imposed initiation ritual or that my mother's story offers a symbolic assessment of the trauma of leaving home to find a mate would have fallen far short of our goal of interpretation.

Interpretation begins with the identification of patterns, continuities, traditions, allusions. Identifying tradition in the personal narrative is not so easy as recognizing as traditional even a garbled version of the ballad "Barbara Allen" or an extremely localized version of an urban legend such as "The Boyfriend's Death" or "The Vanishing Hitchhiker." Nevertheless, the successful effort to do so demonstrates more dramatically than would attention to more conventional genres the unique role folkloristics plays in the study of the human environment. It is the folklorist's charge to identify and describe tradition in the materials and processes of nonprofessional, everyday activities. The continuities they identify may be in abstract terms such as style, content, theme, form, function, or event, or they may be the kind of cultural allusions I identified in chapters 4 and 5. Ultimately the goal of folkloristic research is to demonstrate a continuity or collectivity that can reassure us all that we are each individually connected to the generations of humanity born in the distant past or living even now in unfathomable numbers.

In a secular age, folkloristics is part of a modern academic mythology, an explanatory system even the learned and skeptical can tolerate.[3] By identifying tradition in personal narratives, folklorists affirm the discipline's role in validating this new mythology of culture. Personal experience is transformed to cultural experience through the telling of personal narratives, and folklorists document this transformation. They help the world witness an individual's most fundamental yet difficult task—the momentary "breakthrough" from personal reality into cultural reality.[4] Stories of personal experiences represent one of the most impressive displays of cultural breakthrough. Through them, individuals assert their connection with other people, the social base of even these original accounts of seemingly idiosyncratic experience.

Hearing tradition in personal narratives is a professional response made possible through a literary folkloristic methodology. Only after this step can the researcher categorize the narratives as cautionary tales, as expressions of attitudes or values, or as self-characterizations and offer persuasive interpretations of the meaning he or she hears in the stories. This is the folklorist's contribution to the enterprise of cultural explanation and social philosophy—to hear tradition even in tales of experiences that are *rein personliche*,[5] to listen always with a resonant ear.

Appendix

Here follow transcripts of narratives told or written by Larry B. Scheiber and referred to in the preceding study.

LBS-1: "The Red Velvet Suit." This story was recorded on a Saturday afternoon (February 2, 1974) at the Hotel LaFontaine Lounge. Present were Larry, my sister, Carol, my husband, Mark, and I, and Bob Gnass, who was working as bartender. The setting of the original incident is New Year's Eve, 1973, in the bar in which the story is being told. Reference is made to Larry's friends John Fisher and Bob Gnass and "the town heavy," Doug Hall, who later became one of Larry's good friends.

Larry: New Year's Eve night—see? I've got this maroon velvet suit—[Larry whistles].

Carol: Oh, wow!

Larry: Did you ever see it?

Carol: No, wear it to work sometime.

Sandy: Maroon? Velvet?

Larry: Bob, tell them about my maroon velvet suit. With the pink shirt . . . [pause] [Groans] and the maroon collar and tie. Oh, man, I look super sexy in that dude. I'm not kiddin' you, I just looked like the Christmas fairy or something.

Carol: Oh, yes, did you carry a purse?

Larry: Irresistible with my . . .

Carol: Oh, I forgot about your secret weapon. [Reference to a special cologne he carries in a corked test tube]

Larry: . . . secret weapon splashed all over me. And Certs. And I just smelled so good and looked so good, the women just grabbin' me, man, and I'm just lovin' it, see?

Mark: Sure that's not Brut?

Larry: No, no—At any rate, I come down here in my red velvet suit. I walk up the four marble steps in the lobby. And here comes some dude screamin' at the top of his lungs—AHHHHH! AHHHH!—[growling noises]—tryin' to juke everybody out. I thought, "Oh, gee, it's going to be a bad night." And the night hasn't even started. He tried to hit some old woman! I thought, "God damn, the guy's crazy!"

Carol: The dirty old man.

Larry: So the big hero runs up and I grab the guy, see?—hold his arms. And [more snarling, growling noises]. And he takes his false teeth out—opens his mouth by the nose and he's spittin' all over. There's about six guys hustle us over to the elevator and throw us in there and push the button to the third floor. [Laughter] And here I am minding my own business, and I'm locked in the elevator with this goddamned mongoloid. And he's rickashayin' me around there like a ping-pong ball, man. He's got blood all over just from hittin' the walls. Gosh, I kept duckin' and knockin'—I don't want to hurt him 'cause he—he musta been forty-five years old. But he's stocky—built like a goddamn bull.

Anyway, we got to the third floor and the door slides open. And here's the same six guys, ya know. They're too chicken-shit to ride up with him. [Laughter] They grab the guy, and they got a chair there. And they set him in the chair and hold him down. I help 'em and we carry the chair and all to the room—302. [In breathless voice] We get inside and set the chair down. And I kinda hold him down. Said, "Now, easy, fella, easy. Lie right down there, steady—whew!" [Laughter] The other guys run out, lock the door—click! Said, "We'll be back with a doctor." I said, "Hey, let me out of this room."

Then I heard him comin', and I ducked and his head went ploosh!—knocks all the paint off the door. And I thought, "The only way I'm gonna subdue this dude is just do him in." So I goes around and [motion of encircling the man and lifting] ugh—buddy!—grabbed him by the goddamn throat and powered him over to the bed. He falls on the bed and I'm layin' on top of him, see? And I'm chokin' the shit out of him. I said, "God damn it, I'll kill ya if ya keep messin' with me. Now you're screwin' up my red velvet suit!" [Laughter]

And he keeps [snarling noises]. And his false teeth fall out. Oh, you know how his teeth fell out? Listen, I ain't shittin' ya. [Laughter throughout] He got my *beautiful tie* in his teeth and he's pullin' like—ugh. I'm gettin' all red in the face and so is he. I figure 'bout then I'll choke him 'fore he chokes me. Finally I can't take it any longer 'cause I'm chokin', and I give a big jerk and his teeth fly out. And I thought, "Oh, my God, this ain't real! Hell, I'm just tryin' to be nice."

Anyway, I'm holding the dude down, see? And his teeth are flopped out and my goddamn tie's all bit to hell and my suit's got blood all over. [Laughter] [In a whisper] All of a sudden I hear—click, click—and the door opens and in comes a dude with a doctor bag, see? [Whispering] And he says, "Shhh"—gets this bottle [makes motion of filling a hypodermic needle from the bottle]—and he runs over and goes—plosh—in my ass! [Laughter] They told him there's a crazy guy in there, ya see? I said, "No, ya goddamn dumb-ass—this one!" He says, "Oh, excuse me, excuse me." He gets in his bottle again, goes [motion of filling needle]—shoots the guy in the arm, see? And he says, "You hold him till he quiets down." And he leaves. People keep leavin'

["Yeah"—response to Bob's gesture as to whether he wants another drink.]

And all of a sudden he gets this big smile on his face, see. First time I've seen him smile all night, and his old gums are hangin' out. And he says, "God bless you, son!" I said, "No shit!" And he says, "What's your name?" And I said, "I'd rather remain anonymous if you don't mind." [Laughter] And he says, "I'm going to be all right. God bless you," and all this shit. I says, "Yeah, right. See ya later."

I take off down the stairs, and I come back down to the bar. I still ain't had a goddamn drink! And John says, "You goin' to that party?" And I says, "Oh yeah, I almost forgot." Supposed to go to a party. So John and I go up to this party. We get in there and—John's so cool, he showed everyone this big knife he's got strapped on him there. And everyone—hmm—they're about half scared of him. They don't know what to think of me. We'd been there about five minutes and here comes some little punk in, goin', "F-this, F-that," calling people M-fers.

Carol: Anybody you know?

Larry: And it turned out he's a Scheiber. [Laughter] But anyway, I asked him three times, I said, "Hey, man, people have got their wives here and stuff. Now cool it or I'm gonna break your jaw!" "Who in the hell do you think *you* are?!" So I went [socking motion with fist accompanied by sound of impact]. He sat on a great big high stool like a high chair. And [motion of tall object falling over]—like timber!"

And the lady that owns the place comes out and says, "You son-of-a-bitch troublemaker!" And I says, "Me?!! Didn't you hear what he was sayin'?" "Yeah, I didn't mind." I says, "Well, then you're a damned hog!" She said, "Out, out, out—!!" [Laughter]

So they threw us out of the goddamn party and I said, "John, this is getting to be a terrible evening." He said, "We'll just go down to the bar." I still ain't had a drink. So we come back down here to the hotel. I'm sittin' there on the end and I order a drink. I just get it to my lips and in walks the town heavy—Doug Hall! The place is packed. [In rough, growling voice] "Who's Larry Scheiber?!" I says, "I am." He says, "Outside!" He comes over snarling through his kung-fu mustache. [Laughter] Soon as—soon as he got to my stool, I knew he was going to do something nasty to my bod, so I says, "Bop!" and judo-chopped him in the face, see? And he sorta bopped over against the wall, and I jumped off the chair and grabbed him around the neck. And . . . about sixteen guys got him. They shoved him out the door and shoved me back to the bar. I thought, "Oh, God," ya know. Guy outweighs me ten to one. Ten years younger to boot.

But anyway, I go to drink my drink and he walks in *this* door [indicates door from lobby]. He sits down there and he's starin' at me like this [jaw extended, snarling mouth and ferocious stare]—and diggin' [makes motion of digging fingers into table] his knuckles into the table. Thought, "Man, there's gonna be trouble. Might as well go get it over with." So I come over there and I set down. And I says, "All right, I know how ya feel. Ya got shoved and pushed but ya asked for it 'cause you're *stupid*." Says, "You don't walk up to me and tell me, 'Outside,' and all that shit." I said, "You're just dumb." I said, "If ya think I'm scared of ya, you're wrong." I said, "I just don't want to mess up my red velvet suit." [Laughter] I said, "I tell ya what, go get in my car and we'll drive out to my little Campfire Corner trailer. And I'll get out of my red velvet suit—and I'll fight ya—to the finish if you wish." He says [in a tight repressed voice], "You know something—I'm gonna kill ya, gonna kill ya!" I says, "OK."

So we quietly walked around there—out of the lobby. We get in the car. We no more'n slam the door when rrrr [makes noises of police siren]—flashing red lights.

Carol: Oh, no.

Larry: Ding-dong here [indicating Bob, the bartender] calls four squad cars.

Carol: Ha, this is a friend?

Larry: More cops than we had for the San Francisco earthquake, ya know? They come over and rip the doors open and said, "Out!" And they frisk us all down and ask us what were our intentions. And we said we were going out and *kill* each other. And he said, "Wrong-o." But they made us go home. They said if one blow was swung in Huntington County, we'd both spend forever in jail—maybe longer.

Carol: Aw, you had no fun New Year's Eve.

Larry: No shit! I didn't even get a drink! [Laughter]

LBS-2:   "Koo-Nar, King of the Rats"—Version #1.

Carol: I must hear about Queue-Nar the Frog.

Larry: Koo-Nar, not Queue-Nar.

Carol: OK, who named him Koo-Nar? In the first place?

Larry: Well, we named him after the king of the rats who used to live—

Sandy: King of what rats?!

Larry: You never heard about Koo-Nar—the king of the rats?!

Carol: Nooo, you never told me about Koo-Nar [laughs], the king of the rats.

Larry: OK—when I first got out of the service, I was poverty-stricken. I went through my—my, what-do-you-call-it, separation money like flies on shit, you know? Buying drinks for the whole crew. I'd go into bars and just say, "Give everybody a drink," and throw in a wad of money and go into the next bar and say, "Buy a round for the house," and lay it out. I was really cool!

Carol: You were so glad to be home—

Larry: No, I wanted to make friends—'cause—I'd been out of circulation for so long.

Well, anyway, to compensate for this [pause] obvious lack of thrift, I moved in a guy's—it was supposedly a garage, but it sorta leaned at a forty-five-degree angle and had about an inch slits in the boards—between the sides. And I hung a parachute up for a ceiling, you know, and I parked my MG under there. And I had a *bed*—three innersprings and three mattresses! And—and that's all I had in there for furniture—and then an ironing board, and then I had a vise on the ironing board—and that was my kitchen. Really, I lived in this shack, and I'd wake up with snow drifts on my bed.

Carol: Think how it toughened you, Larry! You're a better person for it!

Larry: Did you ever take a bath in Lake Clare in February?! [High-pitched] Oh, hoho—God! It makes my goodies blue just to think about it. Oh, Lord! So anyhow, where in the hell was I anyhow—?

Carol: King of the rats!

Larry: OK, OK, Koo-Nar, king of the rats—. [Everyone: Right!] OK, when I first moved in there I didn't have money zero. And—and all I had was three pieces of celery that a guy gave me from work.

Carol: Oh, you poor baby!

Larry: —So I made soup out of it in a tin can. [Laughter] I really and truly did, honest to God, that's all I had for all week. And as things got better I bought a loaf of bread and—but listen, let me tell you, before I moved out of there I had money stashed in nail cans, and . . .

Carol: You were a miser!

Larry: Yeah, you could say that! Really! Anyway, this rat lived in there with me, you see? Not by invitation! And, every night I'd hear him in the garbage bag, and I'd flash a light over there, and he'd run like hell. And he was a *big dude!* Well, he got so when I'd flash the light over there, he'd just go [puts thumbs in ears and wiggles fingers while making noise and sticking out tongue], blll-bll-bl. [Laughter] I'm not kidding you, this was a BIG RAT!—looked like a raccoon! [Laughter] And as long as I fed the dude we were on peaceful terms.

Carol: One night you forgot—

Larry: One night I forgot to feed him, and I heard him under the bed. You could hear him running around in the bed springs. Anyway, Koo-Nar got in bed. And I had this terrible nightmare, and I dreamed Koo-Nar was, was chewing on my leg. And you know how you move in slow motion in your dreams? And I dreamed I grabbed him and choked him and choked him, and the harder I choked him the harder he'd bite, you know, and he wouldn't let go. And finally—he just succumbed—as rats do when one shuts off their air. And I dreamed I just *threw* him [makes motion with arm] just as hard as I could, but it was all slow motion in the dream. ('Course, when you got seventeen blankets and a snow drift on top of you, it slows you down too.) But I never really woke up!

And I didn't find out that dude was real till spring! I was gonna move into Momsy's, see? Mom all this time had just been having a heart attack.

Carol: Poor Mom!

Larry: Yeah, poor Mom, one day she said, "Scheib, for God's sake, you've proved you can live through the winter and all that crap in a shack. Now come home!" I says,

"OK, just for laughs." So I'm packing up all my stuff out of the old shack, see? And I pull all my blankets off the bed, which hadn't been changed all winter [groans and laughter]. And when I got down to the bottom sheet— [lowers voice] there's all this rat shit. And I thought, "Oh, my God!"

Carol: Koo-Nar'd been living in your bed.

Larry: All that time I'd been wondering what happened to Koo-Nar. Then I remembered that dream I had that night and I thought, "By God, I got him!" And I saw in a flash: he shit his drawers when I choked him to death. [Laughter] And I got to looking around, and I pulled these mattresses. And between these mattresses and the parachute—which served as a wall between my MG and my bed—there lay KOO-NAR preserved by the cold!

Carol: Poor baby, with your throttle marks on his very throat.

Larry: Well, he was scrawny—and decimated—and he looked as though—he'd *dried* there. But there that son-of-a-bitch was. And I thought, you know, "One plus one equals two." And I looked down at my leg and there was a scar, a big hole. I'd never bothered to look at my leg before. Guys don't look at their legs, you know. But that little son-of-a-bitch had *gnawed me*! And I *got him*, even in my sleep, which proves what a great hunter I really am!

Carol: Right! However, it doesn't prove where the name Koo-Nar came from.

Larry: OK, all the time I lived with Koo-Nar before [pause] his demise, for some reason I just knew his name was Koo-Nar. Because he was the king of the rats, the biggest of all, and it just seemed fitting that I name him Koo-Nar.

LBS-2: "Koo-Nar, King of the Rats"—Version #2.

Larry: Well, when I first got out of the service, I really didn't have anywhere to live, you know. And I didn't want to move into Mom's 'cause that seemed like such a sissy-assed thing to do. So my buddy Brown, he was livin' with his mom—he had no shame— [Laughter] he said, "You can live in our garage!" Well, I actually asked him. (You guys got me tellin' the truth.) I actually asked him if I could live in his garage. And he said, "You're out of your mind!" ya know. And I said, "Well, can I live in there?" And he said, "Hell, yes!—if you can hack it."

But this is not a modern garage. This is an old shabby-assed, fallen-down thing that had a pile of bricks down at one end holdin' it up. And it had half-inch cracks you could see between the boards. I mean it was really sad—leaned at a forty-five-degree angle.

And so I moved in there. And the first thing I did I took all those bricks out from under the garage, which made it lose another ten degrees, but I thought, "Hell, I'll lift it." And I made me a brick floor. And I got two bed springs and put 'em in there and two innerspring mattresses, put those on top of the bed springs. And it was "broing, broing" [makes up-and-down motion with hand]—better than a waterbed!

But, anyway, I lived in this garage. And for the first two weeks, you know, I didn't have a paycheck or anything. See, I was workin' at Wabash Magnetics, and when you work there, you don't get paid at the end of your first week. You don't get paid until the second week. And I did not have shit—I mean literally nil, and I wouldn't accept anything from anybody 'cause I was too damn proud. And good old Louis Shoenauer was eating his lunch one day and he says, "Larry, you want any of this?" He had celery sticks and carrot sticks there. And I said, "No, I'm not hungry." He said, "Come on down and eat 'em, I'm awful full." So I said, "Well, maybe I'll eat them later." So he said, "OK," and he handed them to me, and I put 'em in my pocket.

And I got home that night, and I got a big old coffee can that was in there and I dumped the nails out—it was full of rust. And I filled it with water, and I got it boiling; Brown gave me a little hot plate. And I got this water boiling, and I gingerly and carefully [pause] chopped this celery and carrots into this coffee can and boiled it for two hours. And Brown brought me out some salt, and I put that in there. This had to last me two weeks, ya know. [Laughter]

So I got to cookin' this celery and carrot soup, and it really smelled good. And I thought, "Boy, this is the life!" [Laughter] I had this big parachute; I'd stretched it across the ceiling hoping it would hold in the heat, my body heat, ya know. And I had another parachute halfway through the garage, and I had my MG pulled in it, on the other side of the parachute. 'Cause I was still livin' this old paratrooper role, ya know. Had the strings a-hangin' down, and I'd built a little fireplace and had a big fire cracklin' there. I was really cool. And I had gourds all hollowed out with candles in them.

But anyway, I was hurtin' for chow. Well, this goddamn rat, I don't know if he'd lived there forever or if he just moved in when he smelled the soup or what. [Laughter] The very first weekend I was in there I heard all this rustling around, and I turned on my flashlight and here stood this goddamn rat looked like a cat. And I thought, "Oh, my God, he's gonna eat me!" So I went over there and I took a couple of carrots to him—and a few pieces of celery and put them on the ironing board. (I had an ironing board for a kitchen table; it was the only thing in the garage.) And I put them down and I thought, "The rat'll eat that and he won't get me." Next mornin' I woke up and sure as hell, the old sacrifice was gone, ya know, and the rat hadn't bothered me. Tryin' to make that soup last for two weeks was just a bitch! I got hungry, you know. But still every night I'd have to leave little tidbits on the ironing board for Koo-Nar.

At the end of two weeks I had run out of food—and there was nothing for Koo-Nar. And I heard that son-of-a-bitch runnin' around down there in my bed springs, and he was going berserk 'cause he was hungry! Course I was hungry too. But I thought, "Goddamn, that son-of-a-bitch's gonna get me if I don't give him something." Then I thought, "Oh, the hell with it," he wasn't any hungrier than I was. So I went to sleep. Had this weird dream. I dreamed that Koo-Nar was in my bed and chewing on my leg 'cause he was hungry. And I dreamed that it hurt so bad right on the calf of my leg where he was chewing that I reached down and tried to strangle him. And the tighter I'd squeeze, the tighter he'd bite, ya know? And I thought, my God, I could never last and I would just pass out, but I thought I was *not* dreamin'. But anyhoo, I dreamed that he finally died and relaxed his grip. And the curious part of it is, when you dream, everything's in slow motion. And I dreamed that it just took a gargantuan effort to throw him out of the bed. But I finally got rid of the noxious bastard. [Laughter]

So, I lived out there in that garage all winter long just to prove I could do it. You know, takin' baths in Lake Clare. Goddamn, I'd take out a shovel and break the ice and jump in there, and [high pitch] yaai-ii-ah-ah. Turned blue. But anyway, I made it all through the winter just to prove I could do it. Then I'd wake up in the morning, and there'd be snow drifts on my bed. And you don't really want to get up and go to work. You'd rather just stay there if you know you have five inches of snow to go through just to get up. But I made it that winter.

So when spring came—I went down to Mom's one day, and she said, "Scheib, for God's sake, you've proved your point, you're a big outdoorsman," and all this shit. She said, "We've got a room upstairs that's completely empty. We've got no kids livin' here; why don't you just come home and live with us a while till you find a place?" I said, "Oh well, shit, OK, since it's spring." So I started packin' up all my shit—dumping out all the nail cans, gettin' my money out from under the nails. I was *single*; I didn't have anything to spend money on. Hell, I'd a like to save four hundred dollars in nail cans. [Laughter]

Bob Gnass [from the bar]: Larry [they talk about an unrelated subject for several seconds].

Larry: Well, anyway, I'm packin' up all this shit to go home, see? And I get down to where there's nothing left in the room but the bed. And I pull all my big warm winter quilts off, [pause] and I get down to where it's nothing but sheets. And I take off my top sheet, and down at the foot of the bed is—rat shit! [Laughter] In my bed, man! And I says, "Now wait a goddamn minute. This is too weird cause I know there's no rats in here." After the Koo-Nar episode and I had that bad dream, I bought rat poison and stuff cause I'd been paid. And no one ever ate it, so I knew there were no rats.

Well, anyway, here's all these rat turds in the bottom of my bed, and I thought, "Goddamn that's really strange—except—maybe Koo-Nar really did get in bed with me that night, and maybe I really did choke him." And I thought, "Well, now where would he be?" So I flop down on the mattress and I reconstruct the whole dream, see? And I think, "Ooh, Koo-Nar's hurting my leg," so I reach down and I grab him, and I throw him out of the bed—in slow motion. And I think, "Aha! He would be over by the parachute which separated me from my MG!" And by God, I pulled the old mattress back, and I looked down there, and there's Koo-Nar! Ta-da! Stiffer'n a goddamn board! [Laughter]

Mark: Still frozen, huh?

Larry: Yeah, froze, man! This was like in April, but it was still colder'n a bitch out. And there he was, froze solid, and not a *mark* on him. I checked that dude over and over and over, and not a mark on him.

John Fisher: You killed him in your sleep.

Larry: I did, I kilt the dirty bastard!

John: Without your wakin' . . . ?

Larry: Yeah, it . . .

John: Yeah, it's probably possible.

Larry: Possible, hell! Listen, this is *months* after this had happened. And I thought, "If that's true, then I got a hole in my leg." And I'd never checked before, I hadn't even looked, and I had a GREAT BIG SCAR right here [points to a spot on the back of his leg]. [Laughter] And that son-of-a-bitch really *was* chewin' on me!

John: And you were so drunk you did it in your sleep, huh?

Larry: I was so sleepy . . . [Laughter]

Here follow transcripts of narratives told by my mother, Loretta K. Dolby, and referred to in the preceding chapters.

LKD-1:   "The Barber Shop." This story was recorded on October 13, 1974. The setting for the story was the little shop in downtown Huntington where my father worked as a barber. The date of the incident was 1942. John Thomas was a Huntington resident and a regular at the barbershop.

Mom: Oh, I think Carol was just a baby. I may have been pregnant for Dick, I don't know—it was in about that time anyhow. I'd wheeled Carol downtown in the baby buggy. That's when Dad had the barber shop with the little room in the back there. So, I don't know, I had either changed Carol or something, I don't know just what the deal was, but anyhow I went back in that little back room.

And in the meantime John Thomas came in, and John was quite a storyteller, and it was always kinda rank. But anyway, Dad knew I was back in there, but he didn't know how to get John shut off. John started telling some of his dirty stories. And they laughed and they'd "har-har" and carry on. And finally it just got to be time I just had to leave. And here he wasn't through with John. John was still in there telling more stories. So finally, I put Carol in the baby buggy and waltzed out through there, and John just about died! He shrank down underneath his barber apron. It was really something.

LKD-2: "The Canary, or, The Yellow Dress"—Version #1.

Mom: When I was at Manchester that last summer, Mary Lyons and I roomed together. And we would live a whole week on about three dollars and something worth of groceries between us. And we would live—or we slept in one house, and then we'd arranged with a lady a couple of houses down to cook on a little old beaten-up oil stove in her basement. And we would have—we'd buy a quart of milk for about a dime, and we'd buy a box of cereal, and we could get four bananas for a dime, and that did us for two breakfasts on just a little.

And we could buy a pound of hamburger for twenty-five cents, or no, a pound of hamburger for ten cents, three pounds for a quarter. And we would—out of a pound of hamburger—we'd make our lunch and our supper. And her mother would give us leaf lettuce out of her garden and green onions out of her garden. And she'd pick raspberries along her fence row and bring 'em to us. Sometimes we'd have a peach or two—and I don't know what else. We hardly ever had anything else to eat that whole summer.

That was the same summer that on the Fourth of July I was wearing a wool skirt and a pink satin blouse because that was about the only clothes I had. And my dad had sent me a five-dollar bill in his letter. And so I hurried downtown and—what's the name of that store over there at Manchester now?—advertises so much—German name?—Oppenheim's. Well, they were having a sale, and in the window was a *bright—yellow—dress* for three dollars or two-ninety-nine or something like that. So I went in and bought it. Boy, was it yellow! And then I had two dollars left, so I bought a pair of shoes.

And so I went home, back to the room, and Mary said, "Oh, where did you get such a pretty yellow dress?!" And I said, "Yes, I look like a damn canary!" I hated the thing, but it's the only one I could get for that price, so that's what I got.

That was the same summer—that was the broke summer—but anyway, Mary and I were getting awfully bored and we wanted to go to the show. But between us we had a quarter, and neither one of us wanted to go by herself, so we stayed home. And that night my name had been drawn for a hundred dollars—Bank Night. And I wasn't there to claim it, so I didn't get it—Sad!

That was the same summer we stayed up all night swatting mosquitoes because our screen had holes in it—let the mosquitoes in. We couldn't go to sleep.

LKD-2: "The Canary, or, The Yellow Dress"—Version #2.
Mom: Anyhow, that summer when we stayed there, we *stayed* in one house—and we had a room there, and then about two or three houses down we had a place in the basement. We'd do our cooking there on a little old kerosene stove. [Laughs] And that was really kinda funny when you stop to think about it. But we'd keep an account of how much we'd spent on groceries.

And then we'd get cereal, and that was our breakfast all week. And you could get—I don't know, we'd buy a quart of milk [pause] and that would last us all week. And I don't know, either she would bring some sugar from home or somehow, I don't know how we did with that. But we'd buy a pound of hamburger for ten cents, and then that would—divide that up into four pieces, you know, and you'd have . . .

Sandy: Quarter-pounders.

Mom: Yeah, quarter-pounders. And that would last us for two meals. And we'd get a package of buns. And we'd get, oh, about four bananas. I don't know, we didn't have a great deal to eat. [Laughs] If I remember right, we were pretty hungry.

But then her mother would go picking raspberries along the fence and send us over some raspberries. And we'd get some lettuce out of her garden. I guess I must have lived off of Mary—[Noise of dishes being put away drowns out part of sentence—she repeats.] I must've sponged off of Mary quite a little bit. And green onions—we ate a lot of green onions. But actually I can't remember—we didn't *have* peanut butter. We must have bought some oleo. I can't remember anything else we'd eat, really. Sometimes we didn't eat very much. I think that's when I got real sick of corn flakes. [Laughs]

Anyhow, that was the summer that Mary and I stayed awake nearly all night swatting mosquitoes. We'd start to go to sleep and we'd hear this bzzzzzz. [Laughs] We slept under the covers most of the night.

That was also the time that she and I were so hard up and my dad had sent a five-dollar bill in one of his letters. And of course I wasn't to *tell* anybody that I had gotten it. But I—it was the middle of July, and I was still wearing my wool skirt—and pink blouse I had. I think that's all I had about. So I went down to—what's the name of that place there in Manchester?

Sandy: Oppenheim's?

Mom: Oppenheim's. Anyhow, I had about two-ninety-eight—. They had a yellow dress; oh, it was as yellow as a dandelion. Real yellow, but it *wasn't wool*, so I bought it. And then they had shoes on sale for—oh, it took another two dollars. So there went my five dollars.

So I came home and put on my yellow dress. And Mary says, "Oh, where'd you get that pretty yellow dress?!" And I says, "Yeah," I said, "I look like a damn canary!" [Laughs] She'll tell you that if she sees you, yet—that struck her so funny. She thought it was really pretty. I didn't really like it, but it was the only one I could get for three dollars. But it *was* yellow! Yechh.

That same summer Mary and I were both so poor that we couldn't do anything extra—couldn't even buy a Coke, scarcely. And—uh—one night we were just so *bored* we wanted to go to the show, but we didn't have enough money for the two of us to go. There was just enough for one of us to go, so we neither one went. We only had a quarter between us. You could go to the show for a quarter. And we stayed home that night. And the next morning everybody was telling me, "You should have been to the show last night. You would have won a hundred dollars. Your name was drawn for Bank Night."

Sandy: Huh, they wouldn't let you claim it if you weren't there, huh?

Mom: Huh? No! Huh-uh, I didn't even know I was enrolled.

Sandy: Well, how were you enrolled if you didn't know it?

Mom: Well, I had a date one time, and he went and put my name in and I didn't know it.

Sandy: Huh! How could they afford to be giving away a hundred dollars?

Mom: Oh, that was the big deal!

Sandy: What summer was that?

Mom: The summer of thirty-eight.

Dad [in background]: His name was Puffy.

Mom: No, his name wasn't. His name was Glenn, Glenn Beery.

LKD-2: "The Canary, or, The Yellow Dress"—Version #3.

Mom: But that was the summer that Mary and I both—I bet we had three dresses between us maybe. I had a pink satin blouse that was very beautiful and this *wool* skirt with about five different colors of braid around the bottom of it—a really pretty skirt, but for July it was kinda hot! I mean that was wool! Yechh!

And uh, Dad had sent me a five-dollar bill. And anyhow, he'd inserted a little note to not say anything about it, so evidently he wasn't supposed to be sending me money. I don't know how that happened, but I took the five-dollar bill and we went downtown—to Oppenheim's. In the window was this dress for two-ninety-eight or something like that—and *yellow*—as a pumpkin or canary or something. Boy, it was— it was *nothing* but yellow, didn't have a white collar on it or anything, just yellow! But I bought it, and they had a pair of sandal-type shoes for a dollar-ninety-eight, so I bought those, and there went my five dollars. Good thing they didn't have *tax* or I'd a never gotten it.

So I came home and put on my yellow dress. And Mary came in and "Oh, where'd you get that pretty yellow dress?!" "Yeah, I look like a damn canary!" [Laughs] You'd see Mary tomorrow, I'll bet you she'd tell you that story—'bout my yellow dress.

Oh, I remember the night—it was that same year—that Mary and I fought the mosquitoes all night. Auch! I don't believe either one of us slept all night. We'd sleep, and then bzzzzzzzz. We'd cover up our heads until we couldn't breathe, and then we'd come out and there that mosquito was a-buzzin' around. But, then we got the giggles, of course, but the screens were so full of holes that I'm not surprised.

Notes

1. Introduction

1. For example, earlier works by these two influential folklorists reflect the transitional thinking they were engaged in as "contextualism" emerged in the discipline; see Abrahams 1968, "Introductory Remarks to a Rhetorical Theory of Folklore"; Bauman 1972b, "The La Have Island General Store: Sociability and Verbal Art in a Nova Scotia Community."

2. Hernadi's reference (p. 2) is to Gunther Müller, "Bemerkungen zur Gattungspoetik," *Philosophischer Anzeiger* 3 (1928):136.

3. Matthew Arnold, "The Study of Poetry," an essay first published in 1880.

4. See Tompkins, ed., *Reader-Response Criticism*, 1980; contributors included in the volume are Walker Gibson, Gerald Prince, Michael Riffaterre, George Poulet, Wolfgang Iser, Stanley Fish, Jonathan Culler, Norman Holland, David Bleich, Walter Benn Michaels, and Jane Tompkins.

5. Specifically, this is a response to the interview reported in Burns 1969, "Involving the Introductory Student of Folklore in the Functional Analysis of the Material He Collects."

6. Geertz refers to terminology from Heinz Hohut, *Analysis of Self: A Systematic Approach to the Psychoanalytic Treatment of Narcissistic Personality Disorders* (New York: International Universities Press, 1971).

7. From M. H. Abrams 1981:8, *A Glossary of Literary Terms*, 4th edition.

8. The "contextualists" were so designated by Richard M. Dorson in his "Introduction" to *Folklore and Folklife* (1972:45-47), and they were held responsible for apparent changes in the discipline of folklore during the 1960s and 1970s, reflected most clearly in the collection of essays edited by Américo Paredes and Richard Bauman titled *Toward New Perspectives in Folklore* (1972). A more recent and direct consideration of the role of folklore fieldwork in evoking a more "human" research perspective is *People Studying People: The Human Element in Fieldwork*, by Robert A. Georges and Michael O. Jones (1980).

9. See also my discussion in "The Personal Narrative as Folklore" (1977b:9-30, 203).

2. The Personal Narrative as an Oral Literary Genre

1. Labov and Waletzky's 1967 article represents a turning point in American personal narrative research; works published before that date are generally European studies usually cited as theoretical rather than practical predecessors by American researchers. Two notable exceptions are Richard Dorson's 1952 chapter on the "sagamen" of Michigan's Upper Peninsula and Mody Boatright's 1958 article on the family saga. For a substantial, though not exhaustive, introduction to the range of studies on personal narratives, see relevant Bibliography citations for the following authors: (pre-1967) Bausinger, Blehr, Granberg, Greverus, Honko, Jollés, Neuman, and von Sydow; (post-1967) Abrahams, Agar, Allen and Montell, Bauman, Bennett, Clements, Danielson, Dégh, Dégh and Vázsonyi, Dobos, Graham, Ives, Kalčik, Labov, Langness, Leary, Lockwood, McCarl, McDowell, Mitchell, Mintz, Mullen, Nusbaum, Pentikäinen, L. Polanyi, Pratt, Robinson, Santino, Stahl, Stanley, Titon, and Zeitlin.

2. See my discussion of genre theory in folkloristics in Stahl 1980; this discussion represents a response to comments on the earlier (1977a) article on the personal narrative in its generic context.

3. Also much in the structure Propp identifies for the *Märchen* is particularly reflective of Russian oikotypes of the tales; see Propp 1928, translated 1968.

4. See John Ball's (1954) discussion of varying dimensions of oral narrative style; and one might speculate whether the concepts of "oikotype" and "topoi" have more to do with style than content (cf. Cochrane 1987).

5. The designation and problem of the *Ich-Bericht* form (Ego-Account) is discussed in some detail by Linda Dégh and Andrew Vázsonyi (1974).

6. The narrative was recorded on October 17, 1974, at the Do-Drop-Inn in Huntington, Indiana. Present were Larry, my sister Carol, and I. The time of the original incident was Christmas, 1967. "Dudu," mentioned briefly at the beginning of the story, is Larry's friend Dave Teusch.

7. Reference is to the nineteenth-century German critic Gustav Freytag, *Technique of the Drama* (1863).

8. Information and documentation on Jung's assertion are taken directly from Dégh 1971:56, text and footnotes 2 and 3.

9. See, for example, my discussion of first-person jokes and the intended confusion that results when a fictional account is assumed to be true, in Stahl 1977a: 30-32.

10. Alan Dundes discusses the difference between Propp's "syntagmatic" and Lévi-Strauss's "paradigmatic" structuralism in his "Introduction to the Second Edition" of Propp's *Morphology*, 1928 [1968]:xi-xvii.

3. Interpreting Personal Narrative Texts

1. In discussing anthropological research, Pelto comments further that "a main requirement of the scientific method is that the procedures of the researcher should be clearly (and publicly) specified" (1970:49).

2. I would add *interpretive context* to the six kinds of field context Richard Bauman surveys in his discussion of "The Field Study of Folklore in Context," in the *Handbook of American Folklore*; see Bauman 1983.

3. Elliott Oring makes the point that "function"—a type of interpretation—cannot be considered an explanation for the origin of the folklore item; see Oring 1976.

4. See Dundes and Abrahams, "On Elephantasy and Elephanticide" (1969); Dundes does refer to this article in a footnote (#4) to the "Wide-Mouth Frog" essay (see Dundes 1980a:62-68).

5. Compare Hall's (1977:58-60) discussion of cultural contexting with that presented more generally in folkloristic scholarship, e.g., Toelken 1979 or Bauman 1986.

6. One of the more successful discussions of "the new physics" for a popular audience is Gary Zukov's *The Dancing Wu Li Masters* (1979); Marvin Harris (1968), in reviewing the history of anthropological study, notes the variety of "deterministic" theories that have played a role in the discipline, including his own brand of cultural materialism.

7. The notion of "folk groups" is intrinsic to the field of folklore study, but a particularly helpful discussion of the applied concept is in Abrahams 1978.

8. This version of "Tiny Wires and the Chicken Blood" was offered in response to my request; my sister, Carol, had heard the story before, but I had not. Present at the time of the recording were Larry, Carol, Mark Stahl, and I; it was told on a Saturday afternoon (February 2, 1974) in the lounge of what used to be the Hotel LaFontaine in Huntington, Indiana. The time of the original incident in the story was 1963.

9. For a definition of *idioculture*, see Gary Alan Fine (1979), who first introduced the term into folkloristic studies.

10. Pelto 1979:85. The last prerequisite acknowledges the problems of "confounding the emic/etic distinction" as Marvin Harris has described it; the audience-interpreter, in this case, is both subjective and responsible. See Harris 1968:575.

11. This is a slightly different concern with subjectivity from that implicated in what David M. Hayano (1979) terms "self-ethnographic" studies; nevertheless, it is reflective of the general methodological concern in his paper "Auto-ethnography: Paradigms, Problems, and Prospects"; see as well Lowry 1974 and Kirschner 1987.

4. Koo-Nar, King of the Rats

1. See chapter 10, "The Home Territory Bar," in Cavan 1966:205-33.

2. Distinctions among sex role, sex-role stereotype, sex-role norms, sex-role typing, and sex-role identity are made throughout according to Pleck 1981:10-13.

3. For a discussion of this interesting but esoteric branch of study, see C. Scott Littleton's review of the "new comparative mythology" (1973).

4. See Archer Taylor's study of *The Shanghi Gesture* (1956).

5. See Edward Sagarin's discussion of the growing "toleration of the monosyllables" (1962:168).

6. Legman quotes Abrahams and Dundes to the effect that "the use of voice qualifiers in castration humor is common." Typically, the secondary effect is reflected in a high-pitched falsetto; see Dundes and Abrahams 1969:233.

7. See the "folklorized" personal narratives of the Ray brothers in Biebuyck 1977 and the discussion of "lying" in Bauman 1986.

8. Freud's definition of the term *libido* is: "In every way analogous to *hunger*, libido is the force by means of which the instinct, in this case the sexual instinct, as, with hunger, the nutritional instinct, achieves expression"; see Freud 1963:274.

9. See Susan Stewart's discussion of these four levels of textuality in her book *Nonsense* (1978).

10. Pratt defines *tellability* as a "kind of display-producing relevance," and I think this clearly is the motivation for Larry's presenting the story and including the dream episode—to produce a relevant display; see Pratt 1977:136-40.

11. See the discussion of separation rites in Arnold Van Gennep's *Rites of Passage* (1960:65-115).

12. Dundes says of "folk fallacies": "The folk are normally consciously aware of folk fallacies (though not necessarily that they are fallacious) and can articulate them without difficulty" (1972:101).

5. The Canary, or The Yellow Dress

1. See the discussion of the two place names in Baker and Carmony 1975:96, 119.

2. For a discussion of the traditional practice of separation among American sectarian offshoots of the Huguenots and Anabaptists, see Hostetler 1963.

3. See the "I asked my mother for fifteen cents" rhyme—often known as "Mary Mack"—in Abrahams 1969b:72, 120.

4. The term is my suggestion. Of the scholars who have discussed formulas in folk narrative, few have commented directly on what to call this particular kind of formula. It is not the formula of epic poetry Lord (1971) discusses since it is not in collective tradition; it is not repeated within the work itself as Gray (1971) suggests (nor is it a convention); it is not simply the "personal style" of the teller as Ball (1954) suggests, though if the story were traditional, the formula might be a part of what Ball calls the "style of the tale itself." The formula is essential, but to this story alone.

5. Loretta Dolby, "Castles in Spain," in the *National Poetry Anthology*, by the Teachers and Librarians in the Schools and Colleges (Los Angeles: National Poetry Association, 1959), p. 158.

6. See my discussion of the use of curse words and their euphemisms in Stahl 1977c.

7. Flexner suggests that by 1910, *damned* and *hell* were "not always taken too seriously" (1976:171-73).

8. Compare the simple list of five motifemes with which Dundes represents the basic pattern of African friendship-breaking tales (1971:176).

9. Barbara Babcock (1977) describes the narrative of personal events as the "standard American metanarrational story."

Epilogue: Hearing Tradition in the Personal Narrative

1. Alan Dundes (1969) claims that folklore research has produced mostly devolutionary theories; compare Stocking's (1968) discussion of theories in anthropology and some of the earlier interdisciplinary views excerpted in Feldman and Richardson 1972.

2. A work I found useful in balancing the effects of deconstructionism (a discouraging sense of literary indeterminacy) against those of traditional literary criticism (with its acceptance of "tradition" as a component of content) is Michael Fischer's *Does Deconstruction Make any Difference?* (1985). In addition, I found Werner Sollors's *Beyond Ethnicity* (1986) helpful in balancing a similar sociological dichotomy between inherited culture and culture chosen by the individual.

3. For an interesting discussion of the folklorist's role in "creating" modern mythology, see Friedman 1971; see also Hufford 1983 on explaining "academic belief."

4. Dell Hymes's (1975) notion of "breakthrough into performance"—like Propp's "function," Kuhn's "paradigm," or Pike's "emic/etic" dichotomy—is destined to be variously used and perhaps abused by researchers who are attracted to the inherent ambiguity of the concept; my use here does admittedly take liberties with the term.

5. Von Sydow (1948) uses the phrase *rein personliche* (purely personal) to describe the experience at the base of a nontraditional memorate; see as well my discussion of von Sydow's definition in Stahl 1977b.

Bibliography

Aarne, Antti, and Stith Thompson
    1964. *The Types of the Folktale*. Helsinki: Folklore Fellows Communications, no. 184.

Abrahams, Roger D.
    1963. Folklore in Culture: Notes toward an Analytic Method. *Texas Studies in Literature and Language* 5:98–110.

    1968. Introductory Remarks to a Rhetorical Theory of Folklore. *Journal of American Folklore* 81:143–58.

    1969a. The Complex Relations of Simple Forms. *Genre* 2:104–28.

    1969b. *Jump-Rope Rhymes: A Dictionary*. Austin: University of Texas Press.

    1970a. A Performance-Centered Approach to Gossip. *Man* NS 5:290–301.

    1970b. *A Singer and Her Songs: Almeda Riddle's Book of Ballads*, ed. Baton Rouge: Louisiana State University Press.

    1972a. Folklore and Literature as Performance. *Journal of the Folklore Institute* 9:75–94.

    1972b. Personal Power and Social Restraint in the Definition of Folklore. In *Toward New Perspectives in Folklore*, ed. Américo Paredes and Richard Bauman, pp. 16–30. Austin: University of Texas Press.

    1977. The Most Embarrassing Thing That Ever Happened: Conversational Stories in a Theory of Enactment. *Folklore Forum* 10(3):9–15.

    1978. Toward a Sociological Theory of Folklore: Performing Services. In *Working Americans: Contemporary Approaches to Occupational Folklife*, ed. Robert H. Byington, pp. 19–42. Los Angeles: California Folklore Society.

Abrams, M. H.
    1981. *A Glossary of Literary Terms*. 4th ed. New York: Holt, Rinehart and Winston.

Adams, Robert M.
    1971. The Sense of Verification. In *Myth, Symbol, and Culture*, ed. Clifford Geertz, pp. 203–14. New York: W. W. Norton.

Agar, Michael
    1980. Stories, Background Knowledge, and Themes: Problems in the Analysis of Life History Narratives. *American Ethnologist* 7:223–39.

Allen, Barbara, and William Lynwood Montell
    1981. *From Memory to History*. Nashville, Tenn.: American Association for State and Local History.

Allport, Gordon W., and Leo Postman
    1947. *The Psychology of Rumor*. New York: Henry Holt.

Babcock, Barbara
  1977. The Story in the Story: Meta-narration in Folk Narrative. In *Verbal Art as Performance*, by Richard Bauman, Supplementary Essay, pp. 61–79. Rowley, Mass.: Newbury House.
Baer, Florence E.
  1986. *Folklore and Literature of the British Isles: An Annotated Bibliography*. New York: Garland Publishing.
Baker, Ronald L., and Marvin Carmony
  1975. *Indiana Place Names*. Bloomington: Indiana University Press.
Ball, John
  1954. Style in the Folktale. *Folklore* 65:170–72.
Barbour, Francis M.
  1965. *Proverbs and Proverbial Phrases of Illinois*. Carbondale: Southern Illinois University Press.
Barnes, Daniel R.
  1979. Toward the Establishment of Principles for the Study of Folklore and Literature. *Southern Folklore Quarterly* 43:5–16.
Barthes, Roland
  1974. [1970] *S/Z: An Essay*. Translated by Richard Miller. New York: Hill and Wang.
Bascom, William
  1965. Four Functions of Folklore. In *The Study of Folklore*, ed. Alan Dundes, pp. 279–98. Englewood Cliffs, N.J.: Prentice-Hall.
Basso, Keith
  1984. "Stalking with Stories": Names, Places, and Moral Narratives among the Western Apache. In *Text, Play, and Story: The Construction and Reconstruction of Self and Society*, ed. Stuart Plattner and Edward M. Bruner, pp. 19–55. Washington, D.C.: American Ethnological Society.
Baughman, Ernest W.
  1966. *Type and Motif Index of the Folktales of England and North America*. The Hague: Mouton.
Bauman, Richard
  1972a. Differential Identity and the Social Base of Folklore. In *Toward New Perspectives in Folklore*, ed. Américo Paredes and Richard Bauman, pp. 31–41. Austin: University of Texas Press.
  1972b. The La Have Island General Store: Sociability and Verbal Art in a Nova Scotia Community. *Journal of American Folklore* 85:330–43.
  1977. *Verbal Art as Performance*. Rowley, Mass.: Newbury House.
  1981. "Any Man Who Keeps More'n One Hound'll Lie to You": Dog Trading and Storytelling at Canton, Texas. In *"And Other Neighborly Names": Social Process and Cultural Image in Texas Folklore*, ed. Richard Bauman and Roger D. Abrahams, pp. 79–103. Austin: University of Texas Press.
  1983. The Field Study of Folklore in Context. In *Handbook of American Folklore*, ed. Richard M. Dorson, pp. 362–68. Bloomington: Indiana University Press.

1986. *Story, Performance, and Event*. Cambridge: Cambridge University Press.

Bausinger, Hermann

1958. Structuren des alltäglichen Erzählens. *Fabula* 1:239–54.

Beauvoir, Simone de

1949. [1961] *The Second Sex*. Translated by H. M. Parshley. New York: Bantam.

Ben-Amos, Dan

1969. Analytical Categories and Ethnic Genres. *Genre* 2:275–301.

1972. Toward a Definition of Folklore in Context. In *Toward New Perspectives in Folklore*, ed. Américo Paredes and Richard Bauman, pp. 3–15. Austin: University of Texas Press.

1973. A History of Folklore Studies–Why Do We Need It? *Journal of the Folklore Institute* 10: 113–24.

1976. *Folktale Genres*, ed. Austin: University of Texas Press.

1984. The Seven Strands of Tradition: Varieties in Its Meaning in American Folklore Studies. *Journal of Folklore Research* 21:97–131.

Benedict, Ruth

1968. Continuities and Discontinuities in Cultural Conditioning. In *Every Man His Way: Readings in Cultural Anthropology*, ed. Alan Dundes, pp. 424–33. Englewood Cliffs, N.J.: Prentice-Hall.

Bennett, Gillian

1983. "Rocky the Police Dog" and Other Tales: Traditional Narrative in an Occupational Corpus. *Lore and Language* 3(8):1–19.

Berkman, Susan C. J.

1978. "She's Writing Antidotes": An Examination of Hospital Employees' Uses of Stories about Personal Experiences. *Folklore Forum* 11:48–54.

Biebuyck, Brunhilda

1977. "This Is the Dyin' Truth": Mechanisms of Lying. *Journal of the Folklore Institute* 14:73–95.

Blehr, Otto

1967. The Analysis of Folk Belief Stories and Its Implications for Research on Folk Belief and Folk Prose. *Fabula* 9:259–63.

Bleich, David

1975. *Readings and Feelings: An Introduction to Subjective Criticism*. Urbana, Ill.: National Council of Teachers of English.

1978. *Subjective Criticism*. Baltimore: Johns Hopkins University Press.

Bolte, Johannes, and Georg Polivka

1963. *Anmerkungen zu den Kinder- und Hausmärchen der Brüder Grimm*. Hildesheim: Georg Olms.

Booth, Wayne C.

1961. *The Rhetoric of Fiction*. Chicago: University of Chicago Press.

Brandes, Stanley H.

1975. Family Misfortune Stories in American Folklore. *Journal of the Folklore Institute* 12:5–17.

1980. *Metaphors of Masculinity: Sex and Status in Andalusian Folklore.* Philadelphia: University of Pennsylvania Press.

Brémond, Claude

1970. Morphology of the French Folktale. *Semiotica* 2:247–76.

Brunvand, Jan Harold

1976. *Folklore: A Study and Research Guide.* New York: St. Martin's Press.

1978. *The Study of American Folklore: An Introduction.* 2nd ed. New York: Norton.

Burke, Kenneth

1941. *The Philosophy of Literary Form.* Baton Rouge: Louisiana State University Press.

1950. [1969] *A Rhetoric of Motives.* Berkeley: University of California Press.

Burns, Tom

1969. Involving the Introductory Student of Folklore in the Functional Analysis of the Material He Collects. In *Perspectives on Folklore and Education*, ed. Elliott Oring and James Durham, pp. 13–27. Bloomington, Ind.: *Folklore Forum* Bibliographic and Special Series, no.2.

1984. Doing the Wash: Cycle Two. In *Humor and the Individual*, ed. Elliott Oring, pp.49–70. Los Angeles: California Folklore Society.

Byington, Robert H., ed.

1978. *Working Americans: Contemporary Approaches to Occupational Folklife.* Los Angeles: California Folklore Society.

Cavan, Sherri

1966. *Liquor License: An Ethnography of Bar Behavior.* Chicago: Aldine Publishing.

Cawelti, John G.

1976. *Adventure, Mystery, and Romance.* Chicago: University of Chicago Press.

Chatman, Seymour

1978. *Story and Discourse: Narrative Structure in Fiction and Film.* Ithaca: Cornell University Press.

Cioffi, Frank

1973. Intention and Interpretation in Criticism. In *Issues in Contemporary Literary Criticism*, ed. Gregory T. Polletta, pp. 215–33. Boston: Little, Brown and Company.

Cirlot, J. E.

1962. *A Dictionary of Symbols.* New York: Philosophical Library.

Clements, William M.

1980a. The Pentecostal Sagamen. *Journal of the Folklore Institute* 17:169–95.

1980b. Personal Narrative, the Interview Context, and the Question of Tradition. *Western Folklore* 39:106–12.

Clifford, James, and George E. Marcus

1986. *Writing Culture: The Poetics and Politics of Ethnography.* Berkeley: University of California Press.

Cocchiara, Giuseppe
  1952. [1981] *The History of Folklore in Europe*. Translated by John N. McDaniel.
    Philadelphia: Institute for the Study of Human Issues. Originally in Italian.
Cochrane, Timothy
  1987. Place, People, and Folklore: An Isle Royale Case Study. *Western Folklore*
    46:1–20.
Danielson, Larry
  1979. Toward the Analysis of Vernacular Texts: The Supernatural Narrative in Oral
    and Popular Print Sources. *Journal of the Folklore Institute* 16:130–54.
Dégh, Linda
  1965a. *Folktales of Hungary*, ed. Chicago: University of Chicago Press.
  1965b. Processes of Legend Formation. *Laographia* 22:77–87.
  1969. *Folktales and Society: Story-telling in a Hungarian Peasant Community.*
    Translated by Emily M. Schossberger. Bloomington: Indiana University
    Press.
  1971. The "Belief Legend" in Modern Society: Form, Function, and Relationship
    to Other Genres. In *American Folk Legend: A Symposium*, ed. Wayland D.
    Hand, pp. 55–68. Berkeley: University of California Press.
  1975. *People of the Tobacco Belt: Four Lives*. Ottawa: National Museum of
    Canada.
  1985. "When I Was Six We Moved West . . . ": The Theory of Personal Experience
    Narrative. *New York Folklore* 11:99–108. A shorter version was presented
    as a paper at the Eighth International Congress for Folk Narrative Research,
    Bergen, Norway, June, 1984.
Dégh, Linda, and Andrew Vázsonyi
  1974. The Memorate and the Proto-memorate. *Journal of American Folklore*
    87:225–39.
  1978. The Crack on the Red Goblet, or Truth and Modern Legend. In *Folklore in
    the Modern World*, ed. Richard M. Dorson, pp. 253–72. The Hague: Mouton.
Dement, William C.
  1972. [1976] *Some Must Watch While Some Must Sleep: Exploring the World of
    Sleep*. New York: W. W. Norton.
Denby, Priscilla
  1981. The Self Discovered: The Car in American Folklore and Literature. Ph.D.
    dissertation, Indiana University.
Dohos, Ilona
  1978. True Stories. In *Studies in East European Folk Narrative*, ed. Linda Dégh,
    pp. 169—205. Bloomington: Folklore Institute.
Dorson, Richard M.
  1952. *Bloodstoppers and Bearwalkers: Folk Traditions of the Upper Peninsula*.
    Cambridge: Harvard University Press.
  1957. [1971] The Identification of Folklore in American Literature. In *American
    Folklore and the Historian*, by Richard M. Dorson, pp. 186–203. Chicago:
    University of Chicago Press.

1972. *Folklore and Folklife: An Introduction*, ed. Chicago: University of Chicago Press.

1977. The Legend of the Missing Pajamas and Other Sad Sagas. *Journal of the Folklore Institute* 14:115–24.

1981. *Land of the Millrats*. Cambridge: Harvard University Press.

Dundes, Alan

1962. From Etic to Emic Units in the Structural Study of Folktales. *Journal of American Folklore* 75:95–105.

1963. Structural Typology in North American Indian Folktales. *Southwestern Journal of Anthropology* 19:121–30.

1964a. *The Morphology of the North American Indian Folktales*. Helsinki: Folklore Fellows Communications, no. 195.

1964b. Texture, Text, and Context. *Southern Folklore Quarterly* 28:251–65.

1965a. *The Study of Folklore*, ed. Englewood Cliffs, N.J.: Prentice-Hall.

1965b. The Study of Folklore in Literature and Culture: Identification and Interpretation. *Journal of American Folklore* 78:136–42.

1966. Metafolkore and Oral Literary Criticism. *The Monist* 50:505–16.

1969. The Devolutionary Premise in Folklore Theory. *Journal of the Folklore Institute* 6:5–19.

1971. The Making and Breaking of Friendship as a Structural Frame in Folk Tales. In *Structural Analysis of Oral Tradition*, ed. Pierre Maranda and Elli Köngäs Maranda, pp. 171–85. Philadelphia: University of Pennsylvania Press.

1972. Folk Ideas as Units of World View. In *Toward New Perspectives in Folklore*, ed. Américo Paredes and Richard Bauman, pp. 93–103. Austin: University of Texas Press.

1980a. *Interpreting Folklore*. Bloomington: Indiana University Press.

1980b. The Symbolic Equivalence of Allomotifs in the Rabbit-Herd (AT 570). *ARV: Scandinavian Yearbook of Folklore* 36:93–98.

1980c. Who Are the Folk? In *Interpreting Folklore*, by Alan Dundes, pp. 1–19. Bloomington: Indiana University Press.

1983. Defining Identity through Folklore. In *Identity: Personal and Socio-cultural, A Symposium*, ed. Anita Jacobson-Widding, pp. 235–61. Atlantic Highlands, N.J.: Humanities Press.

1984a. *Life Is Like a Chicken Coop Ladder: A Portrait of German Culture through Folklore*. New York: Columbia University Press.

1984b. *Sacred Narrative: Readings in the Theory of Myth*, ed. Berkeley: University of California Press.

Dundes, Alan, and Roger D. Abrahams

1969. On Elephantasy and Elephanticide. *The Psychological Review* 56:225–41.

Eberhard, Wolfram

1970. *Studies in Chinese Folklore and Related Essays*. The Hague: Mouton.

Eco, Umberto

1976. *A Theory of Semiotics*. Bloomington: Indiana University Press.

Eidson, John R.
    1984. Review of *Life Is Like a Chicken Coop Ladder*, by Alan Dundes. *Anthropological Quarterly* 57:96–98.

Engel, Elliot
    1982. My Turn. *Newsweek* 99 (June 21):13.

Ervin-Tripp, Susan
    1964. An Analysis of the Interaction of Language, Topic, and Listener. *American Anthropologist*, Special Publication, vol. 66, no. 6, pt. 2, ed. John J. Gumperz and Dell Hymes, pp. 86–102.

Federman, Raymond
    1976. Imagination as Plagiarism. *New Literary History* 7:563–78.

Feldman, Burton, and Robert D. Richardson
    1972. *The Rise of Modern Mythology*, 1680–1860. Bloomington: Indiana University Press.

Fine, Elizabeth C.
    1984. *The Folklore Text: From Performance to Print*. Bloomington: Indiana University Press.

Fine, Gary Alan
    1979. Small Groups and Culture Creation: The Idioculture of Little League Baseball Teams. *American Sociological Review* 44:733–45.
    1984. Evaluating Psychoanalytic Folklore: Are Freudians Ever Right? *New York Folklore* 10:5–20.

Firth, Raymond
    1953. The Study of Values by Social Anthropologists. *Man* (old series) 53(October, no. 231): 146–53.
    1973. *Symbols: Public and Private*. Ithaca: Cornell University Press.

Fischer, Michael
    1985. *Does Deconstruction Make Any Difference? Poststructuralism and the Defense of Poetry in Modern Criticism*. Bloomington: Indiana University Press.

Fish, Stanley
    1980. *Is There a Text in This Class? The Authority of Interpretive Communities*. Cambridge: Harvard University Press.

Flexner, Stuart Berg
    1976. *I Hear America Talking*. New York: Simon and Schuster.
    1982. *Listening to America*. New York: Simon and Schuster.

Ford, Julienne
    1975. *Paradigms and Fairy Tales: An Introduction to the Science of Meanings*. Vol. 1. London: Routledge & Kegan Paul.

Frank, Gelya
    1979. Finding the Common Denominator: A Phenomenological Critique of Life History Method. *Ethos* 7:68–94.

Freud, Sigmund

1950. *Totem and Taboo.* New York: W. W. Norton.

1963. *A General Introduction to Psycho-analysis.* Translated by Joan Riviers. New York: Simon and Schuster.

Friedman, Albert B.

1971. The Usable Myth: The Legends of Modern Mythmakers. In *American Folk Legend: A Symposium*, ed. Wayland D. Hand, pp. 37–46. Berkeley: University of California Press.

Frye, Northrop

1957. [1965] *Anatomy of Criticism.* New York: Atheneum.

Gans, Herbert J.

1974. *Popular Culture and High Culture.* New York: Basic Books.

Geertz, Clifford

1976. "From the Native's Point of View": On the Nature of Anthropological Understanding. In *Meaning in Anthropology,* ed. Keith H. Basso and Henry A. Selby, pp. 221–37. Albuquerque: University of New Mexico Press.

Georges, Robert A.

1969. Toward an Understanding of Storytelling Events. *Journal of American Folklore* 82:313–28.

1972. Process and Structure in Traditional Storytelling in the Balkans: Some Preliminary Remarks. In *Aspects of the Balkans: Continuity and Change*, ed. Henrik Birnbaum and Spiros Vryonis, Jr., pp. 319–37. The Hague: Mouton.

1979. Feedback and Response in Storytelling. *Western Folklore* 38:104–10.

1980. Toward a Resolution of the Text/Context Controversy. *Western Folklore* 39:34–40.

Georges, Robert A., and Michael Owen Jones

1980. *People Studying People: The Human Element in Fieldwork.* Berkeley: University of California Press.

Glassie, Henry

1968. *Pattern in the Material Folk Culture of the Eastern United States.* Philadelphia: University of Pennsylvania Press.

1971. "Take That Night Train to Selma": An Excursion to the Outskirts of Scholarship. In *Folksongs and Their Makers*, by Henry Glassie, Edward Ives, and John Szwed, pp. 1–68. Bowling Green, Ohio: Bowling Green University Popular Press.

1973. Structure and Function, Folklore and the Artifact. *Semiotica* 7:313–51.

1982. *Passing the Time in Ballymenone: Culture and History of an Ulster Community.* Philadelphia: University of Pennsylvania Press.

Goffman, Erving

1974. *Frame Analysis: An Essay on the Organization of Experience.* New York: Harper & Row.

1981. *Forms of Talk.* Philadelphia: University of Pennsylvania Press.

Goode, William J.
  1964. *The Family*. Englewood Cliffs, N.J.: Prentice-Hall.
Graham, Joe
  1981. The *Caso*: An Emic Genre of Folk Narrative. In *"And Other Neighborly Names"*: *Social Process and Cultural Image in Texas Folklore*, ed. Richard Bauman and Roger D. Abrahams, pp. 11–43. Austin: University of Texas Press.
Granberg, Gunnar
  1969. Memorate und Sage: einige methodische Gesichtspunkte. In *Vergleichende Sagenforschung*, ed. Leander Petzoldt. pp. 90–98. Darmstadt.
Gray, Bennison
  1969. *Style: The Problem and Its Solution*. The Hague: Mouton.
  1971. Repetition in Oral Literature. *Journal of American Folklore* 84:289–303.
Greene, John C.
  1981. *Science, Ideology, and World View: Essays in the History of Evolutionary Ideas*. Berkeley: University of California Press.
Greimas, A. J., and J. Courtés
  1979. [1982] *Semiotics and Language: An Analytic Dictionary*. Bloomington: Indiana University Press. Originally in French.
Greverus, Ina-Maria
  1968. Die Chronikerzählung. In *Volksüberlieferung: Festschrift für Kurt Ranke*, pp. 37–80. Göttingen.
Haley, Jay
  1967. The Family of the Schizophrenic: A Model System. In *The Psychological Interior of the Family*, ed. Gerald Handel, pp. 271–75. Chicago: Aldine.
Hall, Edward T.
  1977. *Beyond Culture*. Garden City, N.Y.: Anchor Books.
Hanson, F. Allan
  1975. *Meaning in Culture*. Boston: Routledge & Kegan Paul.
Harris, Marvin
  1968. *The Rise of Anthropological Theory*. New York: Harper & Row.
Hartman, Geoffrey H.
  1981. *Saving the Text: Literature/Derrida/Philosophy*. Baltimore: Johns Hopkins University Press.
Hayano, David M.
  1979. Auto-ethnography: Paradigms, Problems, and Prospects. *Human Organization* 38:99–104.
Hellas, Paul
  1981. The Model Applied: Anthropology and Indigenous Psychologies. In *Indigenous Psychologies: The Anthropology of the Self*, ed. Paul Hellas and Andrew Lock, pp.39–63. New York: Academic Press.
Henningsen, Gustav
  1965. The Art of Perpendicular Lying. Translated by Warren E. Roberts. *Journal of the Folklore Institute* 2:180–219.

Hernadi, Paul
  1972. *Beyond Genre: New Directions in Literary Classification.* Ithaca: Cornell
    University Press.
Hirsch, E. D., Jr.
  1967. *Validity in Interpretation.* New Haven: Yale University Press.
  1976. *The Aims of Interpretation.* Chicago: University of Chicago Press.
  1987. *Cultural Literacy: What Every American Needs to Know.* Boston: Houghton
    Mifflin.
Holland, Norman N.
  1975. *Five Readers Reading.* New Haven: Yale University Press.
Honko, Lauri
  1964. Memorates and the Study of Folk Belief. *Journal of the Folklore Institute*
    1:5–19.
Hostetler, John A.
  1963. [1980] *Amish Society.* Baltimore: Johns Hopkins University Press.
Hufford, David J.
  1977. Humanoids and Anomalous Lights: Taxonomic and Epistemological
    Problems. *Fabula* 18:234–41.
  1983. The Supernatural and the Sociology of Knowledge: Explaining Academic
    Belief. *New York Folklore* 9:21–29.
Hymes, Dell
  1960. The Ethnography of Speaking. In *Anthropology and Human Behavior*, pp.
    13–53. Washington, D.C.: The Anthropological Society of Washington.
  1972. The Contribution of Folklore to Sociolinguistic Research. In *Toward New
    Perspectives in Folklore*, ed. Américo Paredes and Richard Bauman, pp. 42–50.
    Austin: University of Texas Press.
  1975. Breakthrough into Performance. In *Folklore: Performance and
    Communication*, ed. Dan Ben-Amos and Kenneth S. Goldstein, pp. 11–74. The
    Hague: Mouton.
Ives, Edward D.
  1976. Common-Man Biography: Some Notes by the Way. In *Folklore Today: A
    Festschrift for Richard M. Dorson*, ed. Linda Dégh, Henry Glassie, and Felix
    Oinas, pp. 251–64. Bloomington: Indiana University Research Center for
    Language and Semiotic Studies.
  1978. *Joe Scott: The Woodsman-Songmaker.* Urbana: University of Illinois Press.
Jacobs, Melville
  1959. *The Content and Style of an Oral Literature: Clackamas Chinook Myths and
    Tales.* Chicago: University of Chicago Press.
Jansen, William Hugh
  1965. The Esoteric-Exoteric Factor in Folklore. In *The Study of Folklore*, ed. Alan
    Dundes, pp. 43–51. Englewood Cliffs, N.J.: Prentice-Hall.
Jason, Heda
  1975. *Ethnopoetics: A Multilingual Terminology.* Jerusalem: Israel Ethnographic
    Society.
Johnson, Barbara
  1980. *The Critical Difference: Essays in the Contemporary Rhetoric of Reading.*
    Baltimore: Johns Hopkins University Press.
Jolles, André
  1930. [1965] *Einfache Formen: Legende, Sage, Mythe, Rätsel, Spruch, Kasus,*

Memorabile, Märchen, Witz. Halle: Max Niemeyer [Tübingen].

Jones, Steven Swann
  1979. Slouching toward Ethnography: The Text/Context Controversy Reconsidered. *Western Folklore* 38:42–47.
  1984. *Folklore and Literature in the United States: An Annotated Bibliography of Studies of Folklore in American Literature*. New York: Garland Publishing.

Jung, C. G.
  1958. *Ein Moderner Mythus von Dingen, die am Himmel Gesehen Werden*. Zurich: Rascher.
  1971. On Synchronicity. Reprinted in *The Portable Jung*, ed. Joseph Campbell, pp. 505–18. New York: The Viking Press.

Kalčik, Susan
  1975. "Like Ann's gynecologist or the time I was almost raped": Personal Narratives in Women's Rap Groups. *Journal of American Folklore* 88:3–11.

Kelly, George A.
  1955. [1963] *A Theory of Personality: The Psychology of Personal Constructs*. New York: Norton.

Kermode, Frank
  1966. *The Sense of an Ending*. New York: Oxford University Press.

Kilmann, Ralph H.
  1985. Corporate Culture. *Psychology Today* 19(April):62–68.

Kirschner, Suzanne R.
  1987. "Then What Have I to Do with Thee?": On Identity, Fieldwork, and Ethnographic Knowledge. *Cultural Anthropology* 2:211–34.

Kramer, Cheris
  1974. Wishy-Washy Mommy Talk. *Psychology Today* 8(June):82–85.

Kroeber, Karl
  1981. Scarface vs. Scar-face: The Problem of Versions. *Journal of the Folklore Institute* 18:99–124.

Kuhn, Thomas S.
  1962. [1970] *The Structure of Scientific Revolutions*, 2nd ed. enlarged. Chicago: University of Chicago Press.

Labov, William
  1972. *Language in the Inner City: Studies in the Black English Vernacular*. Philadelphia: University of Pennsylvania Press.

Labov, William, and Joshua Waletzky
  1967. Narrative Analysis: Oral Versions of Personal Experience. In *Essays in the Visual Arts*, ed. June Helm, pp. 12–44. Seattle: University of Washington Press.

Lakoff, Robin
  1975. *Language and Woman's Place*. New York: Harper & Row.

Lang, Andrew
  1885. [1970] *Custom and Myth*. Oosterhaut: Anthropological Publications.

Langness, L. L.
  1965. *The Life History in Anthropological Science*. New York: Holt, Rinehart, and Winston.

Leary, James P.
  1977. White Guys' Stories of the Night Street. *Journal of the Folklore Institute* 14:59–71.
  1978. Strategies and Stories of the Omaha Stockyards. *Folklore Forum* 11:29–41.
Legman, Gershon
  1975. *No Laughing Matter: Rationale of the Dirty Joke, Second Series*. New York: Bell Publishing Company.
Lévi-Strauss, Claude
  1958. The Structural Study of Myth. In *Myth: A Symposium*, ed. Thomas A. Sebeok, pp. 81–106. Bloomington: Indiana University Press.
  1963. *Structural Anthropology*. Translated by Claire Jacobsen and Brook Grundfest Schoepf. New York: Basic Books.
Lincoln, Yvonna S., and Egon G. Guba
  1985. *Naturalistic Inquiry*. Beverly Hills: Sage Publications.
Littleton, C. Scott
  1973. *The New Comparative Mythology*. Rev. ed. Berkeley: University of California Press.
Lockwood, Yvonne R.
  1977. Death of a Priest: The Folk History of a Local Event as Told in Personal Experience Narrative. *Journal of the Folklore Institute* 14:97–113.
Lord, Albert B.
  1971. *The Singer of Tales*. New York: Atheneum.
Lowes, John Livingston
  1927. [1955] *The Road to Xanadu: A Study in the Ways of the Imagination*. Boston: Houghton Mifflin.
Lowry, Joanna
  1974. The Structure of Subjectivity: Problems in Ethnographic Description. *Journal of the Anthropological Society of Oxford* 10:69–82.
Lüthi, Max
  1976. Parallel Themes in Folk Narrative and in Art Literature. *Journal of the Folklore Institute* 4:3–16.
Lynch, James
  1985a. *The Language of the Heart*. New York: Basic Books.
  1985b. Listen and Live. *American Health* 4(April):39–43.
Marcus, George, and Michael Fischer
  1986. *Anthropology as Cultural Critique*. Chicago: University of Chicago Press.
McCarl, Robert, Jr.
  1978. Jump Story: An Examination of the Occupational Experience Narrative. *Folklore Forum* 11:1–17.
McDowell, John H.
  1974. Coherence and Delight: Dual Canons of Excellence in Informal Narratives. *Folklore Forum, Bibliographic and Special Series*, no. 12:97–106.
Masters, William, and Virginia Johnson
  1966. *Human Sexual Response*. Boston: Little, Brown, and Company.
Mellen, Sydney L. W.
  1981. *The Evolution of Love*. San Francisco: W. H. Freeman.
Merton, Robert K.
  1949. [1967] *On Theoretical Sociology*. New York: The Free Press.

Mintz, Sidney W.
    1979. The Anthropological Interview and Life History. *Oral History Review*
        (1979):18–26.
Mitchell, Roger E.
    1978. *"I'm a Man That Works": The Biography of Don Mitchell*. Orono, Maine:
        Northeast Folklore Society.
Mullen, Patrick B.
    1978. *I Heard the Old Fishermen Say: Folklore of the Texas Gulf Coast*. Austin:
        University of Texas Press.
Neumann, Siegfried
    1966. Arbeitserinnerungen als Erzählinhalt. *Deutsches Jahrbuch für Volkskunde*
        12:177–90.
Nusbaum, Philip
    1978. A Conversational Approach to Occupational Folklore: Conversation, Work,
        Play, and the Workplace. *Folkore Forum* 11:18–28.
Ong, Walter J.
    1975. The Writer's Audience Is Always a Fiction. *PMLA* 90:9–21.
Oring, Elliott
    1976. Three Functions of Folklore: Traditional Functionalism as Explanation in
        Folkloristics. *Journal of American Folklore* 89:67–80.
    1984. Dyadic Traditions. *Journal of Folklore Research* 21:19–28.
Paredes, Américo, and Richard Bauman, eds.
    1972. *Toward New Perspectives in Folklore*. Austin: University of Texas Press.
Partridge, Eric
    1977. *A Dictionary of Catch Phrases*. London: Routledge & Kegan Paul.
Pelto, Pertti J.
    1970. [1979] *Anthropological Research: The Structure of Inquiry*. New York:
        Harper & Row.
Pentikäinen, Juha
    1973. Belief, Memorate, and Legend. *Folklore Forum* 6:217–41.
    1977. Life History and World View. *Temenos* 13:128–53.
    1978. *Oral Repertoire and World View: An Anthropological Study of Marina
        Takalo's Life History*. Helsinki: FF Communications, no. 219.
    1980. Life History: A Neglected Folklore Genre. In *Folklore on Two Continents:
        Essays in Honor of Linda Dégh*, ed. Nicholas Burlakof and Carl Lindahl, pp.
        150–59. Bloomington, Ind.: Trickster Press.
Pleck, Joseph H.
    1981. *The Myth of Masculinity*. Cambridge, Mass.: The MIT Press.
Polanyi, Livia
    1979. So What's the Point? *Semiotica* 25:207–41.
Polanyi, Michael, and Harry Prosch
    1975. *Meaning*. Chicago: University of Chicago Press.
Pratt, Mary Louise
    1977. *Toward a Speech Act Theory of Literary Discourse*. Bloomington: Indiana
        University Press.
Propp, Vladimir
    1928. [1968] *Morphology of the Folktale*. 2nd ed. Austin: University of Texas
        Press. Originally in Russian.

Puckett, Newbell Niles
 1981. *Popular Beliefs and Superstitions: A Compendium of American Folklore from the Ohio Collection of Newbell Niles Puckett*, ed. Wayland D. Hand, Anna Casetta, and Sondra B. Thiederman. 3 vols. Boston: G. K. Hall.
Radcliffe-Brown, A. R.
 1965. *Structure and Function in Primitive Society.* New York: The Free Press.
Renwick, Roger deV.
 1980. *English Folk Poetry: Structure and Meaning.* Philadelphia: University of Pennsylvania Press.
Robinson, John A.
 1981. Personal Narratives Reconsidered. *Journal of American Folklore* 94:58–85.
Rokeach, Milton
 1968. *Beliefs, Attitudes, and Values.* San Francisco: Jossey-Bass.
Sagarin, Edward
 1962. *The Anatomy of Dirty Words.* New York: Lyle Stuart.
Santino, Jack
 1978. Contemporary Occupational Heroes. *Folklore Forum* 11:55–59.
Schachter, Stanley
 1964. The Interaction of Cognitive and Physiological Determinants of Emotional State. In *Advances in Experimental Social Psychology*, ed. Leonard Berkowitz, vol. 1, pp. 49–80. New York: Academic Press.
Scholes, Robert
 1974. *Structuralism in Literature: An Introduction.* New Haven: Yale University Press.
Scholes, Robert, and Robert Kellogg
 1966. *The Nature of Narrative.* New York: Oxford University Press.
Scott, Charles T.
 1965. *Persian and Arabic Riddles: A Language-Centered Approach to Genre Definition.* Indiana University Publications of the Research Center in Anthropology, Folklore, and Linguistics, no. 39. The Hague.
Shibutani, Tamotsu
 1966. *Improvised News: A Sociological Study of Rumor.* Indianapolis: Bobbs-Merrill.
Sollors, Werner
 1986. *Beyond Ethnicity: Consent and Descent in American Culture.* New York: Oxford University Press.
Spradley, James P., and Brenda J. Mann
 1975. *The Cocktail Waitress: Women's Work in a Man's World.* New York: John Wiley & Sons.
Stahl, Sandra K. Dolby
 1973. Structuralism and Three Finnish Runes. *Folklore Forum* 6:25–39.
 1975a. The Local Character Anecdote. *Genre* 8:283–302.
 1975b. The Personal Narrative as a Folklore Genre. Ph.D. dissertation, Indiana University.
 1977a. The Oral Personal Narrative in Its Generic Context. *Fabula* 18:18–39.
 1977b. The Personal Narrative as Folklore. *Journal of the Folklore Institute* 14:9–30.
 1977c. Cursing and Its Euphemisms: Power, Irreverence, and the Unpardonable Sin. *Midwestern Journal of Language and Folklore* 3:54–68.

1979. Style in Oral and Written Narratives. *Southern Folklore Quarterly* 43:39–62.

1980. Narrative Genres: A Question of Academic Assumptions. *Fabula* 21:82–87.

1983. Personal Experience Stories. In *A Handbook of American Folklore*, ed. Richard M. Dorson, pp. 268–76. Bloomington: Indiana University Press.

1985. A Literary Folkloristic Methodology for the Study of Meaning in Personal Narrative. *Journal of Folklore Research* 22:45–69.

Stanley, David H.
1979. The Personal Narrative and the Personal Novel: Folklore as Frame and Structure for Literature. *Southern Folklore Quarterly* 43:107–20.

Stewart, Polly (Deemer)
1975. Style in the Anglo-American Legend. Ph.D. dissertation, University of Oregon.

Stewart, Susan
1978. *Nonsense: Aspects of Intertextuality in Folklore and Literature*. Baltimore: Johns Hopkins University Press.

Stocking, George W., Jr.
1968. *Race, Culture, and Evolution: Essays in the History of Anthropology*. New York: Free Press.

Strelka, Joseph
1978. The Literary Work: Its Structure, Unity, and Distinction from Forms of Non-literary Expression. In *What Is Literature?* ed. Paul Hernadi, pp. 115–26. Bloomington: Indiana University Press.

Sydow, C. W. von
1934. [1948] Kategorien der Prosa-Volksdichtung. In *Volkskundliche Gaben: Festschrift für John Meier*, pp. 253–68. Berlin. Reprinted in C. W. von Sydow. *Selected Papers on Folklore*, pp. 60–88. Copenhagen.

Taylor, Archer
1956. *The Shanghi Gesture*. Helsinki: Folklore Fellows Communication, no. 166.

Taylor, Archer, and Bartlett Jere Whiting
1958. *A Dictionary of American Proverbs and Proverbial Phrases, 1820–1880*. Cambridge: Harvard University Press.

Thompson, Stith
1955. *The Motif-Index of Folk-Literature*. Bloomington: Indiana University Press. 6 vols.

Titon, Jeff Todd
1980. The Life Story. *Journal of American Folklore* 93:276–92.

Toelken, Barre
1978. The Folklore of Academe. In *The Study of American Folklore: An Introduction*, by Jan Harold Brunvand, 2nd ed., Appendix B, pp. 372–90. New York, W. W. Norton.

1979. *The Dynamics of Folklore*. Boston: Houghton Mifflin.

Tompkins, Jane P., ed.
1980. *Reader-Response Criticism: From Formalism to Post-structuralism*. Baltimore: Johns Hopkins University Press.

Toulmin, Stephen
1972. *Human Understanding: The Collective Use and Evolution of Concepts*. Princeton, N.J.: Princeton University Press.

Ulin, Robert C.
1984. *Understanding Cultures: Perspectives in Anthropology and Social Theory*.

Austin: University of Texas Press.

Van Gennep, Arnold
1960. *The Rites of Passage*. Chicago: University of Chicago Press.

Vansina, Jan
1965. *Oral Tradition: A Study in Historical Methodology*. Translated by H. M. Wright. Chicago: Aldine Publishing.

Wallace, Anthony F. C.
1961. *Culture and Personality*. New York: Random House.

Ward, Donald, ed.
1981. *The German Legends of the Brothers Grimm*. Translated by Donald Ward. 2 vols. Philadelphia: Institute for the Study of Human Issues.

Weisstein, Ulrich
1968. *Comparative Literature and Literary Theory*. Bloomington: Indiana University Press.

Widdowson, J. D. A.
1978. Animals as Threatening Figures in Systems of Traditional Social Control. In *Animals in Folklore*. Cambridge: D. S. Brewer Ltd.

Wilgus, D. K.
1971. The Text Is the Thing. *Journal of American Folklore* 84:241–52.

Wimsatt, W. K., Jr., and Monroe C. Beardsley
1954. The Intentional Fallacy. In *The Verbal Icon: Studies in the Meaning of Poetry*, by W. K. Wimsatt, Jr., pp. 3–18. New York: The Noonday Press.

Wise, Gene
1980. *American Historical Explanations: A Strategy for Grounded Inquiry*. 2nd ed. revised. Minneapolis: University of Minnesota.

Workman, Mark
1983. Reading: A Folkloristic Activity. *Motif: International Newsletter of Research in Folklore and Literature*, no. 5(February): 1, 4–5.

Zan, Yigal
1982. The Text/Context Controversy: An Explanatory Perspective. *Western Folklore* 41:1–27.

Zeitlin, Steven J.
1980. "An Alchemy of Mind": The Family Courtship Story. *Western Folklore* 39:17–33.

Zukov, Gary
1979. *The Dancing Wu Li Masters: An Overview of the New Physics*. New York: Bantam Books.

Index

2165381

Made in the USA